Confronting Powerless Christianity

Evangelicals and the Missing Dimension

Charles H. Kraft

Chosen Books
A Division of Baker Book House Co
Grand Rapids, Michigan 49516

Published by Chosen Books
a division of Baker Book House Company
P.O. Box 6287, Grand Rapids, MI 49516-6287

Printed in the United States of America

Library of Congress Cataloging-in-Publication Data

Kraft, Charles H.
    Confronting powerless Christianity : Evangelicals and the missing dimension / Charles H. Kraft.
       p.   cm.
    Includes bibliographical references and index.
    ISBN 0-8007-9314-5 (pbk.)
    1. Supernatural (Theology). 2. Spiritual warfare. 3. Evangelicalism. I. Title.
BT745 .K68 2002
234′ .13—dc21   2002007517

For current information about all releases from Baker Book House, visit our web site:
http://www.bakerbooks.com

Contents

Acknowledgments   5
Introduction   7

1. Spiritual Warfare: A Crucial Issue   11
2. Worldview   27
3. Ten Critical Issues for Evangelicals   46
4. The Importance of Experience   64
5. Misuse of Spiritual Power   83
6. A Science in the Spiritual Realm?   98
7. Three-Dimensional Christianity   115
8. Beyond Conversion to Freedom   138
9. Partnership and Authority   150
10. Using God-Given Authority   161
11. Spiritual Warfare   180
12. Ground-Level Spiritual Warfare   200
13. Cosmic-Level Spiritual Warfare   217
14. I Want to Finish Well   234

Bibliography   247
Index   251

Acknowledgments

I am deeply grateful to God for allowing me to survive heart surgery to finish this book. I also thank my family, Fuller Seminary and ministry colleagues in Deep Healing Ministries for their support and encouragement. Further, my thanks go to Chosen book editors Grace Sarber and Jane Campbell for their considerable help in shaping the final version of this book.

Introduction

My background is in traditional noncharismatic evangelical Christianity. In that context I was converted, brought up and trained. My undergraduate and seminary studies were completed at Wheaton College and Ashland Seminary, two traditionally noncharismatic evangelical schools, and since 1969 I have been a faculty member of the School of World Mission at Fuller Theological Seminary in Pasadena, California. I served as a missionary under an evangelical mission society, and for the first 38 years of my Christian experience was, like most traditional evangelicals, quite skeptical of those groups that claim to work in spiritual power. Up until 1982 I would have considered myself possibly open to contemporary reports of miraculous events but fairly anti-Pentecostal and skeptical of most charismatic testimonies of the miraculous.

But I have changed. Not my evangelicalism. Not my commitment to Jesus Christ. Not my commitment to biblical Christianity. What has changed is my understanding and experience of what biblical Christianity is intended to be. The only kind of Christianity in the New Testament is a Christianity with power—a Christianity quite different from what I experienced during those first 38 years. What I am experiencing now is a Christianity *with* power. And that is what I am writing about.

I write this book with five major purposes.

1. First, I am convinced that, given our commitment to biblical Christianity, traditional evangelicals ought to be in the forefront of any movement to experience and work in spiritual power. Jesus said we would do what He did (John 14:12); and we have become fairly good at doing part of what He did, the part about loving and caring for people in their misery. But we have not learned to work in Jesus' power to release them from that misery. Jesus and His first followers loved and cared for people and also set them free from enemy strongholds in their lives. Thus, my first purpose is to encourage evangelicals to become more biblical than we have been to this point.

2. Second, I and many others are concerned that multitudes of Christians are living in bondage. They desire to experience the freedom Jesus promised (Luke 4:18–19), but they have no idea how to get there. They often go to counselors who employ secular means to analyze their problems but seldom bring real healing. Or they go to pastors who use secular techniques with little effect or who simply advise them to pray harder. Or, worse, they misuse Philippians 3:13 in preaching or counseling, advising hurting people simply to forget those things that are behind, as if when we come to Jesus all past wounds simply disappear. If, as is usually the case, their problems do not disappear, then such preaching or counseling leads them to believe there must be something wrong with them spiritually. If we look at the context of this verse, we find that Paul was not suggesting we forget past hurts; rather, he was advising us to put past *victories* behind us so we can win the present race. I want to help those multitudes of Christians living in bondage know how to experience true freedom.

3. Third, some critics, without looking at the incredible positive results of the "deep healing" ministry in which I have been involved, insist on questioning its validity. These are people who reason from theory, without benefit of experience, that what we are doing must be wrong because we do some things

that are not obvious in the condensed reports in Scripture of what Jesus did. I would like to answer some of their criticisms in a way that is constructive for those not yet "into" spiritual power.

4. Further, I want to discuss the necessity of *experiencing* the things Jesus told us we would be able to do if we have faith in Him (John 14:12). It has been in vogue for traditional evangelical theologians and Bible teachers to warn people against basing doctrine on experience, as if reason is a more sure way of arriving at truth than experience. Yet in the real world experience counts for a lot, and theory that does not work in experience is soon discarded. In addition, the insight of behavioral science in human interpretation of the world weighs heavily on the major part that experience—or lack of it—plays in our conclusions. How we interpret the Bible, then, is strongly influenced by our experience. This fact divides those who have experienced spiritual power from those who have not.

5. Last, I want to suggest that God intends for us to experiment and discover in the spiritual realm, just as we have learned to experiment and discover in the realms of nature and human life. When God put humans into the world, He seems to have told them very little, leaving much to be discovered with regard to the physical world. The same is true of the human world. Likewise I believe scientific laws and principles exist that are not spelled out specifically in the Bible but that pertain to spirit beings and their relationships to humans.

In connection with these five purposes, I have some important concerns about the kind of evangelical Christianity that I have experienced and see all around me.

1. First, what we do in our churches and training institutions is mostly "head stuff." We assume that if people think straight they will behave correctly, so the focus of many sermons is on getting our thinking straight. We insist on this belief despite a mountain of evidence that large numbers of people are not greatly affected by sermonizing or lectures. Nor does learning to think straight automatically result in correct behavior. In addition, focusing on head stuff does little, if anything, to help people who are hurting from deep emotional wounds. And our

congregations are full of a very large number of such hurting people.

2. Second, I observe—both from my own experience and from looking at what is said and done in our evangelical churches—that our primary answers to life's problems are secular ones. When a person is struggling with emotional problems, we send him or her to a psychologist who, though he or she may be a Christian, depends on secular techniques built on secular assumptions, without including Jesus the Healer in the process. In training, even ministerial training, our schools focus primarily on information rather than on Christian behavior, for it is assumed (wrongly) that such behavior will develop automatically as a byproduct of correct knowledge. When a person is sick, though we may pray, our real confidence is in secular medical techniques. We practice a secular Christianity.

3. A concomitant to this kind of Christianity is that it is largely powerless—powerless to heal, powerless to free people from emotional wounds and largely powerless to bring about real-life change. Our churches are filled with hurting people, therefore, who have no understanding of how to gain the freedom Jesus promised us. They think their present state, though uncomfortable, is the best they can hope to attain. They have no idea what this thing called freedom is, since they have never experienced it or anything like it.

It is with concerns such as these that I write what follows.

Charles H. Kraft
South Pasadena, California
January 2002

one

Spiritual Warfare: A Crucial Issue

Behind every book lies a motivation. I stated a good bit of my motivation in the introduction. But in addition I have a deep desire to soberly answer critics who question the attempts of some of us traditional evangelicals to move into the area of spiritual power. Mind you, as members of the same Christian community they have a right—even an obligation—to challenge approaches like ours that they feel are going off track. We are all on the same side, after all. Our critics are not our enemies but our brothers and sisters who see things differently than we do and, whether they intend this or not, are used by God to help us sharpen our understandings and practice. For we all have much to learn in this important area, including how to distinguish spiritual power that is of God from spiritual power that is from the enemy.

Such challenges to our practice and writing are, therefore, neither inappropriate nor unwelcome. It is our right and obligation, however, to answer, especially when we believe their challenges to our positions are based on a lack of the kinds of experience that would enable them to understand our positions, and that their questions can reasonably be answered. In what follows I hope to present some of the perspectives and experiences that answer the most serious questions raised, and also to make clear what motivates me in my commitment to practice and study this area of Christianity so ably modeled for us by Jesus Himself.

A Personal Testimony

As I mentioned, I am a card-carrying evangelical. Until recently I would even have characterized myself as being anti-Pentecostal and anticharismatic. What I thought I knew of those versions of Christianity—which, admittedly, was not much—completely turned me off. What I saw and heard of Pentecostals and charismatics led me to stereotype them as overly emotional, shallow and not-my-type-of-people. I was and still am thoroughly embarrassed by what I hear of many Pentecostal healing campaigns and the kind of programming typical of their television stations. These attitudes kept me from going near churches or people who carried the Pentecostal or charismatic label.

Yet as I read the Scriptures and observed the lives of "renewed" Christians, I remember feeling that there must be more to Christianity than I was experiencing. And as I moved into missiology (a term commonly used among missionaries and mission agencies to designate the science of doing Christian mission), I discovered that the most rapidly growing segment of Christianity worldwide was and is the charismatic segment. I tried to explain this fact as emotional people responding to a type of Christianity that focused on emotion. I soon had to give up that theory, however, and I came to suspect that there must be some quality to charismatic Christianity that my stereotype was keeping me from seeing.

Additionally, dormant in my memory lay the fact that the Nigerian church leaders with whom I worked during the late

'50s frequently referred to their experiences with demonic beings. These references led to embarrassment on my part over my inability, while serving in Nigeria, to teach or minister in the areas of demonism and healing—issues that were at the top of their list of concerns. Neither my Christian experience nor the Christian college and seminary I attended provided any assistance in understanding this part of Jesus' life and ministry, nor any implications it might have for Christian life and ministry. Yet it was clear that for Jesus, dealing with demons was a major theme of healing.

My concern about these issues hardly ever surfaced during my first thirteen years of teaching in the School of World Mission (SWM) at Fuller Theological Seminary (1969–82). When it did I pushed it aside and immersed myself in teaching a secular approach to improving missionary work through better understanding of culture and communication. If missionaries could only learn more about culture and communication, I taught, then they would be more usable by God and, therefore, more effective. As the years went by, though, a question raised by some of the students lodged in my mind. It was, "Where is the Holy Spirit in all of this?" I did not know how to answer that question.

Then in the mid–1970s we became acquainted with John Wimber. He was hired by the Fuller Evangelistic Association, a sister organization to Fuller Seminary, to work with Peter Wagner in promoting American church growth. As I now see it, the church growth movement was largely a secular approach to growing churches. In our discussions with Wimber we found that he, like us, was skeptical about reports of miraculous things happening in our day. He had been influenced by dispensationalism and was quite sure miracles were not for today.

As the '70s came to an end, though, something changed with Wimber—big time. He began a church developed from his wife's Bible class and, through a series of events, came to believe, with Carol, that Jesus meant for His emphasis on healing and deliverance to be passed on to us today. So they began to make praying for healing a major emphasis in their Christian practice. And Wimber's church began to grow.

Though Wimber left the Fuller Evangelistic Association, he continued to be invited by Wagner to teach certain parts of the church growth courses. Increasingly in these classes, Wimber referred to the part healing ministry played in the growth of his own church. By 1980–81 that church had grown to about two thousand attendees, and his emphasis on the importance of a healing ministry had grown apace. So, sometime in 1981, Wimber suggested to Wagner that he teach a whole course on the relationship of healing ministry to church growth.

In 1981 Wagner brought to our School of Mission faculty the suggestion that we offer a course on healing in relation to church growth. Our discussion of this possibility led us into several considerations. One of these was the fact that Wimber was someone we could trust not to be like "those wild Pentecostals." In communication theory terms, he was a "credible witness"—someone enough like us that we could trust him, even though he was dealing with something scary.

A second area of discussion was the fact that all of us on the SWM faculty—about eight to ten people at that time—had failed in this area during our own missionary experience. So we recognized that we needed this kind of emphasis and that, if our students were not to fail as we had, they needed it also.

We arranged to offer this course in the winter term of 1982, with Wagner the professor of record and Wimber as adjunct professor doing most of the teaching. It was attended by about 85 students, plus Pete and Doris Wagner, my wife Meg and myself. A couple of other SWM faculty attended a session or two that first year. Beginning in January we met every Monday night for the ten-week term. The usual conduct of the class involved Wimber teaching on the scriptural and practical aspects of healing, followed by a ministry time during which we saw many of our students healed of physical problems. This was a paradigm-shifting course for all of us.

Attention to this course grew, as did attendance, over the next few years. Faculty concerns, however, especially in the School of Theology, resulted in the discontinuance of the course in 1985. But a group of students gained administrative permission to present the course that year as a student activity for no credit. The following year Wagner and I were permitted to reinstate the course under a different format. The two of us, along with visiting lecturers, taught the course and Wimber was excluded. We have offered that course for credit ever since and have added several other similar courses to the curriculum as well.

Christianity with Power

In 1989 I published a book entitled *Christianity with Power.* In this book I attempted to show what I was discovering about the area of spiritual power neglected by traditional evangelicals. That book enabled me to discuss an amazing paradigm shift that I had experienced, going from a fairly powerless Christianity into what more closely parallels New Testament Christianity.

I describe this shift as breaking through a kind of glass ceiling, out of a Christianity that was essentially a human, even secular, thing into something with the marks of God: connectedness and spiritual vitality. Before that change I enjoyed the fact that I am related to Christ for eternity and that I have the privilege of serving Him, thus making my life much more worthwhile than it might otherwise have been. I considered my Christian experience to be a good way of life. I must say, though, I wondered at times if God was really there and if my connection with Him was real.

Following the events of 1982, a major change occurred. Since then my Christian life has been lifted to a completely new plane. I have experienced the power of Jesus both in witnessing healing and in becoming the conduit of Jesus' healing power, not to mention receiving healing myself. Clearly I have been led into a dimension of Christian experience that previously I never even imagined. This is a Christianity that feels like the New Testament, a Christian experience that is constantly in touch with a close, active God regularly demonstrating His presence, His love and His power in my presence, doing with and through me things I know I cannot do. I believe I have been led by God to break through that glass ceiling into a new dimension in which I am experiencing something close to normal Christianity as defined biblically.

Before 1982 I always wondered if there was more to Christianity than I was experiencing. There was so much of biblical Christianity that seemed out of reach. I felt that I was doing the best I could but that I had to settle for something much less than the Bible promised. Where was the power that Jesus passed on to His disciples in Luke 9 and 10? And what about the promise in John 14:12 that all who believe in Him would do His works and more? "Were the Pentecostals right?" I asked. But, I reasoned, surely God does not expect us to become hyper-emotional like them in order to experience biblical Christianity. So I dismissed looking into Pentecostal or charismatic Christianity.

Now, however, twenty years later, I have been privileged to participate with God in hundreds of healings—mostly "inner" (emotional and spiritual) healings, but many physical healings as well. In each of these experiences, the presence of God is tangible. And I find it almost impossible to explain the aliveness and meaningfulness of my Christian experience to those who live below that glass ceiling and have never experienced what I experience daily. Jesus is really close, both when I am ministering to others and in my day-to-day life. I believe this is normal Christianity and that I had been living subnormally for the first 38 years of my Christian experience.

We are told in John 8:32 that we will "know the truth and the truth will set [us] free." The kind of knowledge intended by the original Greek word is, however, *experiential* knowledge, not simply intellectual knowledge. The correct understanding of this verse, then, is conveyed only when the translation is, "You will *experience* the truth and the truth will make you free." Thus not experiencing Christianity that is "above the glass ceiling" prevents people from understanding the truth of that experience.

I am afraid this may sound arrogant. I certainly do not intend it that way. And I am as surprised as anyone at what God has done in my life by taking me to this level of ministry and intimacy with Him. My career for most of my life has been in left-brain academics, teaching in two universities and a seminary for nearly forty years. Apparently, though, one does not get through what I call the glass ceiling simply by knowing about the spiritual realm and spiritual power. If one is to break through that barrier, he has to experience them in a way that most evangelicals have not.

If you, the reader, are on the underside of that glass ceiling, you may have difficulty with what follows. The critics I cite below certainly do. Like myself during the first 38 years since I met Jesus, they not only have not experienced life above the glass ceiling, but they also probably cannot even imagine what it is like. *All you need to break through the glass, though, is to enter into partnership with Jesus in bringing healing and freedom to others.* You will probably need a mentor to lead you into this new dimension. For some, however, reading and following what is recommended in my books has been enough. Whatever it takes, it is worth the effort.

Criticism

Among evangelicals today, a certain amount of confusion concerning the existence and use of spiritual power is prevalent. For several generations we in the West have not known what to do about spiritual power. And even now, when the issue has become one of wide-ranging discussion, most evangelicals continue to be uncomfortable with the subject.

Some of us have moved strongly into an experience of the power of God in life and ministry. Others stand back asking what the scriptural justification is for the existence and use of spiritual power today. Still others (of course) attempt to ignore the whole matter, preferring the status quo and assuming that only the kooky are concerned about this area.

My concern here is to deal with several of the issues raised by those who criticize the growing understanding and practice of spiritual warfare among evangelical, noncharismatic Christians. Several specific criticisms and accusations are foremost in my mind as I write. In 1994 Robert Priest and two other faculty members from Columbia International University read a paper at the Evangelical Missiological Society. The paper was highly critical of several of us who come from evangelical backgrounds and are attempting to learn about and practice spiritual warfare. The criticism and my response to it were published in the volume *Spiritual Power and Missions* (1995), but the subject deserves a fuller treatment. Though other critics have tackled the subject (e.g., Lowe, 1998; MacArthur, 1992), the array of criticisms covered by Priest et al. represents the most serious. This article is both typical and strident in its accusations, so it serves as the basis of what follows. Furthermore, the authors manifest the most serious problem among critics—the lack of experience with the spirit world and its manifestations.

It is an unfortunate fact that those who criticize most vehemently are, with few exceptions, people who have had little or no experience in dealing with demonic beings. Their criticisms are purely theoretical, therefore, based on interpretations of Scripture and life uninformed by experience with what they criticize. Their approach to these issues also is hampered by the societal blindness to spirit world phenomena that characterizes most Americans, whether Christians or non-Christians.

In addition to the impediment caused by such lack of experience, and in keeping with this societal blindness, critics of the spiritual warfare movement usually exhibit a poorly developed perspective of the supernatural. And such a perspective contributes to a lack of understanding of the differences between Christian and satanic power manifestations. Thus critics with these drawbacks have difficulty interpreting those of us whom they critique and certain portions of Scripture, as well as life experiences that involve supernatural beings and power.

If the critics were to gain a significant amount of experience in dealing with demons, most of their criticisms would evaporate, at least with regard to what I have termed "ground-level warfare." This is the part of spiritual warfare that is concerned with demonic infestation in individual persons. They might still have difficulty, however, with that part of spiritual warfare that takes seriously the existence of the principalities and powers mentioned by the apostle Paul in Ephesians 6:12.

Though I did not welcome the criticism from the Columbia faculty or the need to respond, it served as an important means for forcing me to think through some of my experiences. And the debate provided a good learning experience for me. It is important for those of us who have moved into spiritual warfare to listen to our critics and to answer them, and that learning experience helped me do so.

I set my course to learn whatever I could about the theory and practice of the authority and power given to us by Jesus (Luke 9:1; John 14:12; Acts 1:8). Doing so clearly revealed that there are counterfeits. Our enemy does all he can to deceive us in our concern to experience and minister in the power of God. We are told that Satan masquerades as an "angel of light" (2 Corinthians 11:14). As such he stands behind such cleverly deceptive movements as New Age, Freemasonry, Scientology, Mormonism, each of the world religions (including much of what is called Christianity) and every other occult operation.

Satan is a master of counterfeit. And most of his counterfeits boil down to one or another form of what missiologists call "animism." This is the basis of the faith of perhaps eighty percent of the world's population, including most of those who call themselves Muslims, Hindus, Buddhists and even some Christians (e.g., Latin American Roman Catholics). When we survey the beliefs and practices of the religious and/or occultist faiths of most of the world's peoples, we find amazing similarities. And these similarities suggest a single mastermind behind them.

I want then to carefully distinguish Christianity from animism. This is a crucial distinction since it relates to the Source of power in which we—and the source of power in which they—work. Without understanding this distinction, the above critics and others accuse us of practicing animism, since their lack of experience leaves them unable to discern what is animism and what is working under God in the power and authority of the Holy Spirit.

A Critical Issue in Christianity Worldwide

In our day, whether we are working cross-culturally or in our own backyard, we are increasingly confronted with a plethora of problems related to the spirit world with which evangelicals in the past have not dealt adequately. To be relevant in twenty-first-century America, we need to grow in our understanding of the increasing challenges in this area. Many of our youth are experimenting with spells and hexes in their computer games, or listening to lyrics and rock music dedicated to Satan, or reading and imitating New Age gurus and their spirit guides or even experimenting with Satanism.

All these activities fall under the broad category "animism," a worldwide problem. In fact, from a missiological point of view, animism is the biggest problem in worldwide Christianity. It has always been so in non-Western societies but is becoming more and more a facet in the West. This being true, in order to work effectively for Christ in today's world it is becoming almost a prerequisite to understand how to deal with animistic beliefs and practices. Learning what animism is and how it differs from biblical Christianity is, therefore, a necessary start.

First of all we must recognize that Satan is in the business of deceiving people. Probably his most potent weapon in this deceit is his ability to counterfeit what God does. With this fact in mind, we should not consider it strange if, on the surface, animism looks a lot like biblical Christianity. But let's look at the differences. Though there are significant differences between the systems, *the crucial difference lies in the source of power.* For Christians, the Source of power is God Himself. For animists, Satan is the source.

Animism/Occultism vs. God-Given Authority

It is vital to our discussion to define what I mean by animism, on the one hand, and biblical Christianity, on the other. Animism (including New Age and other occult beliefs and activities) involves a wide range of principles and practices relating to the spirit world. It involves the belief that the world is full of spirits that can hurt or help us, depending on how we treat them. It also involves the practices that go along with that belief system.

Animists may or may not believe in a high god. When they do, he is usually seen as benign and thus in need of little, if any, attention. Most animists agree, however, that spirits—especially evil spirits—are capricious and, therefore, dangerous. So these need to be watched and appeased. In addition, most animists believe that evil spirits can inhabit material objects and places. Examples of these are certain mountains (e.g., Old Testament high places), trees, statues (e.g., idols), rocks (e.g., the Ka'aba in Mecca), rivers (e.g., the Ganges), territories, fetishes, charms and any other object or place dedicated to the spirits. Animists also believe in magic and the ability of at least certain people to convey power via curses, blessings, spells and the like.

Since a major concern of animists is to appease the dangerous spirits lest they cause harm or misfortune, great attention is given to rituals, sacrifices and other acts of devotion in order to please those spirits. Even New Age spirit guides are offered many acts of devotion to keep them "happy." Usually such acts of devotion are understood to be magical, automatically bringing about the desired effect if they are performed properly.

Specialist priests, shamans or gurus usually play an important role in the relationships between people and the spirit world. These specialists preside over many, if not all, the rituals and are consulted whenever difficulties arise that are perceived to be the result of spirit interference in the lives of people.

With respect to the existence of God and the existence of the spirit world, animistic belief is similar to biblical Christian belief. The importance of ritual and sacrifice is also similar in both Christianity and animism. When these facts are recognized, Satan's cleverness in counterfeiting becomes obvious.

Note, however, that the animistic approach to supernatural beings and powers is to pay attention to spirits but to ignore the God who is over all, since He is no harmful threat. In addition, the animist view of how to deal with the spirits is a magical one, aimed at manipulating them by precisely performing certain prescribed activities.

Biblical Christianity, on the other hand, focuses on God and His power to deal with both ordinary human problems and the spirit world. The Bible teaches that the spirit world is real, encompassing both good angels who serve God and evil demons who serve Satan. The biblical way to handle the evil spirits, however, is to appeal to God, not to appease the spirits themselves. Furthermore, the Christian approach to the spirit world is to submit to the God who has power over it, not to try to manipulate either the spirits or God Himself for our purposes.

Christian rituals, then, are directed toward God, not toward the spirits. So were the Old Testament sacrifices and the ultimate sacrifice that ended all blood sacrifices—the completed sacrificial work of Jesus on our behalf. The "inventory" of God, spirits, rituals and sacrifices is, therefore, largely the same for animism and biblical Christianity. But the approach to them is radically different in that the focal point for Christians is God, while for animists it is the spirits.

Recognizing this difference is crucial, whether we are trying to communicate the Gospel to animists in other societies or evaluate the ministries of those who claim to work in the power of God here at home. In recognizing this difference, we must remember that Jesus has given His followers power and authority over demons (Luke 9:1; John 14:12), while the enemy specializes in counterfeiting and confusing. For example, in the case of New Age channelers or animists who worship gods and spirits, it may be clear whom they are serving. But what about counselors and even some pastors who use techniques reminiscent of "guided imagery" and the use of spirit guides to help themselves and their clients?

Much of what the Bible teaches concerning spiritual power recognizes the validity of the power and the power techniques practiced by animists. It also teaches us to use similar techniques based on similar principles, though empowered by a different power Source. The deception is that much of what God does and endorses looks on the surface like what animists do.

For example, just as animists believe that material objects, buildings and geographical territory and features can be inhabited by evil spirits, so Christians believe that such items and places can be empowered by God. In Scripture we see God's power conveyed through material objects such as Paul's handkerchiefs and aprons (Acts 19:12), the Ark of the Covenant, Jesus' robe (Matthew 9:20; 14:36), the Temple, Communion elements ("this cup of blessing that we bless" [1 Corinthians 10:16]) and anointing oil (James 5:14–15), not to mention the flow of spiritual power through our words (e.g., words of blessing and healing). For this reason we dedicate buildings, Communion elements, the water of baptism, prayer mountains and the like to Him.

In areas such as healing, dedicating and blessing, both groups do essentially the same things, but the source of the animists' power is Satan and the Source of our power is God. We learn both from Scripture and from practical experience that many, if not all, of the rules that apply to God's interactions with humans also apply to the ways the enemy interacts with us (see Kraft and DeBord, 2000). For example, obedience to God in prayer, worship, sacrifice and service enables Him to carry out His purposes in the world. Likewise, obedience to Satan in these same ways enables him to accomplish his purposes. This should prompt us to recognize the importance of obedience and the fact that this is indeed a warfare issue.

The relationship between the power itself and the objects and places that are empowered is of concern. One of Satan's deceits is to lead people to believe that items and places are powerful in and of themselves. Animists, for example, believe that objects such as idols or implements used in religious rituals that are dedicated to gods or spirits *contain* spiritual power in and of themselves. Christians believe that objects and places can be dedicated to our God to *convey* His power (e.g., Paul's handkerchiefs, the Ark of the Covenant, anointing oil). On the surface, containing and conveying power look the same, especially since what animists believe to be power contained in objects is, in reality, satanic power conveyed by them.

Another example: Animist diviners, shamans, priests, etc., can heal. So can God. The fact that satanic healing leads sooner or later to captivity and misery is often not immediately apparent to the one healed. Nor is the fact that God's healing leads to freedom and peace. On the surface both types of healing look the same, and people who seek healing rather than the Healer are easily deceived, especially since satanic spirits and gods seem often to work faster in bringing about results than the true God does.

Our authority as Christians versus the authority Satan can give his followers is, at this point, an important issue. Priest and his colleagues, not knowing the difference between God-given authority to work in spiritual power and what animists do, accused us of practicing "Christian animism." But when we exercise the power and authority Jesus gives us to do things animists do—such as healing, casting out demons, blessing people and objects, dedicating buildings, praying for rain or against floods—we are not animists. We are working not in the power of Satan but in the power of God, simply exercising the authority Jesus gave His disciples (Luke 9:1) and told them to teach their followers (Matthew 28:19). We also are emulating the example set for us by Jesus Himself.

In their critique of us, these authors provided no indication of how they understand the authority we have in Christ. Unlike animists we do not try to manipulate God and His power. We, like Jesus, submit to God (John 5:19). It appears that these authors do not understand the difference between the position we have in Christ, which authorizes us to use the authority He delegates to us to convey His power, and the animistic assumption that power is inherent in certain objects and places.

To the extent that these authors speak for other evangelicals, we need to distinguish between animistic practices and true Christianity. The counterfeits are abundant and are luring more and more of those people who feel powerless in today's world—including, sadly, many pastors and psychologists.

To summarize and amplify my points, I present the following chart, designed to highlight many of the contrasts between animism (including New Age) and God-given authority. Note again that the primary expressions of each of these areas look very similar on the surface. It is in the underlying power and motivations that they differ.

	Animism	God-Given Authority
Power	Power is believed to be contained in people & objects.	God conveys His power through people & objects.
Need (in order to utilize spiritual power)	Animists feel the need to learn how to *manipulate* spirit power through magic or authority over spirits.	We must *submit* to God & learn to work with Him in the exercise of power & authority from Him.
Ontology (what is really going on)	Power is from Satan: He is the one who manipulates.	Power comes from God: He empowers & uses us.
God	God is good but distant; therefore, ignore Him.	God is good; therefore, relate to Him. He is close and involved with us.
Spirits	Spirits are fearful & can hurt us; therefore, appease them.	Spirits are defeated; therefore, assert God's authority over them.
People	People are victims of capricious spirits and never escape from being victims.	People are captives, but we can assert Jesus' authority to free them.
Cost	Those who receive power from Satan suffer great tragedy later.	Those who work with God experience love and power throughout life.
Hope	No hope.	We win.

Conclusion

Satan is very good at protecting himself from what he knows to be a power much greater than his. He knows that God has infinitely more power than he has and that Jesus passed this power on to us. His primary strategy, therefore, is to keep God's people ignorant and deceived so that we cannot use God's power against him.

A very important first step for all of us, therefore, is to get to know who we are scripturally and how this is to be expressed in real life. Scripturally we are the children of God, made in His image, redeemed by Jesus Christ to be heirs of God and joint heirs with Him (Romans 8:17). Thus we have all the power and authority Jesus gave His followers to cast out demons and cure diseases (Luke 9:1), to do the works Jesus Himself did (John 14:12), to be in the world what Jesus was (John 20:21) and to participate with God in crushing the enemy under our feet (Romans 16:20). Scripturally, then, we should follow Jesus' example, always using His power to show His love.

The issue of spiritual power is a crucial one for Christians. In exercising God's power, Jesus proved who He was and demonstrated God's great love for us. If we can trust what Jesus said—and we can—then we can know that He passed on to us the same Holy Spirit under whom He worked while on earth, with all of His power and authority.

two

Worldview

We Westerners have a big problem with assumptions when it comes to dealing with the spirit world. The root of this problem lies in our worldview, since it stems from the ways in which we have been taught to interpret life. Ours is what we call a "naturalistic" worldview, in contrast with the many "supernaturalistic" worldviews in the world. Our focus is on the visible, rather than on the possibility that invisible beings and powers affect our lives.

But the Scriptures are full of references to an invisible world of spirits. And until recently Western societies have offered virtually no encouragement for taking the spirit world seriously. Many in our day, however, have perceived that there is more to our universe than what we can see and touch. They are dissatisfied with merely scientific answers to experiences that science does not address. Thus many have unwisely opened themselves up to New Age thinking and Eastern mysticism. On the Christian side, openness to charismatic understanding is occurring in some quarters, stimulating great resistance to such ideas in others. For whatever reasons, those of younger generations especially seem more open to what is not simply visible.

A worldview is a perspective on reality shared by the members of a society or a specific group within a society.[1] It is made up of assumptions that are taught to children before they have the ability to compare these assumptions with other possible assumptions to find out whether they are the most accurate possible assumptions. Worldview assumptions cover the whole of life. Probably millions of them are buried inside each of us and vitally affect every aspect of our lives.

Learning our worldview as infants is similar to the formatting necessary for computer disks to work properly. We can record information on these disks only if they are formatted. Children, as they experience various events, develop mental compartments in which to store the information and feelings accrued in subsequent experiences. These compartments and the assumptions from which they are constructed form the structuring of worldview. Without getting too technical, we can simply say that our worldview consists of the thousands of assumptions we hold concerning time, space, causality, relationships and even how to classify the data of life. We dress because we assume it is improper to go naked. We schedule our activities (e.g., eating, sleeping, going to work) according to the numbers on our clocks because we assume that is the proper thing to do. When things happen to us, we assume that either there was a cause or that they happened by chance. Some life experiences can modify one's worldview but, barring life-altering events, one's worldview changes little.

The Evangelical Worldview

To those of us who study worldview, it is clear that the traditional Western worldview patterns greatly affect the way evangelicals understand invisible reality. Evangelical worldviews

1. See Kraft, 1989 and 1996, for more on worldview.

have been formed within Western worldviews. We have, after all, gone to the same schools as everyone else in our society. These patterns influence us even to the extent that many deny the existence of any invisible beings and power that are not "proven" by secular science (e.g., germs, electricity, radio and TV waves). Though this is changing a bit as at least certain Westerners become more interested in and often involved with the occult, our unfamiliarity with the spiritual realm makes us very insecure in our quest to accept and understand biblical spiritual reality.

Even those who have become aware of spiritual reality may be fearful about the area since it is such unfamiliar territory. We see others overemphasizing spirit things, such as looking for a demon under every bush or believing demons to be the cause of every problem. Thus we shy away from getting into the area, lest we carry things too far. Or we fear the possibility that we will accept insight from the wrong sources, such as animists, and be led astray. We fear this tendency in ourselves and others, and we distrust others if they head further into this realm than we do.

Since we may never have viewed a balanced, sensible way to deal with spiritual phenomena, it may never occur to us that there is such a thing. But there is. And I have written about it in several books (see bibliography), practiced it myself and continue to recommend it in this book.

Disbelief in Spiritual Beings and Powers

Resistance to belief in spiritual beings and powers by evangelicals can be strong, especially by those older in age, those in positions of leadership and those with theological training. Strangely, theologians and those who are theologically trained (e.g., pastors) often seem to have imbibed most deeply the worldview-based skepticism of spiritual things due to the academicism of theological training. Liberals, of course, have long since jettisoned a belief in miracles, demons and most of the cardinal doctrines of the Christian faith. Evangelicals, however, especially those with theological training, also tend to resist embracing a spirituality beyond that grudgingly allowed by our Western worldview.

Even evangelical scholars who claim to be committed to biblical truth often accuse Christians who practice the spiritual authority Jesus gave us of endorsing and advocating an outdated first-century worldview. Perhaps influenced directly or indirectly by the theologian Rudolf Bultmann, who attempted to "demythologize" the Bible, they think somehow that scientific insight approved by Western worldviews is superior to the insights Jesus used and taught. Thus, they contend, secular applications of power (e.g., in physical and emotional healing) should be seen as ordained by God to replace the ways God worked in biblical times. Add to this—as many evangelical scholars and pastors do—a weak sense of how Satan works, even to denying that demons exist, and we have a situation in which our enemy can work freely without being noticed. Such attitudes combine with lack of experience in the spiritual power arena to produce an anemic, powerless Christianity that has become the norm for our society.

Hermeneutics

Theologians define hermeneutics as the science of interpretation. Since all interpretation is strongly affected by worldview, hermeneutics actually is a subcategory of worldview. Interpretation of life and interpretation of the Scriptures and Christian experience go hand in hand. Thus Western worldviews influence the ways Western Christians interpret the Scriptures just as strongly as they influence our interpretation of life in general. Critics of evangelicals who have moved into an experience and practice of spiritual power often miss this point.

Such critics assume they are able to be objective in their interpretations of Scripture. Without realizing it, however, they interpret as everyone else interprets. That is, they are strongly affected by the worldview they learned in childhood and interpret all experience, including the Scriptures, in terms of that worldview. Such interpreters ignore, spiritualize or reinterpret the experiences they read about in Scripture that do not correspond with their worldview. They ignore, spiritualize or discard whatever they see in Scripture that does not fit into the interpretive structure provided by that worldview. If such people have not had scriptural experiences with spirit world phenomena, they are in a very poor position to critique those of us who have had such experiences and have modified our worldviews accordingly.

In their article Robert Priest and his colleagues, like many theologians and pastors, make the mistake of believing they can accurately interpret our experiences with demonization without (by Priest's admission) having had any experience with demonization themselves. They contend that their theoretical understanding of Scripture and life, without the benefit of experience, is sufficient to critique our extensive experience—for me, well over a thousand instances. In their critique, furthermore, they give no credence to the results of the activities in which we acted in the authority and power of Jesus. These results by themselves prove our case if experience is allowed to count—as it does in real life—in evaluating ministry. We have seen hundreds of people freed from enemy activity in their lives, and their lives show the kinds of change that can be attributed only to the hand of God.

Among the crucial hermeneutical issues, then, are:

1. The place of experience in the interpretation of Scripture and life;
2. How we handle experiential data that has no analog in Scripture;
3. How we apply our interpretation of Scripture to our interpretation of experience;
4. How we interpret the relationship between what happened long ago as presented in Scripture and what happens today;
5. How we handle the blinding effects of Western worldviews on our understanding of the spirit world;
6. Whether or not God has left for us to discover at least some understanding of the spirit world through extra-

biblical experience, just as He has done with understanding the material and human worlds.

Let's look at each of these.

1. The Place of Experience in Interpretation

Experience clearly has a prominent place in our interpretation of Scripture and life. We in the West are pervasively affected in our interpretations of life and Scripture by our naturalistic worldview. Without a lot of effort, it is very difficult for us to believe in anything to do with the spirit world. Many of us, with effort, are able to believe in God and some of the things we read about Him in Scripture.

2. Experience and Scripture

Traditional evangelicals, especially those trained in evangelical Bible schools and seminaries, frequently disparage an overemphasis on "experience" as a way of measuring our relationship with God. When such people speak of experience, however, they are really talking about feelings. They teach, then, that we should simply believe what God has said in Scripture as the proof of our salvation rather than trust our experience or feelings. A great deal of truth lies in this attitude as long as we know that it focuses on feelings, not broader experience. But this reaction against extreme emotionalism has led many, especially academics, to discount the value of experience in the interpretive process.

3. Interpreting Scripture and Interpreting Experience

What these interpreters of life do not seem to understand is that all interpretation is pervasively affected by our experiences, whether we admit it or not. Thus with regard to the spirit world, the ways in which those who have had spiritual experiences interpret Scripture and Christian life differ greatly from the ways of those who have not had such experiences interpret Scripture.

Some people without spirit world experience are able to allow for such phenomena, purely on the basis of their reading of Scripture or their trust of reports of those with such experience. In terms of our glass ceiling analogy, these people are able to look through the glass and accept what they see as valid even though they have not had such experiences themselves. I would put myself in this group prior to 1982. Many, however, especially those with academic training, seem not to be that flexible.

Our critics working from below the glass ceiling interpret our ministry on the basis of their lack of experience. Nor are they open to the Scripture-type experiences with the spirit world that we describe. Such experiences are even beyond their imaginations, leading them to mistrust us. Thus they interpret our experiences on the basis of their lack of experience and criticize us with no understanding of what lies on the other side of the glass ceiling. They would need to break through that glass ceiling and experience what we have experienced before they could understand what we are talking about.

4. The Nature of Scripture

In attempting to make sense of the six points listed, we find an important problem stemming from the nature of Scripture. Throughout the Bible we are given only bare-bones, surface-level descriptions of events. These are usually relayed without any attempt to explain the motivations of the people or the underlying spiritual dynamics. We are left to infer both, knowing that God is extremely concerned with motivation and that spiritual interaction is going on behind the scenes. We can look at Peter's denials of Jesus, for example (Matthew 26:69–75), or David's sin with Bathsheba (2 Samuel 11), or the reason for Daniel's praying (Daniel 10) or why Jesus went through Samaria contrary to Jewish custom (John 4:4). We are not told of the motivations behind these events or of those behind hundreds of other scriptural events, nor are we told what was going on in the spirit world.

Except for three events—the conversation between God and Satan concerning Job (Job 1), the indication of satanic interference in delaying the answer to Daniel's prayer (Daniel 10:13) and the interaction between Jesus and Satan at Jesus' temptations (Luke 4:1–13)—we are left to speculate concerning what Satan does in the background. We have little direct information concerning how he operates or the rules by which his activities are governed. Jesus told us that people are in captivity to Satan (Luke 4:18–19), that he is the ruler of the world (John 14:30) and that he has a kingdom Jesus implies is active and well organized (Matthew 12:25–26). Jesus demonstrated that His kingdom and the power He gives us (Luke 9:1) are greater than Satan's, and He called even a physical healing a release from the enemy's grip (Luke 13:10–17). But neither Jesus nor the biblical authors who record the events explained the principles behind them.

Due to the surface, human-level nature of the descriptions, we often can at least infer the influence of human sin in the events. We are shown, for example, that Adam, David and many others disobeyed God and sinned, thus bringing about God's judgment. But when the disciples attempted to infer sin as the cause of the plight of the man born blind (John 9) or of those killed when a tower fell (Luke 13:4), Jesus denied sin as the reason. He gave no insight, however, into the behind-the-scenes spiritual dynamics that influenced these events. Similarly we are not informed as to why curses and blessings work, when they work and what conditions prevent them from working. Proverbs 26:2 helps a little but does not explain most of what we want to know. Nor do the descriptions help us much in understanding the principles in cases such as Jacob's blessings (Genesis 48–49), or the curse God led Elijah to put on Ahab's family because of what he did to Naboth (1 Kings 21:20–24), or the strange dynamics involved in Balaam's activities in Numbers 22–24 or in scores of similar scriptural events.

5. The Blindness of the Western Worldview

One thing clear is that our Western worldview greatly interferes with our attempts to gain insight into the spiritual realities lying behind biblical events. From the perspective of our

Western evangelicalism, we can read the descriptions and easily pick up the human factors. Given our worldview blindness in the spiritual area, however, our instincts are untrustworthy when we try to understand what is going on in that area.

6. New Truth?

Interpreters have long been puzzled by what Jesus said in John 16:13: "When . . . the Spirit comes, who reveals the truth about God, he will lead you into all the truth." Is Jesus saying we can expect to be led into new truth? Or is this simply a promise that the Holy Spirit will help us to understand the Bible? I am afraid we really do not know for sure.

What we do know, though, is that there are many things in the Christian life for which we have very specific guidance. Scripture gives us many commands, such as to love one another as Christ loves us. But transculturally valid behaviors that should be used to fulfill such commands are not given to us. From Scripture we know we are to behave in truth and righteousness. But we are not offered insight into which cultural understandings of such principles are closest to God's understanding. We see this point embodied in the structures we use for worship, communication, church organization and the like. Given that we see no three-point sermons in the Bible, is this a God-ordained new form appropriate for at least some audiences? Are Sunday schools scriptural or not? And what about the different denominational structures?

In the New Testament the synagogue is the predominant form of gathering for those faithful to God. This is nowhere taught in the Old Testament, yet God seems to endorse it. Likewise in the New Testament, the view of the presence, power and activity of Satan and his kingdom is in many ways understood differently, or at least in more detail, than in the Old Testament. And the differences in understanding seem to have been influenced by the views of non-Jews. Can we make a case, therefore, for the continuous leading of God in ways that take us beyond what He has endorsed in inspired writings?

The fact that the Bible is bare-bones revelation plus the complexities of personal and cultural applications of scriptural principles suggests the possibility of discovering things that are new to us. Our unclarity as to how to define the term *new* also bears weight. Is something new if it is simply the outworking of a scriptural principle in new experiences for a person? Or does it have to be something that we can in no way tie to a scriptural principle? Can it be something that, while not tied to a scriptural principle, is not contradictory to any such principle? Or do we require chapter and verse to support everything we do?

Clearly we do many things for which we have no chapter-and-verse support. If such things do not fall outside what is scripturally allowed and also bear good fruit, can we contend that they are legitimate? I believe we can, whether or not we call these things new truth.

I would certainly argue for Sunday schools, though not necessarily for three-point sermons. My arguments against the latter, however, would be on communicational grounds and not because I believe such sermons are against Scripture. I would also argue that our way of weakening demons through inner healing before casting them out is still within what Scripture allows. By being weakened, they are usually not able to throw the person around physically as some of the demons in Scripture did. The person, therefore, is not embarrassed and, I believe, experiences both the power and the gentle love of Jesus in the process.

Is this new truth? It depends on our definition of *new*. In some ways it is new. In some ways it is not.

Dealing with territorial spirits is another subject that has been criticized as "new truth." Certainly Scripture contains precious little that can be used to claim that some of the techniques are scriptural. On the other hand, major documented breakthroughs have occurred in evangelism, church growth and community transformation when such techniques have been used (see Otis, 1999a, 1999b, 2001; Silvoso, 2000; Wagner, 1993, for documentation). Though the combination of techniques may not be overtly advocated in Scripture, many things in that combination cannot be challenged. Among them are forgiveness, repentance, reconciliation, intercessory prayer and unity of spiritual leaders. Perhaps the combination is new, but most of the components are not. And the results appear to be genuinely from God.

Dual Causation

Another important, rarely noticed and somewhat more subtle worldview problem is the fact that Westerners learn somehow that every effect has only a single cause. This leads to "either-or" thinking. Critics of spiritual warfare accuse us of trying to release people from their obligation to take responsibility for their behavior. Since they assume things can have only a single cause, they contend that if we blame demons for any part of human behavior, we are letting people off the hook with regard to their sin. They suggest that we are off-track in looking for spirit-level explanations when, they contend, Scripture puts the blame on human sinfulness.

Our critics, including Priest and his colleagues, contend that we ought to deal with sin and repentance rather than with demons because, they say, it is sin and lack of repentance that cause the real problems. These critics, in keeping with their Western worldview, assume a single cause for any given problem. We should, when people come to us with their struggles, not look for alien beings such as demons, they say. We should, rather, give our attention completely to the single thing (sin) that we know is involved.

If their assumption of a single cause is correct, this is a reasonable position. But what if this assumption is wrong and more than one cause actually exist?

In discussing the problem of demonization, I am frequently asked, "Is the problem caused by a demon or is it simply a psychological problem?" Frequently people are pushed into cognitive dissonance when I reply that if a demon is present, there are *two* causes. Demons cannot be present unless they have something to cling to. They are like rats, and rats cannot exist unless they have garbage to feed on. With demons, the "garbage" is usually emotional or spiritual damage—a type of sin. So with demonization, dual causation exists. We have to deal with both human sinfulness and any alien beings that may live in the garbage produced by the person's sin nature.

Now, not everyone who has problems carries demons. Our first rule, then, is to look for the human problems and address them with inner healing through the power of the Holy Spirit. In the absence of demonic involvement, this approach solves the problems. And if demons are present, taking away the garbage through inner healing weakens them greatly. They are then fairly easy to cast out and can cause no violence. Thus our approach far from oversimplifies things by blaming everything on demons, as our critics charge. If demonic spirits are present, we deal with them by first addressing the human garbage of sin.

So we deal with both the human and the spirit levels, since human problems frequently have a spirit cause as well as a human cause. When demons are present, dealing simply with the human level—as most counselors do—takes care of only half the problem. But dealing only with the spirit level—as deliverance ministries tend to do—also takes care of only half the problem. Taking full responsibility for the problems means dealing with both levels—dual causation.

Had our critics any experience in this area, they might have discovered, as we did, that dealing with the demonic means working at both human and spiritual levels. In keeping with standard evangelical doctrine, Priest and his colleagues emphasize the fact that human problems are rooted in "Satan's influence in the doctrinal, moral and spiritual arena . . . sin and deception" (1995:14) but, they say, not in the enemy's ability to empower curses. What they do not recognize is that Scripture portrays events that imply dual causality. Everything that happens needs to be analyzed at both levels in order to gain a complete picture. Though most events have human causes, influences also come from the spirit level. Thus I contend that we cannot completely analyze any human experience until we have identified the spiritual factors as well as the human ones.

As I mentioned, demons can live in a person only if something exists within that person to which they can attach. This can be sin, though most of the Christians with whom I work already have addressed what is ordinarily thought of as sin. More often it is a sinful condition that is not usually thought of as sin—such as unforgiveness, wallowing in anger or deep feelings of rejection. Such sinful emotional reactions are the result of how others have hurt the person, but they are sinful nonetheless. Dealing with these things requires repentance and the release of damaging reactions to Jesus. Or an inherited satanic grip can stem from vows, curses, dedications or sins made by a person's ancestors (Exodus 20:5–6; 34:7; Numbers 14:18–19; Deuteronomy 5:9–10; Jeremiah 32:18–19; John 9:2–3). In this type of demonic involvement, we employ what we call generational healing. But whatever the garbage that gives demons their rights, we need to speak of two causes—garbage and demons—and not just one.

In all of this I have been speaking of ground-level warfare—the part of spiritual warfare concerned with demonic infestation in individual persons. But dual causation is also true of the relationships between humans and the principalities and powers of Ephesians 6:12. When groups of people usually organized in territorial groupings (e.g., nations, cities), institutions, businesses, clubs and the like are promoting racism, occult involvement, pornography, abortion, homosexuality, gambling or any of a number of other sinful activities, they are giving higher-level spirits legal rights in their society. When dealing with higher-level spirits, then, we must address both the human and the spirit world concomitants to rectify a problem situation. It is critical, for example, for people to repent of racism in order to break the power of higher-level spirits whose job it is to keep that sin active.

We are not guilty of our critics' charge that we are turning people away from the scriptural mandate to deal with the internal stuff. We are simply saying that spirit problems, whether individual or group (i.e., personal or "territorial"), need to be dealt with at both human and suprahuman levels.

Godward and Satanward Perspectives

While it is true that Scripture emphasizes the fact that we are sinful, even to the extent of describing our hearts as deceitful and "too sick to be healed" (Jeremiah 17:9), that is not the only message in Scripture. We agree that God holds people responsible for their sinful choices. Nowhere in Scripture are we released from this responsibility. The need to deal with the human responsibility part of the New Testament perspective is what Lutheran theologian and pastor James Kallas calls "the Godward view" (1966).

But there is another perspective that Kallas claims is even more prominent in Scripture. He labels this perspective "the Satanward view" (1966). This perspective, according to Kallas, presents humans not in control of their lives but tormented and harassed by spiritual enemies they cannot control. The presence in Scripture of these two perspectives side by side is perhaps the greatest paradox of Scripture and the Christian life. One perspective requires full responsibility on our part for what we do about our sinfulness, while the other to a large extent represents humans as victims of an enemy who is too big for us. Both perspectives are present in Jesus' words and works. Though He held people responsible for their own choices—especially those who, like the Pharisees, had studied the Scriptures—He never condemned anyone for being demonized or ill. He simply rescued them as if they were helpless victims. As traditional evangelicals we have learned well the "Godward" perspective. We have, however, remained largely ignorant of and puzzled over the role Satan plays in the universe.

In addition to the human responsibility part, Scripture describes an enemy who is very active and whose commitment is to "steal, kill and destroy" as much as possible in the human context (John 10:10). And we are expected, like the New Testament Christians, to "know what [Satan's] plans are" (2 Corinthians 2:11). When Jesus announces His reason for coming to earth, He speaks of humans as "captives" and "oppressed" (Luke 4:18–19). He later refers to Satan as "the ruler of this world" (John 14:30).

Both Jesus and the New Testament writers were very conscious of Satan's activities in the world—much more so than we are. Paul calls the enemy "the ruler of the spiritual powers in space" (Ephesians 2:2) and points out that "we are not fighting against human beings but against the wicked spiritual forces in the heavenly world, the rulers, authorities, and cosmic powers of this dark age" (Ephesians 6:12). He calls us to be subject to God, the "Father of Spirits," so that we can live (Hebrews 12:9, NASB). And Peter describes the enemy as one who "roams around like a roaring lion, looking for someone to devour" (1 Peter 5:8).

A Complete Analysis: Dealing with Human and Spirit Levels

Again I contend that no spiritual problem is analyzed completely until both the human level and the spirit-level causes are taken into account. Throughout the Bible, especially the Old Testament, whenever a battle—whether group or individual—takes place, it occurs on both levels. An individual is tempted: There are both internal factors, stemming from his or her sin nature, and external factors, stemming from the fact that the members of the satanic kingdom, "the spiritual powers in space" (Ephesians 2:2), are always there to empower temptations. The Israelite army takes on the Philistines at the human level. The God of the Israelites takes on the gods of the Philistines at the spirit level.

A startling example of this need to recognize and analyze causality at both human and spirit levels is recorded in 2 Kings 3:24. Israel was defeating the Moabites to such an extent that the latter were driven back into their walled capital city. The Moabite king, in desperation, took seven hundred of his swordsmen and tried to force his way through Israel's lines (verse 26), but in vain. "So he took his eldest son, who was to succeed him as king, and offered him on the city wall as a sacrifice to the god of Moab," and Israel was routed (verse 27)! Why did the Israeli army run home? On the human level Israel was winning in a big way. The king of Moab, however, through the sacrifice of the heir to the throne, was able to throw so much spiritual power at Israel that they turned and ran. Sadly they did not remember they could have appealed to a greater spiritual Power and won at the spirit level as they had been winning at the human level.

Such an example witnesses, I believe, to a rule of the universe: Humans can partner with spirit beings, enabling them to do more than they would otherwise be able to do. On the Christian side of the fence, we can partner with God in prayer and obedience, thus enabling God to do His will. Those who partner with Satan enable him to get his way—within the limits set by God. There is, I believe, continuous interaction and quite a bit of interdependence between humans and spirit beings on both God's and Satan's sides. When we obey God, He is able to do more of what He wants to do. And when we fail Him, His will may not get done, unless He overrules. Thus Jesus prayed that God's will would be done "on earth as it is in heaven" (Matthew 6:10), because it is not automatic. He does not want any to perish (2 Peter 3:9). But apparently His will is partially thwarted in this matter due to human lack of obedience. Dual causality.

So we recognize the need for something at the human level to enable spirit-level activity. To remain balanced, however, we must recognize that some degree of spirit-level activity is independent of human permission. God can exert influence, for example, on people who seem to have no use for Him (e.g., the conversion of the apostle Paul, Nebuchadnezzar). God can restrain, protect and attack within the rules He has set for the universe. It should not seem strange to us, then, that Satan, working under the same rules, though not with the same degree of autonomy, can exert similar kinds of influence in the human arena. Job is an excellent example. God was protecting him, but Satan requested and received permission from God to attack him, even to the extent of killing his family (Job 1:1–2:10). Thus it was not because of Job's sin that Satan had influence, but because God allowed Satan to interfere. Interestingly the enemy allowed Job's wife to live in order that she could be the vehicle to convey Satan's message to Job: "Curse God and die"

(Job 2:9). This part of the story shows dual causality: Satan gave the words (see his prediction in Job 1:11) and Job's wife spoke them.

Satan also tried to kill Jesus as a child (Matthew 2:16). In order to do this he linked up with a human, Herod, who carried out his will by ordering the killing. God communicated with Joseph and Mary through a dream, however, instructing them to flee to Egypt. In both cases spirit and human components played a part in the events. Dual causality.

I contend that the rules of the universe allow Satan a certain amount of autonomy to exert influence both on those who serve him and, to some extent, on those to whom he does not have rights. With Job he requested and gained more rights than he actually had. With us as sinners, he has certain rights because of our sinful condition. As a part of his right to tempt us, he seems to be able to put thoughts into our minds. Apparently he also has the right to test us and perhaps even, on occasion, to capture us, judging from the words Jesus used in the Lord's Prayer: "Do not bring us to hard testing, but keep us safe [*deliver us*, NIV] from the Evil One" (Matthew 6:13). Satan's ability to influence both "pagans" and the people of God is abundantly clear from Scripture, as well as from contemporary experience. In any event our attempts to understand and analyze must take into account both the human and the spirit influences.

Satan Is an Imitator

A major problem for at least some critics is the difference between what God does and what the enemy does. An issue raised by Priest and associates is the question of whether the practices they criticized are coming from God or from Satan.

Specifically they see similarities between what happens in Christian spiritual warfare and the pagan practices of animism and magic. But they do not look at the results of our ministry to discover that the differences are abundant. We keep ourselves in close relationship with Jesus, claim His presence and power and see the kind of results we would expect if Jesus does the work. And the freedom received by those for whom we pray is consistent with what Jesus promises in Scripture. This being true, agreeing with their contention that we are involved in animism would mean accusing biblical peoples—including Jesus—of animism.

The confusion our critics experience stems from their lack of understanding of the way God has set things up in the universe and the way Satan, who we know is an imitator, works. Our large amount of experience with the spiritual realm brings us to the fairly firm conclusion that the rules of operation for spirit beings are largely the same for both sides (see Kraft and DeBord, 2000), just as they are in the material and human realms. When either God or Satan chooses to operate among humans, for example, both must work in terms of the physical laws, such as the law of gravity that God has placed in the universe. The only exception to those physical laws is when God chooses to contravene them, as when Jesus walked on water (Matthew 14; John 6) or when Philip was on the road to Gaza ministering to the Ethiopian eunuch and the Spirit of the Lord immediately took him to Azotus on the way to Caesarea (Acts 8:38–40).

Both God and Satan also have to deal with people in terms of human laws. One example of these laws is free will. Other examples are the laws of human anatomy and psychology that govern the way human bodies and minds work. Those who help humans to get well (e.g., medical doctors, psychologists) must work within these laws, and whatever either God or Satan seeks to do through those doctors also must fit within the rules God has laid down for such activity.

One of the things our critics assail is the fact that we use certain visualization techniques in the kind of prayer ministry we do. Since similar techniques are used regularly by New Age activists, these critics accuse us of working for Satan. But they have misanalyzed the situation by claiming that the technique itself is satanic. What they miss is that either God or Satan can use the technique, just as either God or Satan can use such things as music, preaching, prayer, historical inquiry or even theological inquiry, or any of the myriad other techniques of human life. The difference is not in which technique is used but in which power flows through the technique. The rules are the same for either side.

It should not surprise us, then, if the activities of Satan in the spirit realm look on the surface deceptively similar to the activities of God, since they operate according to the same rules. To summarize this very important fact, *the major differences in the operation of spiritual principles in the human context lie in the source of the power and in the way the principles and techniques are used, not in the principles and techniques themselves.* In application, the methods and techniques used by Satan and those used by God for blessing, healing, dedication, worship and the like are largely the same, in spite of the fact that the empowerment comes from opposite sources. Though we use such terms as *animism* and *magic* to designate the satanic use of certain spiritual principles, we should not assume that those principles, put into creation by God Himself, cannot be used (with some differences, to be sure) under the power of God for the purposes for which He originally intended them.[2]

Conclusion

The influence of Western and evangelical worldviews is strong on all of us when we attempt to deal with the spirit world. Those with little or no experience with spirit beings and powers are especially governed by Western and evangelical worldview blindness when they criticize those of us whom God has allowed to break through the glass ceiling.

2. See Kraft and DeBord, 2000, for further elaboration of these ideas.

three

Ten Critical Issues for Evangelicals

The issue of spiritual warfare raises some important issues for evangelicals. Ten of these issues are the subject of this chapter and were presented originally to the faculty of Fuller Seminary. The unwillingness of most of the Fuller faculty to deal with this part of our faith is a typical reaction of evangelical leaders, producing one of the crippling diseases of evangelicalism. An important motivation for this book is to try to convince evangelicals, especially leaders, to take the subject more seriously.

1. Both New and Old Testaments portray a context of conflict between God's Kingdom and Satan's domain.

In the Old Testament God wages a constant and largely unsuccessful battle against animism among His chosen people. Whether it is the command that His people prefer none of these other gods to Himself (Exodus 20:5) or His constant condemnation of the kings of Israel and Judah (e.g., 2 Chronicles 21:13; Jeremiah 3:2; Ezekiel 16:15–26) for "whoring after" these other gods, the underlying theme is conflict. The record is more clear about what took place in the human realm, but the clear implication—especially when we factor in Job 1, Daniel 10:13, Isaiah 14 and Ezekiel 28—is that a cosmic battle rages between God and Satan with continual implications for humanity. Given the fact that the propensity of humans to this day is to imitate the unfaithful Israelites, it seems that we should take seriously the spiritual dimension of the Old Testament.

In the New Testament, Jesus and the apostles are in constant conflict with evil personal beings, Satan and demons. Jesus' statement that He came "to set captives free" (Luke 4:18–19) implies that someone out there has put people into captivity. John underlined what Jesus said when he stated that "the Son of God appeared . . . to destroy what the Devil had done" (1 John 3:8). And Paul was so concerned about spiritual conflict that he commanded us to put on full spiritual battle armor (Ephesians 6:12–18). Many more references could be cited, all pointing to the fact that the picture the Bible presents is a battle zone. First and foremost it is a battle for people's souls. But Jesus also portrayed it as a battle to rescue people from demonization and sickness.

It is sad that evangelicals, even those most critical of the "demythologizing" of Rudolf Bultmann, treat anything to do with demons as if they do not exist today. And if they do recognize their existence, these evangelicals would rather not be bothered dealing with them. Thus satanic forces run rampant within our churches and training institutions while few attempt to do anything about them. And those who seek to deal with demonic interference are ignored or severely criticized.

Though this area is of major importance in Scripture, my own evangelical background, including my seminary training, provided hardly a glimpse into dealing with Satan and demons. The only exception was in the area of temptation to sin. And up to 1982 Fuller, in keeping with its commitment to Reformed theology, totally ignored this area. Though most of us offered lip service to the fact that we are in conflict with Satan, we gave no attention to that conflict beyond the need to win souls away from the enemy.

When I experienced the awakening in my own life in 1982, I had many questions: What involvement should evangelicals have in the spiritual warfare part of Jesus' total cause? We have done well to emphasize the winning of souls, but what about the freedom Jesus promised? This freedom lies beyond conversion (as we will discuss in chapter 8) and requires dealing with the spiritual component of warfare. Can we be content simply to deal with things at the human level and ignore the spirit level? Or does our obedience to Christ commit us to do more?

2. A spirit world exists that includes noncorporeal, spiritual entities that serve Satan (Ephesians 6:12). We call them demons.

Though Enlightenment rationalism has succeeded within evangelicalism in demythologizing the existence of Satan and demons, we evangelicals claim to take the Bible seriously. We claim to honor the authority of the whole Bible, and the Bible is quite serious about the issue of spiritual warfare. Presumably, then, we ought to combat Enlightenment influences and take the Bible seriously in the area of spiritual warfare, as in all other areas.

It is not simply a primitive worldview, as some contend, that holds that demons exist. Rather, it is Reality with a capital *R*, as anyone with a little experience with demons will testify. Jesus is not simply a good psychologist, conforming to the beliefs of a primitive people who interpreted psychological ills as the result of demonic activity. Both the New Testament and experience show that demons, unlike psychological problems, are separate, alien beings that live in people. They can talk and be eliminated through the authoritative use of the power of Jesus Christ.

As we might expect from representatives of deceit and the kingdom of darkness, demons are good at hiding and keeping people unaware of their presence. I myself was completely unaware of them for the first 38 years of my Christian experience. When demons are challenged in the name of Jesus Christ, however, they are forced to reveal their presence and can be cast out. I have worked with hundreds of demonized people and have become keenly aware of the presence and activity of these scripturally authenticated beings (e.g., Mark 1:21–45; 5:1–20; 9:14–29). I may have been fooled a few times over the course of the past fifteen years since I met my first demon, but I have not been fooled hundreds of times. Demons do exist, just as Scripture indicates they do, and they do exist today.

Only those interpreting the Bible on the basis of no experience will claim that demons do not exist or that they are not an important factor in human experience. Such people, even though they may be seminary professors and pastors assumed to be conversant with spiritual things, are more influenced by their naturalistic, humanistic, secular worldview than by the clear words and teachings of Scripture in this area.

Some claim that what is called demonization is in reality the psychological disorder now referred to as "dissociative identity disorder" (DID, formerly called "multiple personality disorder" or MPD). But again, experience is the key, as long as it is built on the recognition that demons really exist. I have worked with at least 25 persons with DID/MPD and can testify that demons are quite distinct from dissociated parts of persons. Experience with demonized people and with DID sufferers enables one to differentiate clearly between "person parts" and the alien beings we call demons. One soon discovers, however, that the abusive conditions (usually occurring in early childhood) that result in DID usually also bring about demonization. Thus in nearly every DID client with whom my ministry team members and I have worked, we also have found demonization.

Under conditions of early childhood abuse, a person may dissociate in order to survive. His or her angry and fearful reactions, however, provide fertile ground for the entrance of demons into each of the person parts that respond in that way. Thus, when dealing with DID clients, we look for and almost always find demons in each person part. The demons and the person parts are always quite distinct from each other.

Furthermore, only about 25 to 50 of the hundreds of demonized people with whom I have worked have suffered from DID. Clearly, then, demonization and DID cannot be the same thing.

3. Deliverance and healing were important aspects of Jesus' ministry, and He intends that they be continued by His followers.

Jesus did not ignore the presence of demons, as evangelicals and pastoral training institutions traditionally do. Nor did He treat demons as the cause of every problem. He dealt matter-of-factly with both demons and healing and gave His followers authority over both demons and diseases (Luke 9:1; 10:19). He then promised that we would do the works He did (John 14:12), presumably including the casting out of demons and healing in the power of the Holy Spirit.

In Matthew 28:20 Jesus commanded His followers to teach their followers "everything I have commanded you." From this we can infer that what Jesus taught His followers is to be taught to their followers, coming down to us today. If so, Jesus expects us to both practice and teach healing and deliverance, as He and His followers did.

Jack Hayford stated a simple truth in lectures several years ago at Fuller Seminary: When we look at Scripture and Jesus' expectations for His followers, it is those who do *not* get involved in ministering deliverance and healing who have to justify their behavior, not those who are active in these areas. For Jesus this kind of ministry was *normal*. It should be for us also, if we claim to be following His example. Those for whom such ministry is not normal are the ones who have some explaining to do.

I have been fascinated by the incarnation for more than forty years. Long ago, long before 1982, I set myself to become as much like Jesus as possible. Besides working at this personally,

I began to write and teach what I learned about Jesus as a model for us to imitate, especially in His attitude toward culture and in His approach to communication, cross-cultural ministry and contextualization (see Kraft, 1991, 1996).

Since 1982 I have been learning, teaching and writing about the spiritual power dimensions of the incarnation and dis-covering their high relevance both for cross-cultural work and for the Church in this country. And I have been discovering this relevance both theoretically and experientially through ministry and observation. Shouldn't the spiritual power dimen-sions of Jesus' life and ministry be major subjects for churches and training institutions that claim to be committed to the Bible?

4. If Jesus were on the teaching faculty of one of our training institutions, would He not also be active in setting captives free?

Jesus said He came to set captives free (Luke 4:18–19), and He would not be content simply to talk about setting them free. Through works and words He taught that we live in a world of conflict between God and Satan—a conflict in which we are to be continually involved as He was. The rest of the New Testa-ment supports this view of the Christian life.

Academic work is valid, but faculty members of Christian training institutions usually feel called to some practical min-istry as well (e.g., in churches or parachurch organizations). Freeing students from emotional and spiritual—including demonic—problems is an important ministry, is endorsed by Jesus and, I believe, is meant to be part of the seminary expe-rience. At least some faculty should be involved in this type of practical ministry, especially since it is not adequately handled through secular means or elsewhere in the curriculum of most Christian training institutions.

Those institutions that give a lot of attention to counseling and the incorporation of secular psychological insight into min-isterial training should be especially interested in research and practice in this area. Typically such programs teach almost purely secular insight, with little or no attention to spiritual beings and power. This is terribly sad, given the commitment of such evangelical institutions to the Bible in other areas of their curriculum. If Jesus were invited to work within such a secularized curriculum, He would probably dump most of it and spend His time demonstrating that the neglected spiritual dimension is the crucial part of any help such teaching is expected to bring.

A ministry of spiritual power is thoroughly appropriate to any Christian institution that purports to be training—and free-ing—people spiritually. We should be both teaching and doing such ministry for the sake of our students and for the sake of the ministries in which they will be engaged in the future, whether pastoral, clinical or missionary.

5. Today's church leaders need to know how to conduct spiritual warfare.

Like the world of Jesus' time, today's world is full of evidence that Satan and his demons are active in all areas of human life, including church life. Such problems as violence, warfare, ter-rorism, homosexuality, pornography, divorce, suicide, murder, emotional, physical and sexual abuse, even nominalism and religiosity are *not merely human problems*—though they are that. They also have spiritual and often demonic dimensions.

Church leaders today, just as in Jesus' day, need to learn how to deal with the spiritual dimensions of these problems. It is not enough to teach secular methods. Nor is it enough to teach present and future church leaders to deal only with the human end of such problems. Evangelical training institutions claim to deal with spiritual reality but virtually ignore the spiritual power dimension that for Jesus and the rest of the New Testa-ment was a very important area. And since faculty and admin-istration ignore it, our students go out ill prepared to deal with this dimension—as did nearly all of us who presently teach in such institutions.

Jesus taught by *doing* as well as by talking. It is not enough for us to teach anything, especially spiritual warfare, by simply talking about it. We need to disciple, not just sell information about the subject. We believe that a student needs to practice preaching if she or he is to learn to do it well in ministry. The same applies to spiritual warfare. We do not learn to do it simply by talking about it (and especially by ignoring it). Students, and all the rest of us, learn what church leaders do. If they talk about it, we learn to talk about it. If they ignore the subject, we learn to ignore it. If they observe practice and then practice themselves, we learn to do it.

6. Spiritual warfare—including praying for healing—does not have to be conducted in crazy ways.

The models of "faith healing," deliverance from demons and other types of spiritual warfare of which people are most conscious (e.g., that seen on TV and in healing campaigns) often portray this ministry in a most unfortunate light. Many evangelicals react against such power ministries on the assumption that anyone who gets into such ministry either starts out wacky or gets there before long. They cannot imagine the possibility of a more balanced approach. And they evaluate those attempting to minister in a sane way in terms of their stereotypes, rather than in terms of what we do and write.

Jesus showed none of the hyperemotionalism and showmanship that many contemporary ministries display. He seemed to go about cool, calm and collected, manifesting a most evangelical emotional temperament. I think He demonstrated that such ministry can be done in a reasonable manner. I understand where people are coming from who insist that spiritual power ministries are wacky—I once considered them so myself. But I have found that we can learn to do spiritual warfare in more balanced ways and am trying to prove it in my own practice.

Regrettable in the extreme are such unscriptural doctrines as the "name-it, claim-it" teaching, the "demon-under-every-bush" teaching and the teaching that we do not have to take responsibility for our sinful behavior since demons are to blame. I label these teachings heretical because they are not biblical and regrettable because they are taught by some very visible "faith healers." It is a shame that many, in reaction against such excesses, have turned completely away from this important ministry.

I believe evangelicalism is the proper site for the demonstration of a better way to go with spiritual warfare. For one thing, we tend to have a more solid biblical base than those who fit the stereotype. We also tend to be less emotional and potentially less given to exaggerating the importance of lesser gifts such as speaking in tongues when more important and practical emphases such as healing and deliverance are available. I judge these as more important for two reasons. First, they were important to Jesus, whereas speaking in tongues is not even mentioned as part of Jesus' ministry. And second, healing appears higher than tongues when mentioned in listings of spiritual gifts (see 1 Corinthians 12:9–10, 28–31).

7. What better place is there than evangelical training institutions for Christian leaders to learn how to pray for the sick and cast out demons in a balanced, scriptural way?

Most traditional evangelical institutions have tried over the years to exemplify a balanced form of evangelicalism. But they have been infected by rationalism, by secularism and, in the spiritual power area, by the extreme views of certain Reformed and dispensational theologians (e.g., Warfield, Darby), not to mention by the damaging influence of their stereotypes of Pentecostal and charismatic Christianity.

Pentecostals and charismatics, however, have now been admitted into traditional evangelical organizations and conferences. So traditional evangelicals may be ready to abandon at least some prejudices and open up to their teachings, as well as to our Pentecostal and charismatic brethren themselves. In our day some leaders from Pentecostal and charismatic circles have risen to the top of traditionally noncharismatic evangelical organizations and institutions (e.g., National Association of Evangelicals, Gordon-Conwell Seminary, Fuller Seminary). Unfortunately these leaders have often paid the price of downplaying their distinctives; and I am told by Pentecostals and charismatics that many of their churches have lost their concerns for healing and deliverance. "We might as well be Presbyterian!" one Pentecostal leader once said to me.

Perhaps traditional evangelicals and our institutions can outgrow our fear of the distinctive emphases of Pentecostal and charismatic Christianity, of which we have tended to be suspicious. If so, we ought to demonstrate our new position by dealing with what have been considered "their" issues in a balanced, scriptural way. And we should be mature enough not to worry about our reputation among those whose Christianity is primarily rationalistic and secular.

To date, traditional evangelicalism has promoted largely secular answers to pastoral, emotional and missionary problems. Theologically we are primarily rationalists, a secular form of activity much like secular philosophy. In counseling we advocate secular psychology, even though the practitioners are Christian. In missiology we have become known, at least before 1982, for offering secular approaches to church growth, culture and communication. Educationally we are more like a secular university than the kind of relationally based learning community we see portrayed in Scripture.

One of the questions I heard most insistently from Pentecostal and charismatic students in my first thirteen years at Fuller was, "Where is the Holy Spirit?" Like most evangelicals, I did not know. So I jumped at the opportunity to learn how to combine the best of Pentecostal and charismatic insight and practice with the great scriptural and intellectual foundation that evangelicalism has provided.

I am grateful to Fuller Seminary for the freedom to do this, but note a constant undercurrent of criticism from some colleagues. Though this is to be expected, given their rationalistic perspective and lack of experience, it betrays a disappointing lack of trust in a context that is ostensibly concerned with finding and teaching truth no matter what the consequences. These colleagues criticize but will not come to me to discuss why I focus on spiritual power, or to try to understand my point of view. Their counsel seems to be that we should stop setting captives free because having colleagues who are actually doing these works of Jesus embarrasses them.

With what seems to be a new openness, however, on the part of some evangelical pastors and institutions, we may have more hope today than before that we can see some changes. I receive a steady stream of requests from evangelical churches for seminars on spiritual power. And my courses on spiritual power at Fuller are very well attended. So some evangelical churches and many students are interested. And many faculty dealing with cross-cultural ministry, both at Fuller and elsewhere, are opening up because they see the great importance of expertise in the area of spiritual power to Christian missions in most of the world, increasingly including North America.

Though we can expect church leaders who are in established positions and are not looking for controversy—especially faculty members of training institutions—to be resistant, we may be encouraged that at least some who are struggling with real-world problems are willing to explore this area. So we push on, using whatever freedom we have to teach, write and, hopefully, bring change.

8. Our experience is that demons are attached to spiritual and emotional garbage.

In our attempts to find a balanced way to practice the ministry of spiritual warfare, my associates and I have learned that demonic strength is calibrated to the amount and kind of spiritual and emotional garbage in a person's life. Dealing with the garbage, therefore, is the most important thing to do in any attempt to free people from possible demonic strongholds. So when we minister to a person we spend most of our time—approximately three-quarters of it—dealing with this garbage.

Our ministry involves inner healing counseling with the overt presence and activity of the Holy Spirit. It is a *counseling approach* to setting captives free.

Ignoring demons when they are present, as those who counsel only in a secular way do, leaves a person unhealed and unfree. So we spend part of the ministry time discovering if any demons are present and, if so, getting rid of them. We find that complete healing does not come unless both the emotional and spiritual components of a person's problems are addressed. This means dealing primarily with the emotional garbage but also with the spiritual "rats" (demons).

We have found that most *deliverance ministries* err by assuming that the demons are the biggest problem and that getting rid of them should lead to healing. Ministries that involve only *counseling*, on the other hand, tend to assume that the only problems are human problems. We assume there *may* be both. Since we usually deal with the human problems first, demons are left with little or no ability to fight because the garbage on which they have fed is removed. So we seldom experience any violence when commanding them to leave.

What I refer to as "garbage" includes both *spiritual problems*—such as sin, commitment to occult organizations, dedication to evil spirits or the gods of non-Christian religions; and/or *emotional problems*—such as unforgiveness, hatred, anger, fear, shame, guilt, lust and the like. Though these are problems at the human level, we find that demons are frequently attached to them as well. For the person to receive complete healing, the problems must be dealt with at both human and spiritual levels.

Some challenge the fact that we cast demons out of Christians as well as out of non-Christians. This challenge is based on the theoretical assumption of those without experience that if the Holy Spirit lives in a person, no demon can live there. All of us who deal with demonization, however—though we may start (as most of us did) with the assumption that Christians cannot be demonized—soon discover that we have to evict demons even from Christians. Though the demons in a Christian may be weaker than those in a non-Christian due to the spiritual growth of the Christian, they usually remain until cast out. But since we deal only with what we find present, and since we and everyone else who deals with demonization find demons in Christians, we deal with them as we find them.

This fact challenges us to try to understand this phenomenon. For me the best way to explain it is to suggest a parallel in Christians between the sin situation and demonization. As Christians we have to deal with sin in body, mind, emotions and will. Our new spiritual nature, however, according to 1 John 3:9, is no longer infected with sin. But these other parts of us continue to sin. That new nature, otherwise known as our human spirit, became free from the sin problem when we came to Christ. I believe it also became free from any demons that might have lived there before we came to Christ. That is, if a person carries demons when he or she comes to Christ, the demons can no longer inhabit this person's new spiritual nature. But they can continue to live in the same parts of that person with which he or she has a sin problem—body, mind, emotions and will—at least until they are recognized and cast out.

See my book *Defeating Dark Angels* for a more detailed treatment of this issue and the complications that arise in understanding it, due to the serious mistranslation "demon possession." That term is a mistranslation because the Greek words mean simply "having a demon," and never imply anything as controlling as "possession."

9. In dealing with spiritual warfare, we recognize two levels of spirits. We call these "ground-level" and "cosmic-level" (Wagner's "strategic-level").[3]

Though I deal with this topic in more detail in chapters 11 through 13, I would like to introduce a brief overview of the subject. Ground-level spirits are those that live in people. We theorize that there are at least three types of ground-level spirits: *family, occult* and *ordinary. Family* spirits are those that gain

3. See chapters 11–13 for more on this topic.

their legal right to inhabit a person by dedications of children to spirits or gods, or by being inherited from parents who have been dedicated or have become demonized in some other way. Dedication to gods or spirits is a common practice in most of the world. *Occult* spirits gain their rights through a person's own commitment to an occult organization or religion (e.g., Buddhism, Freemasonry, Scientology). *Ordinary* spirits are those assigned to reinforce emotional problems such as hatred, fear, shame, guilt and anger. Note that we are not saying these emotional problems in and of themselves are demonic. They are not. But if a person wallows in such attitudes, demons gain a legal right to enter the person and to reinforce the human problem.

The term "cosmic-level" spirits comes directly from Ephesians 6:12: "We are not fighting against human beings but against the wicked spiritual forces in the heavenly world, the rulers, authorities, and *cosmic* powers of this dark age" (emphasis added). The subject of cosmic-level spirits is more controversial. From scriptural statements such as Ephesians 6:12 and Daniel 10:13, 20, plus Israel's belief in territorial spirits, plus experiences of apparently effective intercession, we theorize that there is a hierarchy of "spiritual powers in space" (Ephesians 2:2). Many theologians support all or part of this understanding (e.g., Arnold, 1992).

My own tentative analysis defines five categories of cosmic-level spirits. The way I list them is not to suggest a hierarchical ordering or differing levels of power, since I believe their power depends on the amount and kind of human allegiance they receive.

1. **Territorial spirits.** Like the "angel prince of the kingdom of Persia" (Daniel 10:13), these have responsibility to influence the people in nations, cities and other territories.
2. **Institutional and religion spirits.** Most of these influence non-Christian religions and occult organizations, while some in this category are assigned to influence Christian organizations.

3. Vice spirits. These are in charge of vices such as pornography, prostitution, gambling, homosexuality, abortion and the like.

4. Household, geographical and cultural item spirits. These are assigned to specific places and objects such as homes, rocks, trees, mountains, bodies of water and dedicated cultural items such as artifacts and music.

5. Ancestral spirits. These are assigned to deceive people into believing their ancestors are still functioning in human contexts.

What to do about cosmic-level spirits occasions much controversy. This controversy centers on the fact that little or no scriptural evidence seems to justify direct confrontation with such spirits. Yet many in the spiritual warfare movement are involved in various approaches to direct confrontation through the use of such techniques as intercession, developing unity among spiritual leaders, "prayer-walking," "spiritual mapping," "identificational repentance" and even shouting at Satan.

Though sometimes the claims for this kind of activity seem exaggerated and some of its advocates seem to be genuinely "lunatic fringe" in their behavior, some positive things can be said about the movement. For one, a lot of very positive things are going on in Argentina, Guatemala, even in the United States and elsewhere that seem to be associated with this approach (see Otis, 1999b, 2001). Second, the basic value of the approach, whether recognized by its adherents or not, seems to be in what is done at ground level, rather than through any direct challenges to enemy spirits.

The point is that when Christians engage in such ground-level activities as human repentance, righteousness, intercessory prayer and unity of spiritual leadership, the power of the "cosmic-level rats" is lessened and such activities as evangelism are greatly enhanced. A key verse is 2 Chronicles 7:14: "[If] My people who are called by My name humble themselves and pray and seek My face and turn from their wicked ways, then I will hear from heaven, will forgive their sin and will heal their land" (NASB). When these scripturally supported practices are done, cosmic-level warfare seems to be successful. I would suggest that the principle here is the same as for ground-level warfare: Deal with the garbage and the rats have no power.

10. Regularities, rules and principles in the relationships between the human world and the spirit world exist and can be studied scientifically.

Some do not believe we can approach the spiritual realm scientifically, but I firmly believe we can. The research tools we have learned to use in the behavioral sciences also can be used to discover regularities in the interactions between the human and spiritual realms. We cannot expect the kind of certainty, of course, that we are supposed to have in the physical ("hard") sciences. But we have learned a lot in psychology, anthropology, sociology and each of the other behavioral sciences through discovering *correlations* that may indicate causalities (though we try to be cautious in claiming causality).

Such methodology can be just as applicable to the results of spiritual interventions as to psychological interventions. And if it is applied, I predict that we will discover some ways to enhance our psychological practices and to round out our theological thinking. It is obvious to me that our approach has something to teach psychologists and theologians as well as missionaries. We have worked with a lot of people, for example, who have not found spiritual or emotional healing in either psychological counseling or theological reflection but who are now free through inner healing. Science requires experimentation. We have the opportunity to do such experimentation in our evangelical training institutions.

In addition, traditional evangelical theologizing that largely ignores teaching about spiritual warfare and discipling our students in how to challenge the evil kingdom is not adequately preparing our students for the spiritual realities they must face both in this country and abroad. While we carry on intellectual discussions concerning whether demonic influence is real, our enemy has a heyday both in the world at large and in our churches. Where is the serious scientific experimentation and learning in this area that evangelical institutions are uniquely equipped to do? We will discuss this topic further in chapter 6.

Conclusion: A Modest Proposal

Given the place of spiritual warfare in Scripture and in the ministry of Jesus and the apostles, I suggest that we Christian academics back up our claim to be committed to Jesus and the Scriptures by properly emphasizing this area as well. I am not suggesting that we neglect the other important areas, but I believe Hayford is right in his contention that those who do not deal theoretically and practically with spiritual warfare are the ones who need to defend their position. Can we defend our position in the light of Scripture and Jesus' example? And are we mature enough to be able to incorporate into our curriculum courses and emphases that have not traditionally been part of mainline evangelicalism so that we can be more scriptural than we have been in the past?

Do we teach on this topic in our evangelical theological institutions? Does anyone in these schools help prepare prospective pastors and teachers to get involved in a balanced way in spiritual warfare? Or will we continue to be captured by Enlightenment and academic refusal to take this area of spiritual reality seriously? If those who go out from our training institutions never learn to handle the issues arising from this part of spiritual reality, can we expect them to be fully biblical in their ministries?

And given the effectiveness of inner healing approaches to counseling, should we not be doing something to teach the use of prayer power in our evangelical counseling programs? Clients tell me they get more healing in an hour or two of deep-level prayer ministry than they have in years of traditional counseling, even if the counselors are Christian. Yet those who teach professional counseling, even those in Christian institutions, seldom come to find out what we are doing right.

Learning to address counseling issues and demonization with the power of prayer needs to be central to counselor training if our graduates are to be more than simply secular counselors who happen to have a Christian commitment. Why are we not leading a more effective approach to emotional healing, rather than simply imitating secular approaches that counselees regularly assert are much less effective than prayer ministry?

I am not contending that every one of the faculty of Christian training institutions or every staff member of a church should be involved in this kind of ministry. We have different giftings. But someone(s) in each Christian institution should be. For in light of our commitment to Scripture, a glaring discrepancy exists between our lack of emphasis on spiritual warfare and the importance given to this subject in Scripture. The fact that we do not deal with this area in our training institutions likely contributes significantly to nominalism in churches served by our graduates. The fact that evangelical pastors do not know how to handle satanic interference in their churches means that the enemy gets away with a lot in church life without anyone knowing what to do about it.

If it were researched, I suspect that the level of healing brought about by graduates of our Christian counseling programs is usually not much different from that of non-Christian counselors. Both Christian and non-Christian counselors try to deal with deep-level problems that can be healed only by the power of God. Christians have an important advantage since we have available to us the power of the Holy Spirit. All counselors also have to deal, whether they know it or not, with problems created by demonization. Christian counselors should be taught what they are dealing with and how to bring their clients freedom—the freedom that Jesus offers.

I have attempted in this chapter to provide a brief outline of discussion points that I hope will serve both to stimulate dialogue and to provide a bit more understanding of the perspectives of spiritual warfare proponents. Each of the ten topics is discussed further in the following chapters and also in the books listed in the Bibliography.

four

The Importance of Experience

Critics of spiritual warfare are rightly concerned about its implications for the Christian community. Often they are afraid that the whole subject of spiritual warfare will alarm people. Indeed, many of our critics seem to prefer that evangelicals remain ignorant of what our enemy is doing in the false hope that if we do not focus on his activity, it will not affect us. In this chapter I respond to several of the points raised by Priest, Campbell and Mullen (1995) that exemplify concerns felt more widely by our critics.

Overcoming Rationalism

Typically our critics contend that they are not rationalistic. But they convey Western rationalistic bias every time they try to deal with spiritual power. They claim they are biblical, not rationalists. But given the way they treat this subject and in view of their propensity for consistently denying supernaturalistic explanations of our experiences or of biblical passages, that claim has a hollow ring.

Such critics work from below the glass ceiling, having had little or no experience with what the Holy Spirit does today. Priest and his associates even refer to words of knowledge as "Geiger counters"! Spiritual discernment seems outside their experience. And the fact that they cannot distinguish between animism and Christian authority raises the suspicion that their claim to have moved beyond Enlightenment thinking is bogus as well. They allow for supernaturalism in theory but apparently not in practice. That clearly sounds like a variety of Enlightenment rationalism.

One place where Priest, Campbell and Mullen tip their hand in this regard is where, in order to avoid granting validity to our results, they state, "On occasion, God works supernaturally even when the method is clearly wrong" (1995:31–33). This is, of course, true, as they illustrate in the case of Moses striking the rock (Exodus 17:5–6; Numbers 20:7–13). We note in comparing these passages that on the first occasion Moses was ordered to strike the rock, but on the second the command was for him to simply speak to the rock. He disobeyed in the second instance by striking the rock. God gave them water anyway, in spite of the fact that Moses used the wrong method. But God allowed Moses success from the wrong method only once. Those of us practicing spiritual warfare have seen results that parallel those of Jesus' own ministry over and over and over again. To infer that God simply humors us by allowing positive results from "wrong methods" merely underlines the weakness of our critics' case.

Critics even contend that the supernaturalistic methods used by prominent spiritual warfare practitioners like Ed Silvoso and George Otis Jr. have nothing to do with the incredible numbers of people turning to Christ in Argentina and elsewhere. Can we not count on fruit to validate method (Matthew 7:17–18; 12:33; Luke 6:43–44; John 15:5, 8, 16)? Perhaps we should stop doing what leads to such good fruit. Or perhaps we should ask permission of these skeptics before engaging in spiritual warfare so they can advise against it, as Priest advised the Latin American Indian (1995:31f.) who believed demons were involved in his problems and who probably is still living with them.

Priest caricatures the advice we might have given, suggesting that our approach would have instilled fear rather than confidence. But should a demon really be involved, now or in the future, confidence comes from seeking God's protection. And in the example of the Latin American Indian, scheduling an exorcism or telling the man to move out of his house was not the answer, as Priest suggested. Rather, spiritual warfare could be done on the spot. With Priest's rationalistic approach, however, the man did not learn how to call on the power of God. Thus it is very likely that either the Latin American Indian or someone else in his group later did something in secret, related to their traditional spirits, that satisfied their traditional cultural conceptions of the spirit world, but also pushed them more toward animistic practices and gave evil spirits more power over them. Priest missed a golden opportunity to work *within* their categories—whether or not these corresponded with reality—to assist that group in learning to employ the power of God. Whether or not there actually was a demon is, in this instance, really beside the point.

While teaching on these subjects, Priest might have mentioned that even rationalistic American Christians believe enough in the power of God to dedicate their babies and their church buildings. Pastors dedicate their sermons. Some Western Christians even pray over their homes in the belief that God honors such dedication of places. And some, conscious of the fact that Satan is constantly active in a world called his by Jesus (John 14:30), even regularly claim Jesus' protection and obey Paul's injunction to put on God's armor (Ephesians 6:13). Such Christians believe the Scriptures that indicate we are at war with unseen beings whose job is to harass and destroy us, if possible. What an opportunity was missed to work within the Indian's cultural system to teach him something biblical about spiritual power! If Priest had done so, perhaps the man would not (like most of the Christians in the non-Western world) continue to follow the traditions of his ancestors whenever a spiritual power problem arises.

I do not know, of course, that Priest's rationalistic method did not have good long-term results. I pray that it did. Maybe it worked even "for reasons other than those assumed by [the practitioner]" (1995:32). But I do know that the kind of approach Priest recommends has been a major reason for the dual allegiance problem throughout the Christian world, where people who call themselves Christians come to Jesus for certain things but appeal to their traditional gods and spirits when spiritual problems arise. Traditional missionary Christianity has taught them that there is no help within Christianity in dealing with spiritual power. So even Christians deal with spiritual issues in animistic ways, since they have not been taught to handle them biblically.

Thus critics of spiritual warfare allow for supernaturalism in theory but not in practice. Again, this is simply a newer form of Enlightenment rationalism.

Criticisms and Answers

Following are some of the charges of Priest, Campbell and Mullen, and responses to those charges.

CRITICISM: ITEMS BEARING DEMONIC POWER

The Priest article criticizes us for recognizing that material items such as dolls given as gifts to missionaries can bear demonic power. The authors point out that missionaries who dispose of such items for fear they convey evil power might find their ministries hindered because they were insensitive to the goodwill intended through the giving of the gift (1995:12). The authors also express their fear that people who believe this might experience "spiritual insecurity" (p. 14) and devote time and attention to dealing with satanic power that we say can come through curses, objects, inheritance and infected territory. Instead, they say, people should devote their "valuable energies and resources [to] productive reality-based understandings and methods" (p. 15).

I understand their fear. But what if we are right that there is an important spiritual dimension to such problems? Though they buttress their point by giving a couple of illustrations of people who in ignorance overreacted, we could give many more illustrations of people who brought about positive results from acting on our advice.

ANSWER: EXPERIENCE AND RESULTS PROVE WHAT WORKS

Recognizing the dangers of satanic infestation and employing the authority granted us by an all-powerful God works in real life. We think it is important for Christians to learn how to work in that power and authority. We work with the understanding that using the authority Jesus gave us to break enemy power in such items works, whether or not our critics like it.

Those of us involved in ministering to missionaries and others who bring back artifacts from overseas regularly are asked to advise them concerning apparently demonic occurrences in their homes. Such strange events stop when these persons take our advice to either destroy the artifacts or take authority over them in prayer and allow them to stay. One missionary, for example, brought several masks and other such traditional items back from Latin America. During the time when these items were displayed in his home, several events that seemed demonic happened there. After we prayed over the home and the items were destroyed, the strange events stopped and have not recurred for more than ten years. Is there another explanation for such a change? Or have we found through experience an aspect of truth we did not know before?

Working from experience, rather than simply from presuppositions, such as those of our critics, offers one important advantage: We can usually move beyond the fear of the unknown by dealing realistically with that unknown in the authority and power of Jesus. Our critics rightly want to avoid such fear. But ignoring the fear is not the best way to deal with it because addressing the problem takes people beyond their naturalistic assumptions. We do not, as these critics imply, simply scare people by advancing theories without showing what to do about the problems we identify.

A major flaw in the criticisms is that Priest and others cite our experiences as if we can never point to any positive results to support our approach. Not only do they critique our teaching concerning infested objects, but they criticize our approach to such things as curses, the possibility of inheritance of demons, and territorial spirits. But in each of these areas they also ignore the fact that our results are overwhelmingly positive, and they make no suggestions as to why this is true. Are we deluded in the hundreds of cases of demonization and the scores of cases involving curses and territorial spirits in which our methods work? If so, how do they explain the fact that these people were freed from something and have drawn closer to Christ in the process? Are we deluded when we engage in spiritual warfare and see New Testament–like results? If so, what is our critics' explanation of the results?

Another thing our critics miss is that ours is not a hopeless message concerning objects, cursing, inherited demons and territorial spirits. This would be something to be concerned about. Rather, our message is a hopeful one concerning the authority we have in Christ to reverse disastrous experiences or to avoid them in the first place. Our critics often give the impression that we are bent on upsetting the Christian community by propounding theories that will do just that. On the contrary, we are trying to solve problems reported from every side. Our experience proves that there is hope. Spiritual warfare works.

CRITICISM: FEAR OF DEMONIC ACTIVITY

These authors and many other evangelicals who share their perspective are afraid that people who read our materials will become fearful of demonic activity in and around them. This is a very real possibility. Fear of demons is to be expected if one's worldview is naturalistic and one's Christianity is powerless. And it would be tragic if the demonic activity we confront is not true or real, as our critics assert, or if we did not offer an answer to that fear: the power of Jesus Christ. Our experience, however, is that far from becoming unbalanced by our approach to ministry, most of the people to whom we minister find answers to problems they have already been facing. They become free of those problems by the power of a Christ who is like the Jesus of the New Testament, rather than like the powerless One they knew before.

ANSWER: FEAR IS NOT A REASON TO IGNORE TRUTH

It is an unfortunate fact of modern life that books published and lectures given are often only partially digested. For this reason some go off on tangents—just as people did in response to Jesus, Paul, the Bible and any other new information that was spread widely. As Christians we believe we should let the world know the message of salvation—a message that involves the bad news of sin, death and hell. And many misinterpret what we proclaim. Is this sufficient reason to disobey Jesus by refusing to proclaim the Christian message? Of course not. Neither are we deterred from working with Jesus to set the captives free (Luke 4:18–19) by the fact that some people misinterpret, even become fearful, because they have not properly understood the spiritual realm.

As I have written elsewhere (1992:104ff.), it looks as though the enemy's first line of defense is ignorance. And if he cannot keep us ignorant, he tries to get us to fear. Our critics seem to feel we should not teach and write about the subjects they do not like because it might be upsetting to the Christian community. But they do not face—as I do almost daily—people who are struggling in evangelical ignorance to overcome attacks of the enemy coming from each of the areas these critics attack. If they did, they would have to pray hard for the Lord's leading and try some experiments that seem "off the wall" (e.g., that Christians can be demonized and that we can obtain valuable information from demons). In actual experience we see a lot change when we work on the basis of the theories our critics attack. For it is a fact that in the real world, it is how theories prove out in practice, not simply how reasonable alternate theories sound, that carries the day. And we have a mountain of data and experience to support our claims. This is a surer way to "productive reality-based understandings" (1995:15) than their method of picking apart other unfamiliar methods simply because they do not trust the people performing them.

We will continue to be practitioners. We will continue to fight ignorance and seek truth, both through experience and criticism—always, with our critics, holding ourselves accountable to God. As we do this, we will endeavor to teach and write enough to help others through the ignorance and fear barriers, in situations of satanic influence, to the victories that come through the application of God's power and love.

CRITICISM: EXPERIENCE IS UNTRUSTWORTHY

Many of our critics take a standard evangelical position with regard to the untrustworthiness of experience. As I pointed out in the first two chapters, they make a serious mistake by assuming that what we call "experience" is simply feeling. That stance is based on the myth that it is possible to interpret Scripture in some objective way without reference to one's own life situation and experience. This is impossible unless one simply accepts the interpretations of other people based on their experiences.

ANSWER: ALL INTERPRETATION IS CLOSELY TIED TO EXPERIENCE

All interpretation, whether of Scripture or life, is closely tied to experience or lack of experience. The experiences recorded in Scripture are endorsed by God as conveying His truth and are to be regarded, therefore, as authoritative, though not exhaustive. But the understanding we derive from Scripture is subjective and pervasively affected by the perspectives we bring to the process of interpretation—perspectives strongly influenced by experience.

There are at least three kinds of knowledge: intellectual, observational and experiential (1989:94). As Westerners we tend to understand knowledge as an intellectual thing. But the consistent emphasis of both Old and New Testaments is on knowledge based on and validated through experience (see Kittel on *ginosko*). Experience is the measure of knowledge, whether the focus is knowing God in a redemptive relationship, knowing the truth (John 8:32) or knowing what is involved in spiritual warfare.

CRITICISM: "PRIVILEGING THE WEAKER ONES"

Priest and his associates accuse us of favoring the understanding of "the weaker brothers" by "helping to plant such 'weaker brothers' meanings in a mind that did not formerly think in those terms" (1995:33). The critics are afraid we are raising issues for all Christians that are really based on the irrational fears of weaker Christians. This is a difficult accusation with which to deal, for at least two reasons.

First, the accusation flows from the assumption that there is never a problem with things such as foods that have been dedicated to evil spirits. They assume that only "weaker brothers" who do not understand reality would consider such dedication to be dangerous. And since we consider such dedication dangerous, our critics contend that we are foisting on all our readers the fears of a few who really do not understand. According to these critics, therefore, we are siding with the wrong side. In support of their position, they point to 1 Corinthians 8:7–8, in which Paul gives no indication that eating food offered to idols is dangerous. In fact, he states the problem as follows:

> Some people have been so used to idols that to this day when they eat such food they still think of it as food that belongs to an idol; their conscience is weak, and they feel they are defiled by the food. Food, however, will not improve our relation with God; we shall not lose anything if we do not eat, nor shall we gain anything if we do eat.

Our critics contend that in these verses Paul is teaching that food dedicated to idols is not dangerous since the idols are nothing. The problem our critics fail to see in their position is that many other Scriptures contradict their interpretation of 1 Corinthians 8:7–8. For example, 1 Corinthians 10:20–21:

> What I am saying is that what is sacrificed on pagan altars is offered to demons, not to God. And I do not want you to be part-

ners with demons. You cannot drink from the Lord's cup and
also from the cup of demons; you cannot eat at the Lord's table
and also at the table of demons.

It is clear from several other Scriptures as well that God con-
demns those who eat meat offered to idols (see Exodus 34:15;
Ezekiel 22:9; Revelation 2:14, 20). So comparing Scripture with
Scripture, as we need to do to interpret rightly, whatever Paul
is saying in 1 Corinthians 8:7–8, he cannot mean that we should
not take seriously the danger involved in dealing with dedicated
things. Our critics must not take one verse that seems out of
sync with the overall teaching of Scripture as the definitive
teaching on this subject.

Since the preponderance of scriptural teaching on this subject is that the dedication of objects makes those objects dangerous, we who teach this fact turn out to be on the side of
Scripture. Our critics, suffering from a lack of spiritual understanding, cannot support their contention that we are guilty of
raising fears in mature Christians by taking seriously what they
see as the unwarranted fears of immature Christians.

Second, it is difficult to respond to this accusation because
in a sense we *are* attempting to help the weaker ones who are
in difficulty because of fear of the spirit world. They may be
weaker in their Christian growth, but they know that spiritual
power resides in objects dedicated to spirits—including food—
and they respect that power. Centuries of missionary experience have demonstrated that simply denying that power, as our
critics recommend, has not worked; while helping Christians,
whether they be mature or immature, to claim the power of
Christ to protect themselves and to break the power of satanic
dedications does work. This approach is good news for all
because we teach not only that demons are to be respected but
what to do about them. We are not simply raising invalid fears
that have no basis in reality.

ANSWER: BREAKING THROUGH IGNORANCE AND FEAR

In 1 Corinthians Paul's point is that strong Christians do not
need to fear the influence of an enemy kingdom that is infi-

nitely less powerful than the Kingdom we represent. We do not, therefore, need to go around fearing the very real presence and influences of the enemy kingdom. We should recognize the demonic presence enough that we do not partner with the enemy by eating and drinking at his table (1 Corinthians 10:20–21). Nor should we, because of our security and confidence, mislead weaker Christians into putting wrong meanings on our activities and thus falling into sin by imitating us (1 Corinthians 8:9). And we should not let ourselves become fearful and disabled by our awareness of the activities of evil spirits.

Our critics seem to favor allowing weaker Christians to remain ignorant of spirit world realities. I do not believe this is better or more biblical. Nor is it wrong to risk a bit of misunderstanding in order to help the weaker ones discover spiritual authority and move into the kind of security Paul advocates. We are to be secure enough both to claim God's power for protection—whether unconsciously or consciously (i.e., through prayer, 1 Corinthians 10:30)—and to behave in such a way as to be trusted and followed by the weaker and less secure. In this way we handle effectively both the meaning and the empowerment issues. We have chosen to try to help people break through ignorance and fear of spiritual reality to find security in the area of spiritual power.

CRITICISM: USE OF ANECDOTAL EVIDENCE

Our critics are fond of pointing out that we depend on anecdotal evidence to support our claims that God is doing marvelous things in our day. Academics and other skeptics make this accusation as if it is something we should feel guilty about. Presumably what they want us to do is to provide them with enough scientific proof to melt their skepticism.

Their demand is reminiscent of that of the Pharisees in Jesus' day who claimed they would believe if He staged some miracles for them. Jesus rightly refused them, though as soon as He saw someone who needed healing, He felt compassion and used His power, as always, to demonstrate His love. Jesus did not perform for skeptics. He knew their unbelief was a matter of choice, not merely lack of opportunity. They would not believe because they chose not to believe, even though Jesus provided them with many opportunities to observe and believe.

The same is true of modern-day skeptics. Unless they choose to open themselves experientially, to go to where power demonstrations happen, they will continue in their blindness.

ANSWER: ANECDOTES EQUAL EVIDENCE

Are we anecdotal? Of course. But so is Scripture. And so are our critics, at least the few times they point to any data at all. At least we have presented data. That is what makes it possible for those who disagree with us to critique us. But they have not taken us or our data seriously enough to interact with the data that, though anecdotal, exists in abundance.

Do we base interpretations of Scripture and of contemporary events to a large extent on our experience—that is, on our understanding of the interaction between the stories (anecdotes) of the experiences recorded in Scripture and our own? Yes, of course. But so do our critics. And, as I already pointed out, our interpretations and those of our critics—whether of Scripture or of life—are thoroughly affected by experience, even in the face of our critics' frequent claim that their interpretations (but not ours) are "biblical."

As with all scientists, we look for patterns and regularities. When we have experienced a large number of the kinds of things we report (in anecdotes), we see patterns emerge. This is the data from which we work. It would be helpful if we could point to controlled experiments to further validate our work. But we are not yet at that point. I am more optimistic than the critics, however, about the possibility of conducting such experiments in ways similar to behavioral science research. Indeed, as I write we are engaged in such research at Fuller. And this research is already pointing to probabilities, if not yet allowing us to come to precise conclusions. But in the meantime, we describe occurrences in ways similar to how Scripture describes them.

Those of us who have been criticized can point to a mountain of data. Our critics seldom have any, since they work mainly from theory. If they have data, it would be helpful if they would suggest alternate theories and approaches based on that data. The few stories they record, usually of aberrations, are seldom helpful even in supporting their points. In addition, they need to deal with our data. They cannot simply sweep it under the rug—as they have done—because they do not happen to believe that God would fill teeth (Priest, 1995:25) or lengthen legs (footnote 23) or empower objects (1995:6) or work more on one side of a geographical border than the other (1995:28).

Pragmatism may have its flaws, but when all you have to combat it is theory based on skepticism without experience, pragmatism based on experience wins hands down. It may "not seem overly impressive" (footnote 23) for a leg to be lengthened, unless it happens to be your leg, and you no longer have a back problem because God did something. And skepticism regarding whether our God would do such a strange thing as filling teeth is no match for the many reports of such miracles that are there for our critics to check out. Nor can the facts simply be dismissed concerning the great increase of church growth following major prayer initiatives in Argentina; Colombia; Hemet, California; Almolonga, Guatemala; and many other places (see Otis, 1999b).

Can our critics explain the phenomena we describe and the results in a better way? If so, let them do it so we can all learn from their valuable perspective and insights. Given that our critics generally provide no data in any of the areas they criticize, and advance no alternative analyses of our data, it is hard to take them seriously. It is clear that they critique us from a base of little or no experience and, therefore, of little or no knowledge. Simply taking potshots from behind some façade of experience-poor, theoretical understanding of Scripture is not helpful in defining truth. Remember that John 8:32 refers to experiential knowledge, not mere theoretical knowledge, as that which undergirds the truth that sets us free. "You will *experience* the truth and the truth will set you free" would capture the original Greek emphasis better than conventional translations.

With full understanding that experience can be misinterpreted, we look to quantity of experience and consistency of results to bring a measure of protection. When we find that a technique works consistently, the experience enables us to develop a theory based on an interpretation that provides guidelines for the next time we encounter a similar situation.

Having established that, I would like to apologize for the times when someone on our side of the fence relayed a story that turned out to be exaggerated or even untrue. Priest, Campbell and Mullen cite a couple of these and unfairly imply that all our stories are inaccurate. It is not a Christian attitude that prompts these critics to cite only one or two inaccurate stories and to castigate our whole movement on that basis. Nor is it proper to critique our whole movement on the basis of a misinterpretation of the data by one observer, as they have done in the case of Kenneth McAll's analysis of the Bermuda Triangle (McAll, 1991). With a little research Priest could have found out two important pieces of information: (1) that we believe the problems in the Bermuda Triangle were caused by the demons of the slaves who died there, not by their human spirits that had not gone to their eternal resting place (as McAll states); and (2) that whether or not McAll's analysis is correct, no unexplained problems have occurred in that area, to my knowledge, since McAll organized his prayer initiative in 1977 to correct the spiritual problem.

CRITICISM: ASSUMING ANIMISTS RIGHTLY UNDERSTAND SPIRIT REALITY

One of the accusations leveled at us by Priest and his coauthors is that we naïvely "assume that the beliefs about spirit realities held by practitioners of occult and animist/folk religions correspond to reality" (1995:21ff.). This is a serious accusation and we take it seriously. But since these authors and others who join in this accusation have had no experience, one wonders how they would know whether or not their accusation has any validity. Since they have never worked with spirit reality, they have nothing in their experience with which to compare animist understandings.

Answer: We Can Learn from Animists

Nevertheless I can state categorically that none of us assumes that animistic views of reality correspond exactly with God's Reality (what I call "capital *R*-Reality") without testing it. Nor does any one of us assume that the principles we are discovering are the result of satanic revelation (another of their accusations). When things that animists believe or that demons say prove out, however, we take them seriously on the assumption that God is able to reveal things even through enemy agents. God certainly reveals lots of things through non-Christian humans in areas such as medicine, the physical sciences, the behavioral and social sciences and even in biblical studies, when these people are working in areas of their own expertise. Why would God not reveal things through non-Christians (animists) and even demons in spiritual areas? But, of course, we must be careful.

These authors believe that God's principles for the spirit world do not apply in such a way that animists could discover any of them. In fact, they imply, animists are so ignorant that we cannot trust anything they say or believe. Apparently, contrary to our experience in every other sector of life (e.g., science), critics believe that truth in this area comes only from interpretations of Scripture and the spirit world developed by (Western) Christians. Though Priest, Campbell and Mullen are right that beliefs reflect cultural perception, they assume that those of animists cannot possibly correspond with reality. Animists, they assume (without any hands-on experience), are so blinded by sin and darkness that we cannot even look to them for clues concerning spirit world realities. The culturally conditioned perceptions of the authors, however, are assumed to correspond with God's Reality because—they assume—those perceptions correspond with what is taught in the Bible. In addition they assume that biblical peoples who assumed territoriality of evil spirits are wrong and, therefore, not to be taken seriously simply because the Scriptures teach that God is over all (1995:24).

I, and those on my side of these issues, assume that God is indeed over all, but that there is a sphere of influence allowed by God to Satan and his spirit kingdom. Like everything else in the universe, then, Satan's kingdom works according to principles that God Himself has laid down. And many of these principles can be discovered by us or by others. Those of us who have interacted with non-Western peoples with respect to disease and medicine have discovered that animistic peoples have learned some important things about these areas of life. I assume, therefore, that they have also been able to discover some important things about the spirit world and its operations. Not that we can accept their (or our) understandings of the spirit world uncritically. But simply to dismiss those understandings, as Priest and his colleagues have, as totally within the area of cultural perception that does not correspond in any way with God's Reality, is going too far.

Intelligent people in animistic societies have for generations worked with and studied spiritual power. And, like non-Christian—even demonized—scientists in Western societies, they are able to discover important truths, even though they then use them in wrong ways to serve the wrong king. *The problem is not in what animists or other occult peoples understand but in how they use that knowledge.*

So, we believe in going beyond the overt statements of Scripture—though not outside the bounds of Scripture—whether in dealing with the material and human worlds or in dealing with the spirit world. We also believe in experimenting with the insights of others—such as animists, those in Scripture who did not obey God and even (though carefully) demons—in our quest to discover more of what the Holy Spirit wants to teach us in this area.

By studying and experimenting in this area, then, far from giving ourselves to animistic beliefs, we are trying to increase the ability of the Christian community to understand a neglected portion of biblical truth. We are not turning away from the Bible, nor are we as naïve as our critics contend. We are not granting ontological reality to "folk beliefs about spirits" but to the "actual spirit realities" that all Scripture agrees "are active in the systems of worship opposed to God" (1995:24). And we believe animists, though deluded, have as much intelligence as other peoples.

The Need for a Paradigm Shift

Our critics are correct when they assert that "many missionaries have rightly come to realize the need for rethinking their poorly thought through understandings of demonic realities" (Priest, 1995:2). But they have a problem with what results from this rethinking. As they point out, this leads at least some of us to experience a paradigm shift—and, I would add, the even more influential change I call a "practice shift" (see Kraft, 1989). This paradigm shift leads to "a radical reorientation of their understandings of spirit realities and a radical rethinking of ministry strategy in the light of these perceived realities" (Priest, 1995:2).

The fact that such paradigm shifting has led to widespread sharing of the insights coming from new (to us) experiences is what concerns these critics. Instead of lauding the fact that we are writing about our experiences and opening up the subject for public discussion, our critics insinuate that we are doing something wrong. They seem disturbed that we are not conducting business as usual but are, rather, attempting to share, compare and stimulate more creative thinking within the evangelical community, like anyone seeking better ways of doing things. As twenty-first-century missiologists, we have a pretty good idea of the kinds of approaches that do not work. We are seeking approaches that do work, and we believe that such new approaches as we are advocating deserve to be tested. Mistakes will be made. They always are. But continuing to ignore the existence and effectiveness of the satanic kingdom is one mistake many of us have chosen to stop making.

As for the paradigm shift itself, these critics say, "If the paradigm shift being advocated involved an unadulterated return to biblical supernaturalism, we would applaud it. But we fear that such is not the case" (1995:2). The tone of their critique, however, indicates that they probably would not even recognize such a shift if one occurred. They seem a long way from biblical supernaturalism themselves when they misread our approaches to spiritual warfare as advocating animism. And they miss completely the differences between animism and the use of delegated authority when they fail to rejoice with us over the fact that many of those to whom we have ministered are now free, and when they call for a return to "productive reality-based understandings and methods" (1995:15). Judging from this presentation of their stance, the understandings and methods they recommend would be naturalistic rather than spiritual.

The contention that "some missiologists are promoting a prescientific and magical worldview rather than a biblical one" (1995:2–3) is an interesting one, especially since biblical worldviews are themselves prescientific. We are thus accused of advocating one prescientific worldview by those who claim to be advocating another, and with the assumption that a scientific worldview—presumably secular and naturalistic—would be better. The accusation, though a common one among academics, does not make sense and, in any event, is wide of the mark since the discussion involves different understandings of what is biblical, not whether or not we are prescientific. Our critics, in raising this issue, have grasped at the wrong straw.

In the quest to move through that glass ceiling into a better understanding of spiritual reality, we need our critics to attempt to understand what things might look like on our side of the paradigm shift. If they were to do that and then raise their issues (even the same ones) in a context of mutual trust rather than fear and mistrust, we might all get somewhere.

Instead, the critics simply claim that their understanding of what the Scriptures say and imply is better than ours. And in their contention that we are misleading our readers, they assume that they could not possibly be misleading theirs. They claim their understandings and methods are "reality-based," whereas ours are completely off-track because we are pragmatic and experience-oriented. To them results do not count. They are confident the future will prove that our results were merely temporary psychological phenomena, based on the credulity of people who attributed meaning to false understandings of reality. Such denigration of experience and results is, of course, hardly reality-based. In fact, in most areas of life, results are greatly preferred to mere theorizing.

Conclusion

In responding to those who criticize us, we must ask again, On what experience do they base their criticisms? When they speak purely from theory without benefit of experience in the areas in which they criticize us (as nearly all of them do), it is hard to take them seriously. Lack of experience turns out to be a crippling defect, especially when accompanied by worldview blindness and a distrust of those of us with experience in dealing with the spirit world.

five

Misuse of Spiritual Power

One of the reasons many evangelicals turn away from the exercise of spiritual power is the widespread appearance that such power is being misused. Some of the things done in the name of Jesus by those claiming to be working in His power are genuinely regrettable. I have talked to people from a Pentecostal background who tell me they are embarrassed at some of the things they have seen in their churches and on TV. I myself, though my association with Pentecostals has been minimal, have seen enough of such antics to hope that people do not associate me with such behavior.

I once attended a large charismatic meeting in which a prominent healing preacher was teaching. More than 25 people in wheelchairs sat in one section of the auditorium. At one point during the invitation the leader directed his attention to that group, promising that any of them who had enough faith could be healed. "Just exercise your faith and get up out of your wheelchair," he said. Several tried, but I do not remember that any made it—though from testimonies given by people who had been healed of deafness and blindness, it was clear that the Holy Spirit was working in the audience.

My problem with what that preacher did is that it was so *unloving* and, thus, so unlike the example of Christ. The preacher knew that not all those to whom he spoke would be healed. But he promised healing to all of them if only they could generate "enough" faith. Nobody knows what "enough faith" is. And those in the wheelchairs, many of whom must have tried to produce the right amount of faith, were left not only unhealed but feeling guilty that they could not generate the necessary faith. I accuse that preacher of spiritual abuse. I do not care how many people God has healed through him—and I know there have been many. He was just plain cruel to those people in wheelchairs.

We who claim to work in the gifts of the Spirit are accountable to work in the fruits of the Spirit as well. And the first fruit of the Spirit is love. There was no need for that preacher to be unloving. He could have done his job much better if he had said something loving and understanding to these and to others in the audience who were not healed. He could have said something like, "It has been our experience that in an audience like this, the Holy Spirit will choose some of you to be healed. If this happens, we will rejoice with you. But past experience has shown us that it is unlikely God will heal everyone here who has a need. I do not know why that is, but it is a fact. So I want you to know that whether you are healed or not, God loves you very much. He does not have one level of love for those He heals and another for the rest; He loves us all equally. And I do not know why He chooses some to heal and leaves others unhealed." Had he said something like this, just as many healings would have occurred, but many fewer people would have experienced the casualty of spiritual abuse.

A Power Position

When we minister to others, we are in a power position. Whether we like it or not, what we say to a person (or to many persons) to whom we minister comes with the authority of God. It is important, therefore, to watch our words and our attitudes lest we hurt the powerless one(s) we are seeking to help.

When God enlists us to work with Him to bring blessing and healing, He takes us with all of our hang-ups—and most of us have a fair number of these. Many of us, for example, have self-image problems. We may struggle internally to be comfortable in the position God has given us and may, therefore, misuse our authority to lord it over the people we are trying to lead.

I know of pastors, professors, denominational leaders and even ordinary church members who project an attitude of arrogance, as if they are the only ones who hear from God. Such people treat others as if they do not count because these others do not have the education or the gifting they have. They struggle with feelings of inferiority and seek to prove to themselves and others that they are worthy of the position they occupy. When such arrogance is combined with gifting in spiritual power, the results are especially troubling.

In Scripture God is hard on people who misuse power. Perhaps the most prominent offender in this area was King David. In the Bathsheba incident, David had power and misused it to hurt people he was supposed to help. David was, as the prophet Nathan pointed out, like the man who had many sheep but forced another man with only one sheep to turn it over to him so he could slaughter it in order to serve his guests (2 Samuel 12). God's response to David's misuse of power was to chastise and punish him severely.

In a healing ministry we must be careful not to misuse power given us by God. We must do and say everything lovingly. Whenever power is not wrapped in love, it is very dangerous. And situations that were intended to be healing can become situations in which a person is hurt even more.

The "Word-Faith" Movement

Some of those who espouse the so-called "Word-faith" or "name-it, claim-it" doctrine can be accused of misusing prestige and power. The man who spoke to those people in wheelchairs at the charismatic conference belongs to this movement. I believe he and others who make such promises are misusing the power Jesus has entrusted to them.

The message coming from many of the leaders in this group is that Jesus wants good things for all His people. This, of course, is right. But they define "good things" in a rather human, often materialistic way—riches, health, comfort and the like. They say, or imply, that the way to receive those good things is simply to exercise our faith—as if it is the faith in and of itself, rather than God, the object of faith, that brings about good. When they spread such a message, and at the same time encourage people to exercise faith by giving away "seed faith" money, they further misuse God's gifts and power.

I, too, believe Jesus wants the very best for us. But it is up to Him to define what "the very best" is. We have no right to hold Him to what *we* think is best. Surely the apostle Paul and Jesus Himself were receiving the very best from God. But they, and many others in Scripture, also had to endure trials and suffering they did not understand. Although those who were faithful to God always received blessings from Him, many—including Jesus Himself—lived in material poverty.

Word-faith people believe the main operative in healing is a person's faith. They seem to assume that what Jesus meant when He said, "Your faith has made you well" (Luke 8:48; 17:19) was that there is power in the faith itself, as if there is some magic in faith. This cannot be what He meant, since the healing power is in Jesus, not in the faith of the person. Though faith is important for people who appeal to Jesus for healing or for any other blessing, it is *faith in Jesus,* not faith in and of itself, that allows the blessing to happen. What Jesus meant by His oft-repeated phrase was that the persons who exercised their faith had placed that faith in the right Person, Jesus. He did not mean there is some mysterious power in faith in and of itself. He would not have said, "Your faith has made you well" to anyone who had placed his or her faith in someone or something other than Himself.

An especially dangerous aspect of this approach is the teaching that with Jesus' power we can "claim" anything we want and He will do it for us. If we want something, certain of the leaders of this movement lead us to believe, all we have to do is name it and claim it, and it is ours because of our faith. They quote John 14:13–14 (see also Mark 9:23; John 15:16) as if it is an absolute statement of privilege available to all believers. They do not qualify this Scripture with 1 John 5:14–15, which states that we must line up our wills with that of the Father if we are to have our requests granted. Jesus does not present Himself as some cosmic sugar daddy, anxious to do for us whatever our whims lead us to ask. Rather He challenges us to line up our wills with God's will and ask for what God wants us to have, not simply what we think we need.

I know a person who suffers from arthritis. Her hands are gnarled and she has great difficulty walking. But following the "Word-faith" teaching, she asserts, "I am healed," and continues to walk around in pain. I met another woman recently with similar-looking hands who told me she believes she is healed "in the spirit," though not yet in the flesh. These ladies believe that their faith, if it is strong enough, will bring about their healing. But they are not healed; *they are lying* about their condition. And I do not believe God is honored when we lie. I believe with all my heart that God can heal them, but to claim that the healing has already happened, with no evidence that it has, is a serious form of delusion.

One indication that Jesus is not into the more materialistic understanding of the magic of faith was His own example. Comfort and material possessions were not part of His experience, nor were they something He gave His disciples. Jesus was simply not into American materialism or into providing whatever His children decide they want at any time they decide they want it—even if what they claim is healing. We are not to try to control Him, even with a good thing like faith. We are to be subject to Him. I do not understand why He does not give healing whenever we ask for it, nor do I understand why He grants healing when He grants it. I do understand that we have the right to request healing and blessing at any time, but not to demand it or to claim it when it has not happened. And we are to be faithful to Him whether or not He grants our requests.

Blaming the Victim

A major problem of many who believe that the magic of faith makes people well is the tendency to blame the person who is not healed for the lack of healing. If, as Word-faith people believe, anyone who has enough faith will be healed, it is easy to explain the problem if a person does not receive healing. That person, they assume, lacks the right amount of faith. So if the person lacks faith, it is the person's own fault for not being healed.

What tragedies such belief brings into the Christian community! First of all, it assumes that the person leading the ministry makes no mistakes and that it could not be his or her fault that healing has not come. Such leaders assume the position of prophets—those who know the mind of God. They then presume to speak for God concerning the lack of success, though it is unlikely that they really know what the reason is.

Second, even if the person praying has implied no such thing, the assumption that faith is magic leads many of those receiving prayer who are not healed to conclude that the fault is theirs. People have said to me, "I just don't know what's wrong with me. I feel I have enough faith to be healed, but it just doesn't happen." They feel the guilt and blame themselves.

When such people confess such an understanding to me, I try to help them see the error of the teaching they have received. I emphasize the importance of saying, "I don't know" when we don't know. The truth is more complicated than this facile understanding of the problem. None of us knows why God does not heal when He does not, or why He does when He does. We cannot know whether the reason was lack of faith on the part of the person receiving prayer or lack of faith on the part of the person praying, or some other reason.

So when those praying for persons to be healed assert their power, either directly or indirectly, to blame the person for whom they pray, they are abusing the person. They level that blame, when the fact is they do not really know what the reason is. This is a convenient way in which ministry leaders release themselves, whether consciously or unconsciously, from any blame for lack of success. But it is incredibly unkind and unloving toward the person being prayed for. Such behavior on the part of those working in spiritual power constitutes the worst kind of spiritual abuse. It is a blatant misuse of power by those who are in positions of power at the expense of those who are hurting.

The Insecurity Problem

Many of us are insecure. Often we can point to family, personal or cultural reasons for our insecurity. We can also point to satanic beings assigned to keep us off balance. Whatever the reasons, our insecurity is a problem, especially for those who work with us.

Combine insecurity with spiritual power and the problems are compounded. Because of our fears of inadequacy, we may try to promote ourselves at the expense of others. We become more competitive and, therefore, more intent on looking for ways to assert ourselves and to put others down.

The discovery of gifting and the concomitant ability to work in the power of God provide powerful temptations for insecure people to mistreat those to whom they minister. Many gifted people give the impression that their gifts are rewards for their faithfulness to God, and they seem to lord it over those who do not have those particular gifts. They treat their gifting as something they have attained and that they can, therefore, parade before others and brag about. Spiritual gifting, however, is not something one attains, nor is it a reward for faithfulness. Spiritual gifts are the gracious, free offerings of a loving God and are to be used in partnership with Him for purposes He chooses—just as Jesus used His gifts. These gifts do not belong to us. They are loaned to us to be used for God. We are stewards of these gifts, not owners of them. We have no permission to brag about them, therefore, or to think we are somehow better than others who do not manifest these gifts. We are at best what Jesus called "worthless slaves" (Luke 17:10, NRSV) or, in the Good News Translation, "ordinary servants."

Insecurity can persist even after a person has "made it." Well after I became secure in my position as a professor, a student who had come to know me well pointed out to me that I put people down when I answered their questions in class. Though at first I disputed her observation, I watched myself and found that she was right. I was taking the opportunity afforded me by student questions to parade my skill. In dealing with questions I had heard many times before, I would answer in such a way as to lead the class to see the student as not very bright. My aim was to show myself as clever, but at the students' expense.

I have worked hard over the years to overcome that problem in class, and am glad I made considerable progress before learning about and beginning to operate in spiritual power. But I now find a similar problem rearing its ugly head in myself and others on my ministry team. It is easy, given our own insecurities, to develop a competitive attitude toward ministries similar to ours, especially if we feel that people receive more help through our ministry than from theirs. But the fact is, those people are trying their best to fulfill what God has called them to do, even though they may do things differently than we do. And God needs as many groups as possible to be involved in deep healing ministries, since the job is much greater than all of us can do. Our insecurity becomes most obvious when people ask our opinion of these ministries. The temptation is for us to focus on what we feel are their deficiencies rather than on the many strengths embodied in these ministries.

Legalism

A major problem of many Christian leaders is legalism—the attempt to make and keep people spiritual by making rules and regulations they must keep. In the book of Galatians Paul addresses this problem among Jewish Christians who continued to follow the practice of focusing on Jewish law. Through

Abraham God met the Jews in grace and made an agreement—a covenant—with them to be their God and they to be His people. The whole arrangement was to be a close relationship between God and His people. The rules He provided were to support the grace-based relationship, not to become the focal point of it. But the Jews turned from the spirit of the relationship to the rules—the law.

In Galatians 3 Paul chastises the Jewish Christians for falling into the same heresy. He calls them "foolish" (verse 3) and asks if they, having begun their relationship in the power of the Holy Spirit, want to continue that relationship in their own power. He then points to God's relationship with Abraham as the model, saying that it was Abraham's faith, not his adherence to rules, that made him acceptable to God. Paul states that "the real descendents of Abraham are the people who have faith," not the ones who adhere carefully to the rules (verse 7). Indeed, he states, "Those who depend on obeying the Law live under a curse" (verse 10).

In spite of this teaching, many pastors today set forth legalistic guidelines for their people. I have heard of pastors who relate physical sickness to a person's neglecting to pay tithes or have daily devotions. In some congregations it is implied that one cannot expect God's blessing if one dares to think or act outside church rules. I remember many discussions in our church when I was a young Christian concerning whether God could bless or even accept persons who smoked, drank or attended movies. The doctrine taught in many churches that one is filled with the Holy Spirit only if he or she speaks in tongues produces a legalistic basis for dividing people into first- and second-class members.

Many are indoctrinated into theological thinking and denominational practices that, if not followed, carry sanctions purported to be enforced by God. I know of churches that teach that God accepts only one form of baptism, only one translation of the Bible or only one interpretation of what the Bible teaches concerning what will happen in the last days. Their understanding of baptism, of prayer, of the Bible (even the necessity of using a certain version of the Bible), of the efficacy

of certain words and rituals may even border on magical thinking—that if we do and say certain things in certain prescribed
ways, God is obligated to bless us. If we do not do and say those
things properly, then we cannot expect them to convey God's
power and blessing.

Combine such legalistic thinking and practice with spiritual
power, and the results can be brutal. When an ill person is given
the impression that he or she cannot expect God's favor unless
certain arbitrary rules are followed, scriptural truths concerning God's love, grace and primary concern for motivation are
lost. And pain and self-blame are added to the lives of people
who are already hurting.

Unfortunately even pastors who know better often give the
impression that obeying the rules gives us favor with God.
Though some do not intend to give this impression, others are
rules-oriented themselves and, therefore, purposefully load
their hearers down with similar burdens. This was the exact
focus of Jesus' criticism of the Pharisees who failed to see that
relationship, not rules, determines our position with God and
our service for Him.

Perhaps a major part of this problem, as with many other
problems, is the fact that we usually perceive and present Christian messages in intellectual and legal terms rather than relationally. If, for example, sin is viewed primarily as the breaking of a law rather than as being unfaithful to a relationship, it
is normal for people to conclude that obeying rules is what God
wants most. So we are given the impression that attending
church, giving tithes, having daily devotions, spending time in
Scripture and doing good things for other people will bring
blessing to us because these are the rules of our religion. These
are considered to be good things in and of themselves, we are
taught, whether or not we really meet God in any of them. And
when we are told that God wants obedience, not sacrifice
(Psalm 40:6–8), our minds focus on these rules.

But obedience, commitment and service are meant to be relational. Whatever rules are attached develop from relationship
between the persons involved; they are not imposed by an organization or its leaders. In true Christianity rules are always to

serve relationship, not themselves to be the focus. When our Christian faith is reduced to a religion, it becomes rule-governed. *But our faith was never intended to become mere religion.* Jesus came to bring life, abundant life (John 10:10), not religion. He demonstrated relating to a God who is on our side, not obeying rules about things that are supposed to make a reluctant God more favorable toward us. Unlike the religions of the world, true Christianity is not about gaining favor with God by doing things. True Christianity is about walking with a divine Friend who starts by accepting us and then invites us to cultivate and develop our part of that friendship in relational—not legalistic—ways.

When the personal or spiritual power of Christian leadership is misused as a way of enforcing legalistic belief and behavior, people are brought into captivity by the very ones who are charged by God to set captives free. This is spiritual abuse.

Prophecy

I believe God still gives genuine prophetic gifting. Prophet Cindy Jacobs, however, calls some prophecy "flaky" (1995). Some even conduct seminars to teach others to prophesy. Could this be a flaky practice? Does God want everyone to prophesy?

Genuine prophets do give genuine prophecies today, but the prophecy movement gives ample opportunity for abuse. People are frequently told things that do not come true. When people receive a false prophecy and trust that it is a word from the Lord, great disappointment and confusion follow. On several occasions I have run into people who were very sick with long-term problems and received false prophecies that they would soon be well. Though the prophecies did not come true, they probably came from well-meaning people who intended to encourage the persons with what they thought were messages from God. The results, however, were just the opposite—great discouragement when the prophecies turned out to be off track.

In one such situation a prophecy was given that a severely ill person would be healed if her whole church gave itself to prayer and fasting for several weeks. But it did not work. The disappointment and puzzlement were great. On at least two occasions I have prayed for people who received such prophecies. They died. Most likely those who gave the prophecies were not hearing from God. Their prophecies, though undoubtedly well intended, were probably mere wishful thinking or even attempts to read God's mind or to coerce Him into obeying human desires.

Unfortunately the occurrence of inaccurate prophecies is so frequent that it makes one suspicious of the whole prophecy movement. And the emotional damage to those whose expectations are raised and then dashed is so great that one is tempted to actively oppose the activity. I myself have received prophecies from flaky prophets and easily discounted them. I also remember a prophecy I received a few years ago from a person I very much respect as a genuine prophet. But so far none of it has come to pass. I am puzzled myself.

On one occasion, however, I received a word of knowledge that was similar to a prophecy, and I knew immediately it was right on target. On many occasions I have received such insight myself in ministry. So I am a firm believer in the fact that God does give direct revelations to people today. One thing I have learned, however, is to present such insights in as loving a way as possible—not saying categorically, "This is what the Lord says," but rather suggesting gently, "I am getting an impression that . . ." or asking, "Is _____ a problem you face?" Presenting words from the Lord in such a way frees the person receiving it either to agree or deny what is said without embarrassment. It also saves embarrassment on the part of the person giving the word if the word happens to be wrong. I am very glad my mentor, John Wimber, taught me this before I made any serious mistakes. On one occasion early in my healing ministry, just as I was about to pray for a woman, a clear thought came to me that I was sure was a word of knowledge. It was, "She is having a problem with her grandchildren." Fortunately, instead of stating it as the thought had come to me, I asked her, "Are you a grandmother?" She said, "No," and I learned a lesson.

I like to apply what I call "the Rule of Three" to prophecies. I first heard of this from a mission administrator who found over the years that whenever the mission acted on a single prophecy, they were often misled. And when they acted on agreeing prophecies from two independent sources, they were sometimes right and sometimes wrong. But when they followed the advice supported by three independent prophecies agreeing on the same thing, they were never wrong.

The Apostolic Movement

A fairly recent movement that has dangerous implications is the identifying of certain leaders as apostles. An apostle is one who leads leaders (such as pastors) and is accountable only to God. The New Testament landscape is dotted with those to whom God granted the gift of apostleship. If one assumes, as I do, that all the spiritual gifts are still available to the Body of Christ today, one should have no difficulty in accepting the validity of the claim that there are those in our day who have this gifting. The problems come with misuse of this (or any other) gift.

One thing I wonder about is just how certain people got to be called apostles. Were they authorized by God or by humans? If by God, how did the authorizing come about? Did God-led human beings offer some sort of confirmation of their right to call themselves apostles? And are there any checks and balances to their activities? Are they accountable in any way to others who may be just as close to God as they are? And would they be subject to any discipline if they misused their office?

Having raised these questions, I observe that lots of people are calling themselves apostles these days. And there are reports of serious abuses of that status, probably because some of these apostles fit into the insecure, controlling or legalistic categories highlighted in this chapter. As always, when such people misuse power, it is the "little people" around them who become hurt. These may be secretaries, administrators or members of a congregation. Typically the decisions that hurt such people are justified by the apostle as having come from the Lord. It is particularly sad if someone claims the right to blame the Lord for what is arguably more a human problem than a divine instruction.

Control

A problem that interweaves through all these areas is the issue of control. Christian leadership is often used, whether consciously or unconsciously, to control others. And the more spiritual power that is claimed, the greater the temptation to make use of that power to control.

Insecurity and the fear that usually accompanies it push people to seek control over situations and people, lest the insecure person find himself or herself unable to cope with what is going on. Combine insecurity with such things as pride, heady giftedness and the power of position, and the mix is lethal. Such a combination often leads to domination and manipulation by leaders who, because of their misuse of power, come under the strong influence of our enemy, Satan.

What, Then, Should We Do?

As always, we need to follow Jesus' example. Many healers and exorcists lived and operated in Jesus' day. Though many were charlatans and fakes, some of them probably worked in genuine spiritual power. When people accused Jesus of casting out demons with satanic power, He pointed to the fact that His accusers' followers also cast out demons, presumably using power they received from God (Matthew 12:27; Luke 11:19). Though some used power correctly, it is clear that Jesus was hard on those who misused it, whether that power was spiritual or temporal. Jesus especially condemned those who used their power to oppress.

Yet He risked the abuse of power by giving authority and power to the twelve disciples and then to the 72 (Luke 9–10) while He was on earth, then to hundreds more on the Day of Pentecost. He Himself did not shy away from using spiritual power among a power-oriented people, even though He was misunderstood and accused of being in league with the devil (Matthew 12:22–32).

We should take special note of the risk He took in giving power to the disciples. They had already proven that trusting them was risky. That Jesus would take such a risk by trusting them with His authority and power is surely one of the greatest acts of grace in all of history. If Jesus was willing to risk using and passing on the power of God to ordinary human beings, we should not be afraid of the risk either and should not follow the counsel of those who seek to suppress the use of God's power.

Likewise we should not turn away from the exercise of spiritual power simply because of the widespread appearance that such power is being misused. What we see in some churches and on TV should not hinder us from seeking genuine gifting in spiritual power. We should not throw out the baby with the bathwater. Although, as we discussed, some things done in the name of Jesus by those claiming to be working in His power are genuinely deplorable, many other things done in His name by those with genuine spiritual gifts bear much fruit for the Kingdom of God.

(For further insight into the problem of spiritual abuse, see Ken Blue's [1993] excellent treatment of the subject.)

six

A Science in the Spiritual Realm?

Through the ages people have speculated continually about the ways in which God relates to humans. This discussion often has centered around whether God determines events or whether we as human beings are left to our own devices. How we deal with this issue is of great importance to our discussion.

I was told about a Christian man of Dutch Calvinistic background who was diagnosed with cancer. He reported this to the members of his men's group, who said they wanted to pray for him. The man demurred, saying God would take care of him. But the men insisted and prayed over him for his healing. Several days later the man underwent another examination that revealed no cancer at all. When he reported this to his men's group, they praised God for his healing. The man, however, simply said, "I told you I didn't need you to pray for me. God is taking care of me."

This man clearly believed God has things all worked out ahead of time, that we simply play out our lives without knowing how He has planned things and with little or no say over our fate. If this is true, what is the point of praying for healing—or for anything else, for that matter?

Does God "need" us or not? Does He just do what He wants to do, or does He work according to rules?

None of us would contend that God is obligated to obey rules made by someone or something else. But do rules exist that He Himself made and according to which He runs the universe? I believe they do—rules He has made and that He obeys, at least most of the time. Some of these rules, at least, can be derived from a scientific approach to the world.

Physical scientists, through theorizing, experimentation and sharing information with each other, have identified such rules in the material world and codified them into sciences. We call them the laws of physics, chemistry, geology, etc. The law of gravity is one example. Social and behavioral scientists, using similar processes of theorizing, experimentation and comparing insights, have identified such rules in the human world. We call them principles of human behavior or the rules of psychology, sociology, anthropology, communication, etc. The aim of science, whether the physical sciences or the social and behavioral sciences, is to discover these regularities.

God has revealed very little about either physical or human regularities. He has left most of these, whether in the physical or the human realm, for humans to discover, analyze and apply. We find precious little in the Bible to help us work out scientific regularities. And often those who have interpreted the Bible without experience have stood against what turned out to be scientific fact—for example, the discovery by Galileo and others that the earth is round.

The question I raise is whether the spirit world also operates according to rules. And if so, do we get all the information we need concerning these regularities from the Bible? Or might it be that, as in these other areas, God instituted rules and principles and expects us to experiment and to discover them?

If God-made rules do govern the spirit world, we should not be surprised if those without experience have not discovered them.

Studying Spiritual Reality: A Science

Fairly recently a new development has occurred in the area of spiritual warfare. A number of us who have begun to practice in this area are also studying the phenomena. This results in a good bit more writing on the subject, new issues for discussion and helpful critiques of one another's positions and experience. The article by Priest and his coauthors is a case in point. They claim to have read the writings of myself and others (though I question how carefully they read these writings) and have critiqued our positions, supposedly on biblical grounds. Such critique is welcome, though I question the spirit in which these authors presented their perspectives and the fact that they have no relevant experience in the areas they criticize most sharply.

Even so, we traditional evangelicals who have begun working in spiritual power agree with Priest and others—such as Lowe, MacArthur and other evangelical critics—on many topics. We share a commitment to Jesus Christ, for example, and a basic belief system. These include a belief in the authority and trustworthiness of Scripture; the existence of the spirit world and its constant interaction with human beings; the inadequacy of our Western worldview to enable us to fully understand the spirit realm; the need to seek understanding in this area; and the need for those concerned to compare notes and thereby enrich each other. We also share a deep concern for adhering to biblical principles, though we often disagree on what the Bible allows in areas that are not explicitly addressed.

Another area on which we tend to agree is our basic method of dealing with our subject matter. Probably due to the influence of Western schooling, we tackle our quest in a structured, organized, rational manner, as scientists do. We look for regularities—things that can be predicted. And when we observe such regularities, we articulate principles and tentative rules that condition our expectations the next time we find similar conditions.

Among the hermeneutical, or interpretive, issues is the problem of how much we are limited to Scripture in seeking to understand our universe. Prior to Galileo's time, most Christians assumed that all God wants us to know about the universe is embodied in the Bible. Those who, like Galileo, claimed otherwise were treated harshly by the Christian establishment. Nevertheless they persevered in the conviction that humans could learn much about the physical universe through scientific study, quite apart from and beyond the small amount of information provided in Scripture. And they proved their point.

Now we laugh at the naïveté that restricted those who sought to explore, theorize, test, compare and replace old understandings with newer ones. Though we do not accept every theory that scientists advance concerning the universe, we honor the process of discovery—a process that has resulted in an incredible amount of insight into and control over the universe.

The same is true regarding the quest for understanding human beings. Again, we do not accept every theory coming from psychologists, sociologists, anthropologists, political scientists, historians, communication specialists, linguists and the like, but we do recognize the great value of many of their insights, even when they go far beyond what the Bible says about humans. Could principles and regularities in the spirit world exist, just as they do in the material and human worlds? And has God left us to discover such principles outside of Scripture? If so, could this be why one of the Holy Spirit's assignments is to lead us into further truth (John 16:13)?

I believe that all parts of the universe—the material part, the human part and the spiritual part—are governed by God according to rules and principles that He embedded in His creation. Some, but not all, of these principles are indicated in the Bible. The rest are left for us to discover. Since the time of Galileo people have learned that it is profitable to explore the material and human dimensions of the universe. Similarly we are learning to explore the regularities in the spiritual world.

Much criticism of the way we contemporary evangelicals approach spiritual warfare comes from those like Priest who assume that all truth in the spiritual area—unlike that in the physical and human areas—must be derived from Scripture. This is the attitude the medieval Church took in opposition to

Galileo and other advocates of the round-earth theory. Those who opposed Galileo assumed God had revealed everything about the physical universe. They believed, therefore, that any search for understanding based on experiment and experience was invalid. They were proven wrong. In the same way, we assume God has not revealed all there is to know in the spiritual area. So we experiment in this area and, like scientists who work in other areas, develop and test theories in order to gain greater understanding.

Two possible attitudes can be taken toward the use of Scripture. We can contend that ideas or practices are scriptural only when they are explicitly condoned or taught by Scripture—according to one's own interpretation. Or we can contend that ideas or practices may be scriptural as long as they are not condemned by Scripture. Our critics often take the first position; we take the second. We experiment and develop theories on the basis of those experiments in an attempt to go at things scientifically. And we welcome interaction even if it knocks down some of our theories. All of us would welcome attempts beyond our own to measure the effects of our ministry and spiritual warfare activities—as long as it is not done simply to knock down ideas that do not happen to fit a critic's paradigm. The scientific process involves give-and-take, the advocating and testing of positions and the questioning of them by those with a different point of view and experience.

The amount and kinds of experience separate opposing sides of this dialogue in major ways. For example, *principles derived from a study of the Scriptures without actual experience of the phenomena to which the principles refer are likely to be quite different from principles based on experience with those phenomena, even for people equally dedicated to following Scripture.* Priest, for example, is critical of the ways we deal with demons and the possibility of curses being inherited. His criticisms have little validity, though, since he has no experience either to disprove our techniques or to advocate another way of understanding such spiritual phenomena. By his own admission, he has never, even once, confronted a demon, whether the demon was invited by or inherited by a victim. Thus he has not had the experience that would qualify him to test either his or my theories. If he were to test his theories in confrontation with demons in, say, twenty-five or thirty deliverance sessions, I would be glad to discuss whatever differences might remain between us. But we are not on even footing until he discovers in practice that to be successful in confronting demons, he must do and say a lot of things not explicit in Scripture.

Experience and analysis both are required in order to discover which regularities and principles apply to the various aspects of spiritual warfare. Prior to the current upsurge of writing and discussion on this topic, there have been many practitioners but few analysts. Now we see both, but some of the analysts suffer from lack of experience. They are still on the other side of the glass ceiling, not having moved through the paradigm and practice shifts necessary to understand the experiential side. They can, through a study of Scripture, see some of the things on the other side of the glass, but their view is vague, partial and distorted by such things as a Western worldview that doubts or denies supernatural beings and powers. Only through valuable discussion between Scripture-oriented Christians with personal experience in spiritual warfare can the scientific process truly take place in the spiritual area. Valuable discussion can take place, however, between those who, though Scripture-oriented, also have personal experience in spiritual warfare, thus enabling the scientific process to take place in the spiritual area.

Up to now, those of us from traditional evangelical, noncharismatic backgrounds generally have not dealt with the kinds of issues before us. Personally I tended to ignore them, as did my seminary professor who allowed my systematic theology course to end before we got to the section in the textbook that dealt with Satan and demons. Those from Pentecostal and charismatic backgrounds often function in this area but without a major concern for comparing notes in a systematic way or analyzing the broader issues involved. But a new day has dawned. For one thing, some of us noncharismatic evangelicals with as strong a biblical orientation as Pentecostals and charismatics but with behavioral science training and orientation have entered the arena. And some of us have garnered considerable hands-on experience in addition to our propensity for analysis. In addition, an increasing number from Pentecostal and charismatic backgrounds are developing an interest in analyzing and comparing notes.

These factors, plus the increasing openness of both sides to each other's perspectives, put us in a better position than ever before to develop the kind of dialogue that could produce a science in the spiritual area that parallels the existing physical and human sciences. If we recognize, as I think we must, a third area of reality—the spirit realm—parallel to the reality of the material and human realms, then we can also expect to find a large number of regularities within that realm. These regularities can be studied to produce insight into the rules—"laws"—by which the spirit realm operates. The process through which we discover these rules, and the subsequent results of that process, will someday constitute a much more complete science of the spirit realm. But at this point we who seek to understand the spiritual aspect of reality are probably several hundred years behind those who study the material world.

If we are to make progress in working together to develop such a science, we need to monitor our attitudes toward one another. The first and most important requirement is *trust*. We need to trust each other even to the extent of trusting the validity of each other's experiences and analyses. Whether or not we ever come to agreement, we should listen to each other in an attitude of trust and openness to learn. An adversarial position, motivated by distrust and fear, cripples any discussion from the start.

Discovering Spirit World Principles

The worldview of theologians and Bible scholars produces special problems. Academic disciplines embody their own worldviews. In addition to the basic assumptions of the Western worldview held by all Western academics, each set of academic disciplines holds specific assumptions. And disciplinary groupings retain certain major differences.

A major distinction exists, for example, between the world-view assumptions lying behind the physical sciences (e.g., physics, chemistry, biology) and those lying behind the humanities (e.g., philosophy, history). Though theory construction is important in each, the sciences focus on experimentation and replication as the primary means of proving or disproving theories. In the humanities, however, logic and reasoning are the primary techniques leading to acceptance or rejection of theory, since philosophical conclusions in real life are seldom demonstrable. The ideas and concepts of the humanities are not amenable to the same kind of testing that chemists or physicists consider crucial in the process of discovering and applying their theories.

The kind of research conducted by those in such disciplines as philosophy and history might be labeled "thinking research." Academics in such fields do most of their work in libraries, focusing on ideas, without the necessity of proving anything in real life. The "thinking research" tradition and the worldview assumptions that lie behind it have dominated the approach of most Christian scholars in their quest for greater understanding.

Theology and biblical scholarship, working within the "thinking research" methodology of the humanities, are given to discussion and argumentation concerning ideas and concepts that often are not capable of empirical proof. Theories concerning the nature of human beings, for example, are constructed without actually testing to see if people really behave in the way the theory suggests. The same is true with theories of sin, language, revelation, spiritual power and most other aspects of Christianity.

Though some experiential testing of theological theory does happen, conservative circles maintain a widespread fear of basing any theory on experience. Experience-based insights are likely to be condemned, therefore, if they seem to fall outside specific biblical interpretation or what is for conservative Christians politically correct tradition. With respect to conversion, for example, evangelicals are warned not to trust experience and feeling (the two are often equated) over a reasoned faith based on politically correct interpretations of certain Scriptures. Though I recognize the danger of putting too much trust in experience alone, such warnings often have the effect of dismissing the usefulness of experience as even partially valid in assessing the quality of one's relationship with God.

To cite two of many possible Scriptures usually interpreted without reference to experience, we can point to 2 Corinthians 5:17 and 1 John 4:4. The usual interpretation of 2 Corinthians 5:17 is that once a person becomes a Christian, all things in his or her life become new. Experience tells us, however, that this is far from the truth. The fact is that many, even all, people find that coming to Christ does not solve all their problems, as the traditional interpretation of that verse implies. Conversion often means a lot more problems internally in emotional and spiritual areas and externally in relationships with others. First John 4:4 is often interpreted to mean that, since He who lives in us is greater than Satan, demons can never live within those who truly belong to Christ. The problem with this interpretation is that it does not stand up to experience. Those of us who work with demonized people find that we frequently have to cast demons out of Christians.

The point is that the true meaning of those verses needs to be determined by taking into account both logic and experience. They cannot be interpreted apart from the testimonies of thousands of people whose experience contradicts the wishful thinking of armchair expositors.

In place of recommending at least a balance between Scripture-based knowledge and experience, traditional evangelicals tend to focus almost entirely on knowledge. And from our Western worldview conditioning, we (and the Bible scholars we follow) understand the knowledge in focus to be theoretical knowledge—the kind of information-oriented knowledge that we learn to accumulate in school. This is contrary, however, to most biblical usage of the term *know*. In Scripture, knowledge is experience-based. When the Bible speaks of knowledge and knowing, it normally refers to knowledge gained through and confirmed by experience. As I pointed out previously, John 8:32 should be translated: "You will *experience* the truth and the truth will set you free."

Working in terms of this humanities tradition, with its focus on theoretical knowledge and disdain for experience, many of those studying the Bible and theology assume they can theorize accurately without the benefit of experiential testing. In addition, since they are dealing with sacred matters and claiming God's guidance, many assume their ideas are biblical even though untested. This is especially true with regard to spiritual power, an area in which our Western ignorance adds fear to the above hindrances to experimentation.

The fairly new factor that makes the above discussion relevant is that many of us within evangelicalism now are experimenting with spiritual power from the research methodology of science, rather than that of the humanities. We have been influenced by the behavioral sciences (e.g., psychology, sociology, anthropology) to test whatever can be tested in real life. And we believe that the operation of spiritual power can be tested.

We recognize that dealing with people—and especially dealing with spiritual reality—does not allow us to tie things down as tightly as those in the physical sciences do. We can, however, work toward correlations in the same ways in which psychologists and anthropologists do—correlations between human behavior and what appears to be activity in the spirit world. With this perspective, then, we look for regularities and principles in the interactions between the spirit world and the human world.

Spirit World Principles and Rules

In my book *Behind Enemy Lines* (1995) and in greater detail in *The Rules of Engagement* (2000), I attempted to outline several of the regularities and principles that seem to govern interactions between the spirit world and the human world. If, as I contend, a science in this area does exist, then many more such rules and principles also exist. Though dealing with all of the principles and rules would be impossible even if we knew them, I will attempt here to list some of the principles and to suggest some of the rules that spin off from these principles. For a more complete treatment, including scriptural bases for the various assertions, see *The Rules of Engagement*.

1. God built rules into the interaction between the spirit world and the human world. We observe throughout the Scriptures that when people do things on earth, they often affect what God does. On the negative side, we are told that as we live our lives on earth, we are engaged in a wrestling match with evil spirit beings (Ephesians 6:12).

2. There are two sources and dispensers of spiritual power: God and Satan. These sources of power are, however, far from equal. All power originates with God, even that used by Satan. Thus Satan can use his power only to copy, counterfeit or pervert what God has done. According to the first chapter of Job, God set certain limits within which Satan had to work. God can, however, extend those limits, as He did when He gave Satan permission to attack Job. We see in the world around us, then, that Satan has the ability to hinder God's workings. He does this through spirit beings that serve him, called demons. These beings are very active in the human sphere, as are God's spirit servants, the angels. Though Satan and the other angels (both good and evil) are below humans in the created order (see Psalm 8:5, correctly translated as in the Good News Translation), Satan gained authority over creation at the Fall (see Luke 4:6).

3. A very close relationship exists between the spiritual and human realms. If this is true, any action in the human realm has at least some repercussions in the spiritual realm. Thus any analysis of an event, if it is to be complete, must take into account both the human and the spiritual influences. God seems to have made rules that limit His activities within the human realm. The rules God set up to govern the interaction between human and spirit realms seem to be essentially the same for both the Kingdom of God and that of Satan. The choices made by humans seem to govern their relationships with God or Satan and grant power to spirit beings over the people who make these choices, and even to their property and territory. The effects of the allegiances initiated or reinforced by these choices are carried down to succeeding generations as blessings or curses. In accordance with such choices, God has limited His ability to protect us from the evil one.

4. The good news is that there are major differences between how God and Satan operate. We have already mentioned that Satan is limited to using and damaging what God created, though he can use the laws and rules God established, plus the power God allows him. Satan apparently cannot create anything from nothing, as God can, and seems to be limited in the area of creativity to that of the humans who serve him. God works with integrity, leads His people to freedom, can be trusted and offers His followers a "true self," leading them to adopt His character. Satan, on the other hand, works by deception, leads his followers into captivity, cannot be trusted, offers only a counterfeit of what God offers, including a "false self," leading his followers to adopt his character. In addition God gives His followers the Holy Spirit to live inside them. The best Satan can offer is a fallen angel—a demon.

5. Obtaining and exercising spiritual power and authority by humans flows from allegiance, relationship and obedience to whichever master they choose to serve—God or Satan. Either spirit being can invest people, places and things with power. But each has certain limits related to the cooperation each receives from his followers. God and Satan ordinarily work in the human realm through partnerships with humans (see chapter 9). These partnerships grant them legal rights in human life. Such rituals as sacrifice (especially blood sacrifice), worship and prayer seem to empower the object of the ritual. Human authority relationships are recognized and used by God and Satan. Either God's Holy Spirit, demons or both can obtain legal rights to live within humans. Either God or Satan can provide protection for followers. The amount of human support attained by either God or Satan relates directly to the ability of each to successfully attack the other. People can use a variety of methods to transmit the spiritual power delegated by either God or Satan. And people have the right to switch from one allegiance to the other.

6. Cultural forms can be subject to spirit power through dedication to either God or Satan. Words, physical objects, buildings, music, even animals can convey spiritual power and exert spiritual influence. Blessings and curses carry the power of the one under whose authority they are uttered—God or Satan—to release reward or punishment in the human realm.

7. Territories and organizations also can be subject to spirit power through legal rights given through such means as dedication by those who serve either God or Satan. Higher-level spirits (e.g., principalities and powers, Ephesians 6:12) seem to exert a "force field" influence over territories, buildings and organizations. The rules for breaking the power of higher-level satanic spirits are parallel to those for breaking the power of demons (ground-level satanic spirits) over individuals. Principalities and powers seem to wield their authority over territories as defined by humans (e.g., Daniel 10:13, 20). They also seem to be assigned to human organizations, institutions and activities. Rules must be followed either by God's people to launch attacks on satanic spirits or by Satan's people to launch attacks on God's angels that are assigned to territories and organizations.

On What Do We Base Such Conclusions?

These are some of the regularities we infer from our experience concerning the interaction between the spirit world and the human world. People often ask where we get our information. Much of it is through the scientific process of experiencing, analyzing, theory-making and testing. As with all science, though, we work from certain worldview assumptions (especially those derived from our study of the Bible) that we continually test and modify in order to arrive at tentative conclusions.

In my own case, I have worked with God to release well over fifteen hundred persons from emotional and spiritual problems using techniques ordinarily referred to as inner healing (see chapter 12). I have found and cast out demons living in well over a thousand of these persons. We sometimes refer to this kind of ministry as ground-level spiritual warfare. My own body of experience, plus at least an equal number of such experiences on the part of close ministry colleagues, provides a large amount of data to analyze and from which to theorize.

In these ministry sessions we learn a lot about how the enemy works. We learn, for example, that the key to his working lies in the obtaining and exploiting of his legal rights. We also learn that when we work in partnership with Jesus to remove those rights, people become freed. Rights are obtained by the enemy through inheritance (e.g., from ancestors who have been dedicated to enemy spirits) or when a person does such things as pledging allegiance to an occult organization or wallowing in some sin, emotional problem or unforgiveness. These rights give demons the opportunity to live inside people. When we work with Jesus and take these rights away, it is usually easy to cast out the demons.

We also learn such things as the power that can be wielded through words empowered by Jesus or by Satan; the power embodied in objects dedicated either to Satan or to God; the importance and effectiveness of blessing; and the danger of curses. We learn of Jesus' willingness to participate with us in bringing healing to past and present wounds and in bringing freedom from demonization. We learn that when we work under the power of the Holy Spirit to deal with demons, we can learn much of what we need to know from the demons themselves. Indeed, when they are under pressure by the Holy Spirit, they regularly supply even the information that enables us to break their power.

In addition, we obtain clues concerning spirit world realities from those with the closest and most intensive contact with enemy spirits: animists. As I pointed out in chapter 1, the vast majority of the world's peoples are animists. Animists interact with evil spirits regularly in their attempts to live their lives free from demonic interference. They have learned much, therefore, about how the spirit world works. Though much of what animists think they know is inaccurate, either in the way they understand it or in the ways they apply it, we can gain some insight from their perceptions into how the satanic kingdom works. Basic animism, since it embodies views and practices very close to Judeo-Christian understandings, is one of Satan's cleverest counterfeits. This is one reason the Jews fell into animism throughout the Old Testament when they neglected their relationship with the true God.

Most animists of the world know, for example, that there is a supreme God who lives above the evil spirits and is more powerful than they are. But they misanalyze what to do about this fact. They usually reason that the supreme God will be good to them, so they need pay little or no attention to Him. They also reason, on the other hand, that the way to keep the evil spirits from harming them is by sacrificing to them to appease them, rather than (as in Judeo-Christianity) obeying the God who is above these evil spirits and seeking His protection from them. They know that sacrifice and worship directed toward those spirits are effective in appeasing or empowering them. They seem to know from long experience that such worship and sacrifice enable the spirits to exercise more of their power among humans—always, of course, circumscribed by what God allows. Such acts of devotion may also quiet or appease an angry spirit, deterring it from vengeance.

Animists' belief and behavior are based on correct understanding of an important principle, and that position is logical. But it embodies a serious misunderstanding of how God intends humans to respond to the very real interference of evil spirits in human life. Nevertheless we in the West who have been blinded by a worldview that eliminates the spirit world from our perception can learn important things from a study of animism and animistic peoples. Some of these insights are embodied in the above rules and principles.

Our use of insights from our own experience and from that of animists has earned us the criticism of some armchair critics. Priest and his associates (1995) accuse us of falling into what they call "Christian animism." Since they know little of the authority and power Jesus gave us (Luke 9:1; John 14:12), they accuse us of magical thinking. Though these accusations are easily refuted, as I have attempted to do in *Spiritual Power and Missions* (1995), they represent the typical concerns of those without experience in the spiritual realm who observe that much of what God does looks similar on the surface to what Satan counterfeits. Since the rules God has set up for Himself are the same rules the enemy has to obey, the main differences lie not in the activities observable at surface level but in the sources empowering those activities.

Animists and others may observe, for example, that certain objects and places seem invested with a great deal of spiritual power. Whether these are objects or shrines dedicated to a satanic spirit or, on the Christian side, anointing oil or a building used by Christians for worship, an observer may see spiritual power manifested in many of the same ways. A major difference, however, lies in the fact that in one case the power comes from Satan, and in the other it comes from God.

At this point animists often make a mistake in the way they analyze the power and its operation. They usually conclude that the object or place *contains* the power in and of itself, and that it is necessary to perform some magical ritual precisely to activate or protect against that power. What they often fail to see is what our Bible tells us—that behind the power they observe are spirit beings. Thus, in actuality, the items or places are *conveying*, not *containing*, the power observed. As Christians we should have this straight (though many of us do not), since we can see from Scripture that spiritual power comes from either God or Satan, never from objects or places in and of themselves.

Words, anointing oil and other items that might be used only *convey* the power that either God or Satan invests in them—as did the words of Jesus, the Ark of the Covenant, spit and mud in Jesus' hands, and Paul's handkerchiefs and aprons, among other items in Scripture. Contrary to the perception of animists themselves, they do not *contain* that power. Our critics need to learn the difference between the empowerment of words and objects that God and, unfortunately, Satan give their followers the authority to convey, and the magical concept that things may possess power in and of themselves. By looking only at the superficial, surface-level similarity between the way animists use artifacts and words in magical practice, and the fact that we, like Jesus, use cultural forms to convey God's power, our critics miss a crucial distinction. *Unless our critics take note of this distinction, they will be found to be accusing Jesus Himself of magic and animism for speaking words and using material elements to convey God's power!*

seven

Three-Dimensional Christianity

The year was 1958 and I was in northern Nigeria. Meg and I were pioneering missionaries assigned to work in a tribal setting where the Church of Jesus Christ was nearly new.

The church leaders there had become acquainted with a kind of Christianity that I recognized—a Christianity centered around Sunday lectures called sermons. These sermons were listened to dutifully by those in Nigerian society who came to church. But they focused on doctrine and reason and had little carry-over into the rest of their lives.

As my experience with these people grew, I began to realize I was seeing in relief a Christianity that seemed to be less than what I read about in the Scriptures. I began to wonder if this was all that Christianity was meant to be.

The Nigerian church leaders with whom I worked wondered why we missionaries were typically so distant from them. And as I grew personally close to these leaders, I began to pride myself in the amount of time I spent with them. But they told me, even though it was more time than other missionaries spent with them, it was not enough. Though I taught that the aim of our missionary work was to incarnate Christ in their setting, they saw Jesus as much more relational than I was. If the way I portrayed Jesus was accurate, surely He would have spent more time with them if He had been there.

And they raised a second issue: Why was I, their missionary, not able to help them with what was the most important question in their minds: What do we do about evil spirits?

Theirs was a society that was pervasively relational, where interaction within the extended family was nearly a full-time occupation. To them all meaningful social activity outside the family involved drumming and the sharing of local beer. Most missionaries, however, instead of relating to the people, spent the bulk of their time administering an organization and teaching in an impersonal way in classrooms. Had they spent their time with the people, they might have found out the meaning of the drumming and beer drinking, not to mention the importance of family.

And in a society riddled with fear of evil spirits and dominated by the advice of shamans, missionaries did their best to avoid thinking or talking about this area. We had learned nothing of this dimension of Christianity. And we feared the possibility that activities in which drumming and drinking are prominent involved satanic power. So missionary Christianity condemned what we did not understand (e.g., such activities as funerals, weddings, monthly dances), then taught against such practices and later invited the people to make their own decisions with regard to them.

To fulfill their desire for social activity and to keep alive their relationships, Nigerian Christians would sneak off to dances, funerals, planting and harvest festivals, and other family and clan activities. To meet their need for power to deal with spiritual reality, they went in secret to the shamans because there was no power in missionary Christianity. The result was an anemic, nominal Christianity, disturbingly similar to what we had experienced in the States: strong on information about our faith but weak in the relational and power areas.

We treated the relational aspects of our faith as byproducts of our knowledge about our faith—just as we had learned in seminary. We worked on the totally discredited assumption that if people think straight, they will behave right. Relationships with God and others, we assumed, would grow properly at a personal and informal level if people focused on theological theory.

And when it came to spiritual power, we were clueless and even negative. We reasoned that those who experimented with such things as praying for healing and deliverance from demons "got weird."

The Nigerians with whom I worked asked me, "What do we do about evil spirits?" I did not know how to answer them. I remembered that in seminary a section of our textbook dealt with Satan and demons. But we never got to that section before the term ended.

My Nigerian experience left me with an unconscious agenda for my life: to discover what is in Christianity that I was not trained to experience. I began to seek what was lacking that could help my seminary students present a more whole Gospel than the one I took to Nigeria.

This chapter summarizes some of the results of that quest. These thoughts are not brand-new. Many other Christians have come to the same conclusions I have, at least in part. The way I put them together, however, may be new or at least thought provoking. And the conclusions have major implications for the way we practice Christianity and train our leaders to serve both at home and abroad.

The Three Dimensions of Christianity

In 1991 I published an article that focused on the need to encounter the adherents of non-Christian faiths in three areas: allegiance (or commitment), truth and power. As I have reflected on that theme over the intervening years, I have come to the conclusion that these three encounters represent three—

perhaps the only three—crucial dimensions of Christianity. Each of these dimensions has a starting point and an aim. I define the dimensions as:

1. Allegiance/commitment leading to relationship;
2. Truth/knowledge leading to understanding; and
3. Spiritual power leading to freedom.

Though for analytical purposes we can separate these dimensions, they are intended to function together, enhancing and supporting each other as they did in Jesus' ministry. Jesus, for example, while continually focusing His ministry on allegiance to God and to Himself, spent a good bit of His time and energy teaching and demonstrating truth. In addition He frequently employed His God-given power to show His and the Father's love. Though He taught truth and knowledge and frequently demonstrated God's power, He did so with growth in allegiance and relationship with Himself and God the Father as the intended aim.

Thus it is the relational dimension that is the most important of the three. Though Jesus taught truth and knowledge, His teaching method—discipleship—was relational. As I have pointed out, the knowledge and truth Jesus focused on were to be *experienced,* not simply accumulated. When He healed and freed people from demons, His aim was a relational aim: He healed to show God's love. This fact becomes clear in accounts such as that of the man born blind (John 9) and of the leper who returned to thank Jesus (Luke 17:11–19).

Thus the truth/knowledge dimension and the spiritual power dimension play supporting roles to the relationship dimension. Jesus heals people so they can relate properly, and He teaches people so they can understand what this relationship is all about. In all, the growth to maturity in the relational dimension is the defining characteristic of our Christian experience.

It is possible for us to know but not grow. Indeed, as James points out, Satan and his dark angels know and believe (James 2:19) but will not be saved. We could also be healed, experiencing Jesus' mighty power to free us from satanic bondage, but not respond to our Healer for salvation and spiritual growth. Neither truth/knowledge nor spiritual power, then, is efficacious in and of itself. Both, however, are crucial to our faith as supports for the relational dimension.

The "Knowledge-About" Problem

As one who has been a committed Christian for more than half a century and involved in theological reflection and teaching for more than thirty of those years, I have come to question a number of our emphases. Primary among these is our focus on "knowledge about" rather than on the experiencing of our faith. Both in church and in Christian college and seminary, my head was filled with information—called "truth." Much of this information was useful, at least in teaching others information about God and His works. But although I was sincere and dedicated to experiencing the reality of my relationship with God, I had to do most of that experiencing with very little assistance from either church or school.

In personal reading of the Scriptures, for example, I learned mainly to extract information ("truth") rather than listen to God. And though we were encouraged to follow the example of Jesus' ministry, no one even hinted that we could actually do what Jesus promised we would do in John 14:12: His works. I was not consciously aware that these things were problems, however, since this kind of knowledge and information orientation was the norm in the evangelicalism in which I grew up. The deficiency of which I speak only became apparent to me in the early 1980s, when I was privileged to move into profound spiritual transformation that took me to the other side of the glass ceiling.

From this vantage point I conclude that the evangelicalism in which I was brought up was a rather secular Christianity—knowledge-based and without power. As evangelicals we considered our relationship with Jesus Christ central, but cultivated it largely as a byproduct of the knowledge we were continually fed. Not that this knowledge was unimportant! It was very important, but incomplete, especially since we were taught to distrust our experience. We equated experience with emotionalism. The truth, we were taught, lay in the rational statements of belief (the propositions), not in the experience.

What I took to Nigeria as a missionary focused mostly on leading people to Christ, and from then on loading them with information that we equated with scriptural truth. There was more to our ministry than that, of course, but the theory behind it gave what I now see as an overbalanced prominence to the knowledge dimension of Christianity. In my teaching as well, both in Nigeria and in my position at Fuller Seminary, the contextualization of the theological knowledge has been my primary emphasis.

Those of us who pioneered the contextualization emphasis—the technical term for the emphasis on adapting Christianity to local cultures—had fallen into the habit of focusing almost exclusively on what I call a *knowledge-about* approach to Christianity rather than a *practicing-of* approach. We focused on contextualizing theology, not behavior, and certainly not spiritual power. We showed a major concern for truth, but truth defined theoretically and academically, rather than truth as something that is lived and that can be experienced in spiritual power.

We had been carefully trained in our Western school system to be preoccupied with knowledge. And, whether consciously or unconsciously, we continued to emphasize theoretical knowledge in our seminary or Bible school training. So this is what we took to other societies in the name of Jesus Christ, both in our witness and in the schools we set up to train church leaders. We had bought this information, often at a high price in the schools we attended, as if that information were valuable in and of itself, apart from its usefulness in ministry or in other parts of real life.

Much of the information we were given in our classes could be useful if it were applied to real life. But real life is hard to demonstrate in classrooms or even in information-oriented sermonizing. And the ability of people to apply classroom information in real-life situations is not great, whether they are students in Christian institutions of higher learning or parishioners who sit in church pews every Sunday. Most of the information just sits there, stored as information rather than applied.

Imitating our Western school–based approach to learning, we have unwittingly fallen into a misunderstanding that goes back as far as the Greek philosophers: *that the thing wrong with humans is ignorance and the antidote is to provide more and more knowledge.* This is the theory on which our school system is based; and we have taken it right over into our Bible schools and seminaries, not realizing that this assumption has never worked in the West. And it has been a disaster cross-culturally, leading to widespread secularization in the name of Christ.

Such an approach is not wrong because it is in error, but because it contributes little to helping and enabling those to whom God has called us, those for whom Christ gave His life. With such an influence in our background, we missionaries established schools in other societies to pass on this "knowledge-about" Christianity to the church leaders we sought to train.

How different might things have been, both in our home countries and abroad, if we had imitated Jesus' approach to teaching? He approached things *relationally,* not academically. Discipleship is a relational, experiential, practical approach to passing on ability. It is ability-based, not information-based. Information is important, of course, as well as the theoretical truth that comes with it. But Jesus' form of discipleship focuses on experiencing and using that information and truth, not simply on attaining it.

The Knowledge/Understanding Dimension

I criticize our preoccupation with knowledge and understanding not because those are unimportant but because we have overdone it. To use an analogy that has been applied in other contexts, knowledge is like manure; it helps things grow if it is spread in small doses over a wide area. But it sure can stink when it is all piled in one place! Not to mention that it will kill most anything that tries to grow in it.

Sometimes we have used the word *truth* as a label for the knowledge/understanding dimension, as in the phrase *truth encounters.* This usage makes sense to Westerners since we often associate truth with information, facts, explanations and the like. But scripturally, truth—like knowledge—is something experienced, not merely something thought. It is not a theoretical thing; it is an experiential thing. When Jesus says, "I am the way, the truth and the life" (John 14:6), I believe He is saying, "I am the One who will be true to you as you follow Me, the way, and participate in My life."

There are at least three kinds of knowledge in human experience: observational knowledge, intellectual knowledge and experiential knowledge. *It is the third kind, experiential knowledge, that is usually in view in the Scriptures.* Furthermore, when the words for *knowledge* are used in Scripture, those words strongly imply a moral obligation to live up to that knowledge.

So when teaching in the Scriptures takes place, it is done relationally, in interaction with disciples and mentorees. Students are guided into *experiential knowledge.* Furthermore, those who learn something are expected to obey what they know in response to their relationship with the Giver of that knowledge. Knowing the truth carries a moral obligation to practice it in real life. A proper English rendering of John 8:32, then, would be: "You will experience and obey the truth and the truth will set you free." *It is not biblical simply to understand any part of the Gospel theoretically without obeying it.*

Following is a chart of my take on the knowledge/understanding dimension:

The Truth/Knowledge/Understanding Dimension

Primary Concern: *Experiential Understanding*

1. This dimension involves teaching led by the Holy Spirit (John 16:13).
2. Scripturally both truth and knowledge are experiential, not simply cognitive, assuming obedience to what is known.
3. Truth and knowledge are learned by doing them, not simply by thinking them.
4. Truth provides antidotes for ignorance and error.
5. Though spiritual truth is pervasively relational and experiential (John 8:32), it also has a cognitive and informational dimension.

6. This dimension embodies truth and knowledge of all aspects of Christian experience.
7. We are to learn in this dimension about the contents of the other two dimensions.
8. We are expected to grow in this knowledge dimension as in all other dimensions of Christian experience.
9. Satanic and human lies are to be countered with God's truth.
10. Under this dimension the Church is to be experienced as a *teaching place* (mentoring, discipling, classroom).
11. Theology is primarily experiential, with an important cognitive component.

The Relationship Dimension

A glance at the Scriptures shows us a different sort of Christianity than that taught in our classrooms. Biblical Christianity is not merely informational; it is primarily relational. Whether in Jesus' approach to teaching or in either Old or New Testament expressions of faith, the major focus is not on knowledge-about but on what I call a *relationship-with* response to God and His commands. Scripture focuses on relationships with God and with brothers and sisters in the faith; and this "relationship-with" Christianity is something quite different from "knowledge-about" Christianity.

In Scripture the primary requirement of our Gospel is that people commit themselves to God in a new allegiance. Jesus taught the primacy of such a relationship, as did Paul and each of the other New Testament authors. Our Christian message contends that without a relationship with God through Jesus Christ, there is no salvation, no meaningful life, no eternity with God. We are to start our faith with a commitment to a relationship with God, and to continue to grow spiritually through strengthening and deepening that commitment. If there is one dimension of Christianity that is more important than all others—and I believe there is—it is the relationship dimension.

Not that we have ignored this dimension completely. As evangelicals we have been strong on the need for a relationship with Jesus Christ. Without this there is no salvation. We talk a lot

about conversion, love, forgiveness and a myriad of other relational things; we work at practicing them. Many churches even
get relational in their worship, singing their love and commitment to God and relating to other worshipers as they do.

Yet we have often contented ourselves in our organized activities—whether in church or in our training institutions—with
merely increasing our knowledge about our relationships with
God and His people. We have left the development of the relationships to happen informally. We also tend to treat our relationship with Christ as *a byproduct of our knowledge about Him*
when, in fact, relationship is an entirely different dimension
from the knowledge-about dimension. We can seldom, if ever,
get to a relationship through simply gaining information about
relating. *We can learn relationship only by relating.*

Relegating the relationship dimension to the status of
byproduct has resulted in a tragedy widely recognized in American Christian circles. When seminary and Bible school students
are inundated with information about Christianity, many
neglect or even lose the very relationship with Christ that they
came to our schools to nurture. They die spiritually even as
they grow intellectually. This happens to many in our information-oriented churches as well.

God started with a covenant, not with a book of doctrine.
Jesus came that the world might be saved through relationship,
not through information-oriented theology, as important as it
is to think biblically. The intended purpose of theological truth
and knowledge is for these to serve relationship. This priori-
tizing is what we should be practicing and taking to the world.
If we are to be scriptural, we need to focus on *culturally appropriate relating to God,* not simply culturally appropriate thinking about God.

A focus on the relational aspects of our faith has to become
a major focus of our teaching, writing and witnessing. We need
to be at least as intentional about experiencing relational activities such as fellowship meetings, ministering healing, the
Lord's Supper, baptism, repentance, reconciliation and relational teaching and preaching as we are about information-oriented teaching and preaching.

In order to further describe and elaborate on what I am saying, I present the following chart:

The Allegiance/Relationship Dimension

Primary Concern: *Relationship*

1. This is the most important of the three dimensions.
2. This dimension starts with conversion—a commitment to Christ—to establish a saving relationship with God through Jesus Christ.
3. Its aim is to replace any other allegiance/relationship as primary. All other allegiances are to be countered with commitment to Christ.
4. All other allegiances are to be secondary to this one.
5. It continues as growth in one's relationship with Christ and with others. It is expressed as loving God with one's whole heart and one's neighbor as oneself.
6. It includes practicing all that the Bible teaches on subjects like love, faith(fulness), fellowship, the fruits of the Spirit, intimacy with Christ (e.g., John 15), forgiveness, repentance, reconciliation, obedience and all other major doctrines.
7. True intimacy and relationship should not be confused with *knowledge about* intimacy and relationship.
8. Knowledge is to be experienced and obeyed in relationship.
9. Under this dimension the Church is to be experienced as *family*.
10. Witness to one's personal experience is key to communicating this dimension.
11. Discipleship is the way to teach this dimension.
12. Relationship is learned through relating.
13. Theology is experienced in discipleship, fellowship in which people experience being true to each other, worship and submission to God (Romans 12:2).

Experiencing Relational Intimacy with Jesus

Perhaps most of what I have said about the allegiance/relationship dimension is familiar. But some may be experiencing a glass ceiling between them and Jesus in their attempts to gain relational intimacy with Him. For years I sought a closer relationship with Jesus by praying and reading Scripture—as we are advised to do within traditional evangelicalism—and usually felt that the level of intimacy I attained was far below what

I and Jesus wanted. But I consoled myself by recognizing that I am a left-brain (i.e., cognitive) type of person and assumed that greater levels of intimacy are reserved for the right-brained, feeling-type people. I felt cheated but decided to be as content as possible with what I had.

Then, after 1982, I became involved in ministering deep-level healing in the power of God to the emotionally damaged and broken. This has led to an amazing discovery: Even I can experience closeness with Jesus to a much greater degree than I ever imagined. I am still not as expressive as many of the "touchy-feely" type people I know. But I have moved into a calm and deep satisfaction with the progress I am making in experiencing—not just knowing—Jesus.

This progress has come from two primary sources. The first is ministry, the second worship. These two streams are separate, but they interact with each other regularly.

The way in which ministry has contributed to achieving intimacy with Christ is embodied in the fact that He keeps using me to set captives free. This fact blows me away! I never anticipated that life—even life in Christ—could bring such satisfaction, not to mention such assurance that Jesus is real and willing to use even me to free hurting people. Every time I participate with Him in ministering to the broken, and watch Him heal their brokenness, my spirit leaps with joy. And I—the unemotional left-brained scholar—shed tears of gratefulness (as I am doing now as I write) over the privilege of being involved with Jesus in doing things I know I cannot do, such as healing people.

In following chapters I will discuss the topic of partnering with Jesus in doing His work. It is this partnership that enlivens both my ministry and my daily life and that produces feelings of deep intimacy with my Lord. That He has accepted me not only for salvation but into partnership in ministry is at the same time mind-blowing and deeply satisfying.

The second source of my newfound intimacy with Christ is worship. My experience of worship has changed because my relationship with Him has changed. Though I have great difficulty in raising my hands when singing contemporary worship songs, due to my upbringing as a traditional evangelical, the meanings of those songs affect me deeply. So do traditional hymns. Because of the closeness to Jesus that I now feel, I can no longer get through a worship service dry-eyed. (It is often embarrassing!)

I offer these reflections concerning my own experience in developing a closer relationship with Jesus in hopes that they may help you in a similar quest. Become involved in ministering to people in need by working in the power of Jesus to set captives free, and you, like me, will probably be blown away by the experience. And Jesus will be really close to you both in worship and throughout your days. As an important side benefit, you probably will find, as I have, that you are not just reading the Scriptures but *experiencing* them, not merely reading the accounts of things that happened long ago and far away. The Gospels especially have become brand-new to me ever since I began to work with Jesus to do the kinds of things He did while on earth.

Jesus promised in John 14:12 that we would get to do the works He did while on earth. When we obey Him by partnering with Him in such ministry, the byproduct is the intimate relationship with Him that we have sought.

Spiritual Power—An Ignored Dimension

Beyond the relationship dimension that we have neglected and the knowledge-about dimension that we have overemphasized, another dimension to Christianity exists: the dimension of spiritual power. We traditional evangelicals have ignored this dimension almost completely in our own lives, and as missionaries have crippled the churches we have planted and nurtured by not dealing with it.

My Nigerian church leaders read in the Bible that Jesus worked powerfully to heal, deliver and set captives free. They also read that He passed this power on to His followers. But they saw none of this power in missionary Christianity. Nevertheless they hoped I could help them in dealing with their battles against evil spirits. But I could not because I had never experienced or even learned cognitively about this dimension in my Christian pilgrimage. Oh, I believed in Satan and demons, *sort of,* but I was very happy to ignore the whole subject—just as my seminary professors had.

As we study Scripture, however, we quickly become aware of the fact that Jesus, though totally relational, also concerned Himself with whether or not people were free. When He stated His mission in Luke 4:18–19, He quoted from Isaiah 61:1–3, and His focus was on setting captives free.

Jesus was very conscious that life and ministry in His Kingdom involve a constant concern for dealing with the devastation brought about by our enemy, Satan. Jesus dealt with that devastation by using the power and authority given Him by God the Father to bring freedom. And He initiated His disciples—in a relational way—into the use of that power and authority. He also taught them that down through the ages, "whoever has faith in Me will do what I do"—that is, will work in that same power and authority (John 14:12).

This power dimension is not the primary dimension; relationship is primary. But if the power and authority dimension was as important to Jesus as Scripture shows, it should play a much greater role in evangelical Christianity than it has— unless, of course, we give up our contention that we are trying to be biblical. This emphasis into which some of us have now moved is not a fad that will pass. It is an attempt to rectify an omission by bringing scriptural balance to an unbalanced evangelicalism.

What we evangelicals often miss is that Jesus' use of the power and authority of the Holy Spirit had two important purposes beyond simply helping people to feel better. The Satanward purpose (to use James Kallas's term, 1966) was to destroy the works of the enemy (1 John 3:8). But the Godward purpose was to express the love of God in very tangible ways. *Jesus always used His power to show His love.* Thus in Jesus' ministry, power, like knowledge, was used to support relationship. We should not ignore something so prominent in the ministry of Jesus and His early followers.

Obviously, as I indicated in chapter 5, some ministries that exercise spiritual power do so in excess. But given the amount of doctrinal heresy in existence, might I suggest that there is at least as much excess in knowledge-oriented approaches as in power-oriented approaches to Christianity? If we ever hope to experience and proclaim a balanced and fully biblical Christianity, we dare not point to those excesses as a reason for ignoring something that was so much a part of scriptural portrayals of what Christianity ought to be. *If Jesus was not afraid to risk the distortions and perversions of power ministry, neither should we be,* especially since He made it clear that His followers were to do what He did (John 14:12).

We note from various Scriptures that all the world lies under the strong influence of our enemy, Satan. For example, 1 John 5:19 says, "The whole world is under the rule of the Evil One." Second Corinthians 4:4 speaks of the fact that people "do not believe, because their minds have been kept in the dark by the evil god of this world." Ephesians 2:2 refers to Satan as "the ruler of the spiritual powers in space, the spirit who now controls the people who disobey God." And Ephesians 6:12 says, "We are not fighting against human beings but against the wicked spiritual forces in the heavenly world." Despite some teaching and writing that deemphasizes the spiritual warfare aspect of Scripture, we cannot avoid this theme if we take Scripture seriously.

The presence of these statements in our Scriptures suggests that bringing people to freedom should be as high on our list of priorities as it was on Jesus' list. Again, this focus on spiritual power should not be seen as a tangent or fad. Rather it is a sincere attempt at a corrective to deal with an information-oriented, powerless Christianity.

If we take seriously Paul's statement in 2 Corinthians 4:4 about the blindness of normal people, we have to ask ourselves, How can people whose minds have been blinded think well enough to respond to Jesus Christ for the purpose of entering into a saving relationship with Him? We have assumed that people can think freely, hear the message and respond appropriately. But, whether at home or abroad, it is often *not a lack of knowledge that hinders people from coming to Christ but a lack of freedom.*

The people to whom Jesus ministered recognized that the biggest hindrances to a well-ordered life are evil spirits. Most of the peoples of the world today, including many Americans, also know this. This fact makes dealing with spiritual power a major issue for anyone who takes Scripture—and real life— seriously. It is certainly a major problem for millions of people worldwide.

Throughout the world people hear or read of a wonderful Miracle-Worker who once lived and did spectacular things. They are attracted to this Jesus who heals, delivers and sets captives free. So they come to Christ seeking that freedom. All too often, though, they are disappointed, seeing little or none of this activity in most Christian churches, whether here or abroad.

Those who do join and stay with our churches usually practice what I have called "dual allegiance Christianity." They go to church on Sunday to express their allegiance to Jesus, but their allegiance is to secularism or to enemy spirits the rest of the week. That is, when they have problems, it seldom occurs to them to go to church leaders since they find no power in churches to deal with these problems. In America we go to doctors, psychologists and other secular specialists. If we go to a pastor, the chances are high that he will recommend secular rather than spiritual answers. Overseas—and increasingly in America—even Christians appeal to occult practitioners to deal with the problems of life. They know they are not free, and they know there is little or no help in the church.

Jesus demonstrated for us and passed on to us a Christianity with power. He showed us a faith with a living, active, concerned, loving, healing and freeing God. *This is quite a contrast with what we see in most of our churches at home and abroad where knowledge is prominent, relationship is a byproduct and spiritual power is a mystery.*

Following is a summary chart of the spiritual power/freedom dimension:

The Power/Freedom Dimension

Primary Concern: *Freedom*

1. This dimension focuses on spiritual power (e.g., not political, personal, etc.).
2. This dimension recognizes that humans are held captive by Satan.
3. Jesus worked in the power of the Holy Spirit to set captives free (Luke 4:18–19); He did nothing under the power of His own divinity (Philippians 2:6–8).
4. Jesus passed this power on to His followers (Luke 9:1; John 14:12; Acts 1:4–8).
5. Satanic power must be defeated with God's power. It cannot be defeated simply with truth or a correct allegiance, though these help.
6. Under this dimension, the Church is experienced as a *hospital* where wounds are healed, thus freeing people, and an *army* that attacks the enemy, defeating him at both ground level and cosmic level.
7. Awareness of the power dimension of Christianity needs to be taught both cognitively and, especially, experientially (as Jesus did).
8. Working in Jesus' power is learned through working in Jesus' power.
9. Theology is experienced as confronting and defeating the enemy in warfare, resulting in freedom to grow in relationships and understanding.

Christianity in Three Dimensions

A maturing evangelicalism needs to learn to express our faith in at least these three dimensions both at home and abroad. We will not fail to teach theology—the knowledge-about dimension. But we need to learn to teach it relationally, as Jesus did. And we need to balance our handling of this dimension by making relationship central, as our Bible does, and adding a major concern for spiritual power. Since the knowledge/truth and the power/freedom dimensions are to serve the relationship between God and humans, both our theorizing and our training should put the primary focus where the Scriptures put it, on relationship—not knowledge about relationship but actually relating to God and to each other.

Evangelicals practicing this approach will not be content to ignore (as the Western Church has largely done) the power dimension. People are often not free to properly hear and respond to an invitation to relationship. Often, even as Christians, they are not free to grow as they ought. *Something must be done, not just theorized, to enable people to be free.* So again we are talking about something that is *done,* not just thought about.

We must learn to practice and to theorize our faith in three dimensions, not just one. We need a clear and pervasive focus on relationship with self, other people, spirits and God. We need to confront old relational patterns experientially with Christian patterns in each of these four areas. To break old patterns we must learn and experience the power of Christ in setting captives free (see chapter 12).

In each of the three dimensions of Christianity, encounters or confrontations need to take place as people grow toward greater Christlikeness. False allegiances and the relationships that flow from them need to be confronted with a growing and all-consuming allegiance to Jesus Christ. Lies, deceit and misinformation need to be encountered continually with the truths of God. And counterfeit uses of power under the influence of our enemy, Satan, need to be confronted by the true, freeing power of a loving God. The object of three-dimensional Christianity is balanced, well-rounded, scriptural growth toward maturity in Christ—as opposed to an unbalanced and partial growth mainly in one dimension.

What I view is not a static Christianity that seeks orthodoxy in adherence to a set of unchanging cognitive propositions but a dynamic faith grounded in a life-transforming relationship with the eternal God. This faith is alive in all three dimensions, growing and confronting anything less than a totally scriptural perspective and experience. But, as in Scripture, God is willing to start where people are and to work with them patiently in moving them toward His ideals. As they grow, however, God will at some point want to confront their primary relationships (usually to family) with the need to relate primarily to Him—as He did with the Jews. He will also want to confront the powers that blind and bind them with His power to set them free. And He will, of course, want to confront their truths with His truth.

Each of these encounters with the world, the flesh and the devil has a different purpose. The truths with which people have lived in their pre-Christian state or even within some sub-ideal form of Christianity are to be confronted experientially with God's truth. This is the antidote for ignorance and error. But the confrontation itself is to be done in a Christian way—patiently, lovingly and understandingly. Any sub-ideal allegiances are to be confronted by the need for a proper and growing relationship with the true God. This is the antidote for false allegiances. And any power sources not from the true God are to be confronted by the true Source of power. This is the antidote for captivity to satanic power. Scriptural balance requires all three of these dimensions and continual confrontation in each.

Unfortunately some in the West set a bad example. They try to confront everything with knowledge. Though knowledge and truth are proper antidotes for error and ignorance, we cannot effectively confront power with knowledge. Nor can we be assured that relationships will be changed, improved or healed simply by providing knowledge. Nor can we come to proper understanding of the truth simply by having the right relationships or by working in the right power.

The problems addressed by each dimension are separate problems and need to be dealt with from within each dimension, not with a one-size-fits-all cognitive knowledge approach. People often change or increase their knowledge without changing their allegiance or their relationships. And they often change their allegiance without being really free, due to a lack of the use of God's power to free them. They may work even in God's power without correctly understanding what they are doing.

What This Approach Could Help Correct

Countering a Weak-Relationship Christianity

Learning to work in all three dimensions could help us deal with many of the problems of our weak-relationship, knowledge-centered Christianity, both at home and abroad. A focus on gaining information rather than on nurturing faith (relationally) produces a rationally satisfying but *secular* Christianity—a Christianity with impressive growth in knowledge but little growth in the all-important relationship-to-God part. Such secular Christianity misses the spiritual reality that can be gained only through intimacy with Christ—an intimacy of relationship that leads to living the kind of life He modeled for us.

Jesus was keenly conscious of the spirit world and spiritual reality. The Pharisees were at least conscious enough of the spirit realm to fast regularly and to deal with demons. The Sadducees appear to have been totally secularized. We may be somewhere between the two.

We have bought into a Greek, knowledge-seeking approach, mentioned in 1 Corinthians 1:22, where it is noted that the Greeks were committed to the quest for knowledge. Because the Greeks theorized that the thing wrong with humans is lack of knowledge, their answer to human problems was to supply information—a system that those with perception can clearly see to be bankrupt. But our whole schooling system, including ministerial training, is based on this misleading theory plus its corollary—the assumption that if people have the right information, they will behave rightly.

Training programs and sermonizing that focus people's attention on information rather than on behavior deaden faith. People lose their faith in evangelical churches and training institutions not because the knowledge is wrong or theologically off track, but because an overload of knowledge without putting it into practice deadens relationships.

Such overemphasis on doctrine also leads many people (especially academics) to be suspicious of experience. This is strange, since it is precisely experience that is necessary to enable knowledge to be valuable. Virtually the only kind of knowledge advocated in Scripture is experiential knowledge, not simply theoretical or academic. As I have said, John 8:32 should be translated, "You will *experience and obey* the truth and the truth will set you free."

Countering a Powerless Christianity

Learning to work in all three dimensions could also counter the powerlessness of evangelicalism, both at home and abroad.

We seek to help people. But without spiritual power, our only answers are secular ones. We can recommend only secular medicine and psychology to those who hurt. We can only imitate secular approaches to poverty and homelessness. Thus, *even Christian missions have been more effective in secularizing than in promoting a truly biblical Christianity.*

Most of what Jesus said had been said before. It was His authority and power that set Him apart from other religious teachers of history. *The majority of His message was in who He was and what He did.* And He specifically taught that we are able, with the Holy Spirit, to follow His example (John 14:12). It is this authority and power that proved His relationship with the Father. He said He did nothing on His own authority (John 5:19, 30). He had set aside His own divinity (Philippians 2:6–8). His works were empowered and endorsed not by Himself but by the Father and the Holy Spirit.

It is this authority and power that made His relationship with His followers life-transforming. They went out fearless, taking on the whole Roman Empire because of the transforming power of that relationship. An important concomitant of that relationship, then, was that Jesus gave them the same Holy Spirit who had empowered Him. A Christianity without this authority and power has little to offer a world that Satan claims is his (Luke 4:6). We cannot fight Satan's power with rational, theoretical truth. You can fight error and ignorance with truth and knowledge. But *you have to fight power with power.*

We know and practice a good bit of the power of love but often with little of a spiritual dimension to it. Jesus used spiritual power as an exciting way to *demonstrate* God's love. A lack of such demonstration makes most of evangelical Christianity spiritually lifeless and unable to deal with the spiritual realities of which Jesus, Paul, Peter and the rest of our New Testament authors were so conscious.

We act as if Satan is a toothless lion, not the roaring lion Peter describes (1 Peter 5:8). We treat those who take Ephesians 6:12 seriously as if they are loony! We act as if demonization, common in Jesus' day, is a thing of the past; and as if those who deal with demons are simpleminded, weird or hyperemotional—all in spite of an increasing amount of evidence that demons are alive and very active today in American society.

We may criticize liberals for leaving out certain sections of the Scriptures, but we evangelicals do the same thing when it comes to issues of spiritual power. If we are going to be scriptural and realistic about our Christianity, we are also going to have to join Jesus, Paul, Peter and the others on the lunatic fringe. As Jack Hayford said in his lectures at Fuller, we should regard as strange those who *do not* deal with such spiritual realities, not those who do.

Our enemy does not go away simply because we do not take his activity seriously enough to learn how to deal with it. And he rejoices that we have neglected, both in the Church and in our training institutions, to learn how to deal with him. We criticize those in popular culture who contend that the only reality is what we create for ourselves, but we side with them when we create a theology without recognizing that Satan and his demons are alive and very active today.

A Message Truly Scriptural and Relevant

Monodimensional, knowledge-about Christianity is only partially scriptural and only minimally relevant to needy people around the world. To many of these peoples, both at home and abroad, it would come as a surprise to learn that following Jesus is relevant to our relational and spiritual power needs. The kind of Christianity they have experienced would not lead them to that conclusion.

This being true, many have either abandoned the faith or become merely nominal in their practice of Christianity. Often they find more satisfying relationships outside the Church, and certainly they find more ability elsewhere to deal with the pressing problems of life. Some seek power in New Age deceit—power offered by our enemy to those who do not find it in the Church. Many are content with secular answers. Powerless, dead Christianity is the norm.

Few can say with Paul that our "faith does not rest on human wisdom but on God's power" (1 Corinthians 2:5; 4:20). And many in our congregations are both captives of the evil one and relationally immature.

For ourselves and to pass on to others, we badly need a three-dimensional Christianity.

eight

Beyond Conversion to Freedom

Jesus said He came to set captives free and to release prisoners (Luke 4:18–19). Traditional evangelicals have usually interpreted *freedom* to mean freedom from sin—that is, salvation. I believe, however, that Jesus had more than salvation in mind.

When Jesus commanded us to "go, then, to all peoples everywhere and make them my disciples . . . and teach them to obey everything I have commanded you" (Matthew 28:19–20), He definitely had more than just conversion in mind. He foresaw a prolonged process of teaching and learning—a process I assume involves coming into the full freedom Jesus promises to those who come to Him with heavy loads (Matthew 11:28).

The enemy has a scheme, I believe, whereby he moves new converts right into prisoner-of-war camps to keep them from interfering with his activities. It is from such camps that Jesus wants to free us.

Our Main Focus—And What We Ignore

Growing up an evangelical, I learned that the people of the world who do not have a saving relationship with Jesus are going to hell. I still believe this with all my heart. This belief was a major factor in my feeling called to become a missionary, and it has remained an important factor in my continuing service to the Lord.

The focus on conversion is a strong point of evangelicalism. It results in an impressive commitment to obey Jesus' Great Commission by witnessing for Him to the ends of the earth. Jesus said we are to go into everyone's world to communicate His message of good news. We are to tell everyone that a relationship with Him can help them reach the fulfillment He intends for time and eternity (Matthew 28:19–20; Mark 16:15; Acts 1:8). A focus on witnessing to people to bring them into a relationship with Jesus results in the execution of much of Jesus' command.

Although we Christians have not always been as good at helping people grow to maturity in Christ, this has been an additional important focus. As we ourselves seek to become more and more Christlike, we attempt to lead others in that direction as well. But our definition of Christlikeness stops short of being complete. It focuses almost entirely on becoming loving, patient, forgiving, able to resist temptation and faithful to God the Father—as Jesus was. This definition is fine, as far as it goes. I would not suggest we drop a single bit of it. But in spite of some emphasis on progressing to maturity in Christ, we have given the impression that salvation is more an end than a beginning. Whether coming to Christ ourselves or bringing others to Christ, we have focused on this entry point of a saving relationship much more than on what comes after that decision. We even interpret Jesus' words concerning the freedom He came to bring as if those words refer simply to salvation.

But even when focusing on becoming Christlike, we evangelicals have largely ignored another important aspect of Christlikeness. We seldom advocate becoming more like Jesus in working in the power of the Holy Spirit to fight Satan. When we mention dealing with the enemy at all, it is largely in terms of defending ourselves against temptation. Little or nothing in our churches or our personal lives looks like going on the offensive against our enemy.

Indeed, we have reduced the message of Jesus to something like this: Receive Him into your heart and receive, in return, a rocking chair in which you sit until the Rapture. We seldom see ourselves as warriors, except when we send out a few professional Christians into missionary work that is characterized as going into battle for the Lord. We may sing Luther's great battle hymn, "A Mighty Fortress Is Our God," but assume that the theme concerns protection, not attack. We may belt out "Onward Christian Soldiers" or "Stand Up, Stand Up for Jesus," which have attack themes. But the attack thinking so prominent in these hymns (and a few others) is far from our minds and even farther from our behavior.

We have the salvation message straight. And our focus on becoming like Jesus has most of the components right. But the example of Jesus also included attacking the evil one. We have missed that part—the part that Kallas claims constitutes eighty percent of the synoptic gospel narratives (Kallas, 1966). Whether the percentage is that high might be debated, but we cannot debate the "Jesus as Warrior" theme that is so prominent. A major reason for this lack of attack thinking: We evangelicals practice a Christianity without power (see Kraft, 1989).

Prisoner-of-War Camps

This Christianity without power has caused us to fall into a major part of Satan's strategy. Our enemy, of course, does all he can to keep people from coming to Christ. But if he fails at this, he has a backup plan to move converts into prisoner-of-war camps.

What do I mean by prisoner-of-war camps? In wartime, when soldiers are captured by the enemy, they are kept in camps that typically are walled or fenced in and surrounded with armed guards to keep the prisoners from escaping. The prisoners, though they have been trained, equipped and sent out to conduct warfare, become disabled and useless. They are captives and no longer a threat to their enemy.

Several characteristics of evangelical Christianity suggest to me that most of us are prisoners of war. The first characteristic, as mentioned above, is that we are so focused on the salvation message that we do not move on to what I believe is Jesus' intended second step: freedom from past wounds and bondages. I will discuss this further in the next section.

A second characteristic of evangelicalism is the apparent lack of recognition that Jesus called us to warfare. We have been so influenced by the secular worldview around and within us that we, like non-Christians, consider the invisible spirit world fiction rather than fact. Though the authors of Scripture and Jesus Himself clearly assume the presence and activity of Satan and his demonic helpers, we act as if that part of Scripture is not to be taken seriously. We seem to skim over those Scriptures that portray the world as being under the strong influence of our enemy, Satan.

So at the practical level—whether or not we say we believe such Scriptures—we see no war, no active enemy and no demonization. We regard Jesus' conflict with demons as something He experienced in history, probably because He was the Son of God. We ignore the issue. Or, like liberals, we even rationalize that He adapted to the concepts of the people of His day, acting as if He were casting out demons when, in reality, He was simply dealing with psychological problems. What a shame that our strong commitment to Scripture ignores this important emphasis of Jesus!

A third disturbing characteristic of evangelicalism is the fact that many of us believe Satan is real but teach that all we have to do to defeat him is to study Scripture and pray. Often we misinterpret 2 Corinthians 5:17 and Philippians 3:13 as indicating that since we are new creatures, God simply blots out whatever we did in the past under satanic influence. God will simply make all well. When we find that those memories are not erased and that they still influence our lives, we often develop tremendous disappointment with God. Then we either drop out of Christianity or else continue in our bondage (prisoner-of-war captivity), feeling that is the best we can expect from life.

I want to assert again that coming into a relationship with Jesus is crucial, but this is only the first step. We are correct that without this step, no following step is valid. This is where liberal Christianity makes its greatest mistake. Many liberal churches do many good things, things that Jesus wants His people to do. But they ignore the salvation step. So they are doing good works without a saving relationship with the One who commanded us to do such things. Evangelicals, on the other hand, do not make this mistake. We have learned to do "good works" while not ignoring the saving faith step.

What Satan fears most, however, is not occasional conversions or the good things we do in Jesus' name. *What he fears is that we will discover we are supposed to be an army and begin to act like it!* If we would start liberating Christians from the prisoner-of-war camps, putting uniforms on them, arming them and teaching them how to fight, the enemy would become very concerned. Indeed, churches that have done this find that Satan begins to attack them strongly, proving he is afraid of Jesus' power.

Freedom: A Step Beyond Salvation

I have spent more than fifteen years in healing ministry to people deeply committed to Christ but broken and in bondage. In this time I have been privileged to help hundreds take a step beyond salvation that they usually did not know was necessary. This is a step into freedom. In taking this step, hurting persons usually work with an anointed prayer minister who operates in the power of the Holy Spirit and uses the approach commonly known as inner- or deep-level healing.

The people who come to me are often able to fool others into thinking all is well with them. They put on a good front, but underneath are badly crippled due to unresolved issues in their past. They carry such problems as rejection, abuse, betrayal and unforgiveness—problems rooted deeply in the past, often in childhood. These hurts and the pain associated with them rob these persons of the joy they should be experiencing in their relationship with the Lord.

I and the ministry partners who work with me have found that these people are not free enough to grow as Jesus intended them to grow, nor are they free enough to live in the kind of intimate relationship with Jesus that He intends. Spiritual maturity is rare among them. And they do not know how to mature because evangelical Christianity, while advocating growth toward maturity, has said virtually nothing about how to overcome the deep hindrances to such growth. We have assumed that everyone who comes to Christ starts on an even playing field. We assume, therefore, that if they do not grow in Christ, they must not be working at their spiritual life as God wants them to work at it, and that they themselves are to blame for their lack of growth. Not knowing the freeing power of Jesus, we assume this kind of life is the best we can expect from our Christian commitment.

What I have learned, however, is that more intimacy with Christ, more spiritual maturity and more freedom than evangelicals ordinarily recognize are available to believers. Jesus is willing to come right into our present lives to bring healing in the form of freedom from the past wounds and bondages that keep us from experiencing all we expect in our Christian lives.

Deep-Level Healing

A concern to see people experience this freedom soon leads us into the areas where people are most bound—the emotional and spiritual areas of their lives. Recognizing the importance of these areas has led many pastors to either specialize in psychological counseling or to refer people regularly to psychologists. In keeping with our secular evangelicalism, however, such counseling—even by Christians—seldom employs any power beyond a casual prayer asking Jesus to do something. These prayers often make some difference but seldom provide enough power to truly free the person.

An example of the greater effectiveness of pairing traditional counseling with prayer came to my attention while listening to a presentation by Judith MacNutt, wife of Francis MacNutt. If I remember the story correctly, Judith was working in a secular counseling center but praying for her clients outside of the actual counseling time. Her supervisor became aware of the fact that her clients were improving more than the clients of the other counselors, and asked her what she was doing differently. She confessed that she was praying for them outside of the counseling sessions. Her supervisor then reprimanded her and ordered her to stop doing that. He said it was against hospital policy.

Even when conducted apart from the counseling session, prayer for clients makes a difference. But would more prayer make more of a difference? If, for example, the whole session were conducted in an attitude of prayer, with the presence and power of Jesus invoked at every turn in the counseling, would even more change occur?

During the charismatic movement of the 1960s and 1970s, a practice arose that is ordinarily referred to as inner healing. In this approach a counselor, often referred to as a prayer minister, invokes the presence and power of Jesus throughout the ministry session—and with much greater effectiveness than either secular or "Christian" counseling. Though some have misused inner healing, its value and success have been overwhelmingly demonstrated. Such practitioners on the Protestant side as David Seamands (1981, 1985, 1988), John and Paula Sandford (1982, 1985), Rita Bennett (1982, 1984), Betty Tapscott (1975, 1987), Mike Flynn and Doug Gregg (1993), and on the Catholic side as Dennis and Matthew Linn (1974, 1979, 1985) and Michael Scanlan (1974) have done a responsible job of practicing and writing about this approach.

Having practiced this kind of healing ministry myself for more than fifteen years, I can testify to its effectiveness in bringing people the freedom Jesus wants them to experience. Although we must learn from charismatics in order to work in such ministry, I do not believe we have to move beyond a solid scriptural and evangelical base to do so. Such ministry does, however, require some creativity and experimentation consonant with the recognition that Jesus is willing to be present and active in human life if we invite Him to be. Indeed, we find that He is willing and anxious to partner with us in attempting to set captives free from emotional and spiritual bondage.

Deep-level healing is the term I use for this type of ministry to distinguish it from physical healing, or "surface-level healing." Deep-level healing is a ministry in the power of the Holy Spirit that attempts to bring healing to the roots of a person's surface-level problems. This approach uses tools derived from secular counseling combined with the power of the Holy Spirit throughout the counseling sessions. The result is the healing of Jesus at the deepest level.

Since the majority of people's problems are emotional or spiritual, we focus our attention there. We have found that the healing power of Jesus is effective in freeing people from problems such as anger, bitterness, resentment, shame, guilt, fear, hatred, unforgiveness, a desire to die and even suicide attempts, lust, rebellion, feelings of inadequacy and self-condemnation, perfectionism, occult involvement, physical or sexual abuse and a host of other crippling problems.

It is a well-recognized fact that even physical problems have emotional or spiritual roots. It is my practice, therefore, always to look for such roots, even when the presenting problem is physical. When a person comes with a physical problem, I routinely ask two questions: "When did the problem start?" and "What else was going on in your life when the problem started?" The answers to these two questions usually enable me to identify the roots of the physical problem.

The deep-level healing process is fairly simple. I usually interview the person briefly about his or her contemporary problems and more intensively about such things as early childhood memories, since that is where the roots usually lie. As we get more into the person's story, we begin to take each hurtful event to Jesus. In so doing, the person himself or herself gives the hurts to Jesus and forgives, if necessary. The usual way of doing this is to ask Jesus to show the person His presence in the hurt-ful events so that the person can experience the fact that Jesus was there. He or she then gains the freedom that comes when problematic feelings and especially unforgiveness are given to Jesus—a freedom far beyond that available through traditional counseling methods.

This practice, which I call "experiential exercises" or "faith picturing," has been the focus of some criticism. But it is based on real-life experience and scientific study. People who have experimented with teaching through what is sometimes referred to as "game theory" have found that by approximating real life in games or experiential exercises, they are able to help people "get out of their heads" and into their feelings. Through this type of learning, the material presented has a deeper impact on the person than is possible if we deal with it only at the cognitive level.

There is a reason. Those who study the way memory is recorded in our brains (e.g., Schacter, 1996) describe three kinds of memory: an "operations" memory, a "word" memory and a "picture" memory. The operations memory handles how we do things like riding a bicycle, driving a car and typing. Although this part of our brain's memory function is very impor-tant in life, it has little to do with how we relate to one another. The other two types of memory are, however, of great impor-tance to our topic.

Word memory is the part of our memory system that stores concepts that come to us in words, whether spoken or written. This is the part where we deal with logic, reasoning, linear thinking and most other intellectual activities. It is the part of our minds and memories most in focus in our schooling. The picture memory, on the other hand, stores things in images. In this part we deal with total experiences, including our feelings, reactions and intuitions. This is where most people live most of the time. The things stored in this part of our brains are usu-ally more influential in our lives and more easily retrievable when we want to recall them. It is even true of intellectuals that things pictured, such as sermon or lecture illustrations, are recalled more easily than things presented in logical propositions. This is why Jesus almost always spoke in pictures rather than propositions.

In ministry we make use of this insight. In order to bring about emotional healing, we frequently take hurting people back to their unpleasant memories and invite them to picture a part of those memories they were unaware of when the events happened: the fact that Jesus was there with them in the events. In this way people are able to experience both the truth that Jesus was there when they were being hurt and the fact that emotional healing can take place when they give their anger to Jesus and forgive the perpetrators. We teach that the facts of the hurtful events cannot be changed, but that transactions with Jesus can happen, resulting in freedom and healing from the hurt. Such freedom and healing result over and over. For more detail on this approach, see my book *Deep Wounds, Deep Healing*.

Thus counseling becomes a transaction between the person and Jesus Himself, and healing comes not so much through human ability as through the power of Jesus. The counselor, or prayer minister, is really only a facilitator of this interaction between the client and Jesus. This contrasts with secular counseling, in which only human power is available. If in traditional secular counseling the person is whole enough to take advantage of the considerable insight of secular psychology to bring about self-healing, that process can work. If the person is not that whole, however, he or she may be well aware of the problems but unable to effectively gain healing of them. Clients who have experienced both approaches frequently tell me that working with Jesus in deep-level healing has for them resulted in gaining more freedom in a couple of hours than was accomplished in years of secular counseling.

Frequently demons are attached to the damaged emotions. If so, in order for the person to be completely healed, it is necessary also to get rid of the demons. Many who have experienced a good bit of healing through secular counseling have reported to me that, in spite of the progress made, the job was not complete until we dealt with the demons—usually through deep-level healing. On the other hand, clients who have been freed from demons but who have not dealt with the garbage find that they are not fully healed either. Most of the people who come for ministry suffer from both human problems (e.g., emotional and spiritual) and spirit problems (demons). Complete healing is not attained when only one set of problems is addressed.

Demonic strength is calibrated to the amount and kind of emotional and spiritual garbage to which the demons are attached. The existence of such garbage gives demons a legal right to be there. Taking away that garbage through deep-level healing leaves them with no legal right and, therefore, no power. They are then fairly easy to cast out.

I will deal with demons more completely in chapter 12 and have written a detailed treatment of demonization in *Defeating Dark Angels* (1992). I have addressed deep-level healing in detail in my book *Deep Wounds, Deep Healing* (1994), so I will not go further with that topic here. Suffice it to say that God has showed us an effective approach in which to work with Him to set captives free.

Freedom and Power

What I advocate, then, is that evangelicals discover and begin to work in spiritual power not only to get people saved but to set captives free. The captives in view are the people who fill the pews of our churches each Sunday and the seats in the classrooms of our Christian institutions. Jesus said He came to free "His people" (Luke 4:19). We are to do no less.

Like Jesus we must always use His power to demonstrate His love. What is more loving than bringing freedom to those who are bound by things deep inside that they do not know how to handle?

How would our own Christian lives be different if we focused on freedom beyond salvation? And how would our churches be different if they were full of free people? It is my contention that each new member of our churches should be required to go through deep-level healing.

Sadly the condition I call "unfreedom" is so prevalent in evangelical Christian circles that most do not realize they can do any better. They have never been victorious over their inner hurts and have never met anyone else who is, either, so they think what they are experiencing is the best Christianity has to offer. Some, from reading the Scriptures, feel that more freedom and joy are out there. They are able to see this part of what is on the other side of the glass ceiling, but not to get through it. So, since they have never met anyone with such freedom nor anyone who could lead them into it, they give up the hope of finding anything more in their faith.

Meanwhile our pastors continue to focus on knowledge, since that is what they have been taught in our training institutions, and they also cannot imagine how to achieve anything more. They continue to be unfree, experience-poor leaders of unfree, experience-poor congregations.

I am here to tell the evangelical world that there is more! It is possible to move from salvation into freedom. *But to get through that glass ceiling, we need to learn to work with Jesus today in His power.* We cannot be content to merely recount the stories of what He used to do as if basking in biblical history is all that Jesus requires of us. He is still willing to use that power to bring people into the freedom and love we see in the lives of biblical heroes. God did not turn off that power when Jesus left the earth.

nine

Partnership and Authority

In chapter 6, which dealt with the possibility of a science dealing with the spirit realm, I outlined seven spirit world principles and rules. I consider one of these to be incredibly important. It is the fifth principle I listed, the one that relates to the necessity of relationship and partnership in the obtaining and exercising of spiritual power. That principle states:

> Obtaining and exercising spiritual power and authority by humans flows from allegiance, relationship and obedience to whichever master they choose to serve—God or Satan. Either spirit being can invest people, places and things with power. But each has certain limits related to the cooperation each receives from his followers. God and Satan ordinarily work in the human realm through partnerships with humans. These partnerships grant them legal rights in human life.

Through a study of Scripture informed by years of life experience in ministry, I have become convinced that God has made a rule that neither He nor any other spirit being can operate in the human sphere without a human partner.

The Principle of Partnership

This principle is evident throughout Scripture, but perhaps most clearly in the prophets. God's search for a partner is overt in Isaiah 6 where He says, "Whom shall I send? Who will be our messenger?" (verse 8). God would not do or say certain things until Isaiah agreed to participate. The same was true of Daniel, Jeremiah, Ezekiel and all the rest of the prophets.

Can there be limitations to what God can do? Many are fond of saying things like, "God always gets His way," or "God can do whatever He wants to do whenever He wants to do it." I used to make such statements, but no longer.

For one thing, 2 Peter 3:9 asserts that God "does not want anyone to be destroyed, but wants all to turn away from their sins." But the New Testament makes it clear that many will perish, lost in their sins. Furthermore, Jesus prayed that God's Kingdom would come and His will be done on earth as in heaven (Matthew 6:10). If God's will is automatic, why would Jesus pray such a prayer?

An enormous amount of data also indicates that God has not gotten His way in situation after situation in the course of human history. A radical Calvinist would point to Romans 8:28 and assert that God has a purpose in everything He allows to happen. But this verse has at least three translations:

1. All things work together for good to them that love God (KJV).
2. In all things God works for the good of those who love him (NIV).
3. In all things God works for good with those who love him (TEV).

The first of these translations is not based on the best manuscripts, and also seems to endorse a fatalism that leaves God out rather than recognizing that God is active in working for good. The second and especially the third translations are better, both because they represent the Greek more accurately and because they put things in the hands of God, not of fate. The third of these translations rightly shows God to be working *with* humans, not just above them.

Observing how God works with humans, both in Scripture and in contemporary life, enables us to understand that this verse is to be interpreted as an "after-the-fact" statement. That is, whether the events that have already happened are good or bad, God is working with us to bring good out of them. He has a magnificent ability to work in our lives for good, both with the things He desires and with the things He does not desire.

Bad things happen regularly—things that God does not want to happen. But He has limited Himself in dealing with them by granting free will to humans. This free will enables good people to do good things and it allows people who wish to do evil to do evil things. God, choosing to abide by the limitations He has set on Himself, refuses to make a sham of human free will by interfering—though I believe He sets limits on what the enemy can do. (If He did not, none of us would be alive.) And God retains the right to work through circumstances to move people in directions He chooses and, of course, to use His own people to accomplish His desired ends.

The story of Joseph in the Old Testament provides a good illustration of the teaching of Romans 8:28. Joseph was treated very badly by his brothers. Because of his faithfulness to God, however, God was able to "partner" with Joseph and use him in the midst of the events of his life—even things God did not desire (his brothers' mistreatment of him)—to bring about good. Through the various events of Joseph's life, God and Joseph worked together, wresting good from some difficult events. Looking back at those events in light of the fact that he could now rescue his family from famine, Joseph could say to his brothers, "You plotted evil against me, but God turned it into good" (Genesis 50:20). Earlier he had told his brothers, "It was really God who sent me ahead of you to save people's lives" (Genesis 45:5). God did save their lives, but only because Joseph was willing to partner with God to work with Him both for Joseph's good and for that of his family—not to mention for the good of Egypt.

Starting back at creation, I believe God had a partnership in mind when He assigned Adam to rule the earth. That part of God's plan was frustrated when Adam chose to partner with Satan to disobey God. Then various humans came along between the times of Adam and Noah, some who partnered with God and others who partnered with Satan.

God's relationship with Abraham was another of His partnerships. Other important biblical partnerships included Isaac, Jacob, Joseph, Moses, Joshua and David. God partnered with common people, kings, prophets, poets, rich and poor.

Some of God's partnering with humans seems fairly normal, some more spectacular. When He partnered with Joshua to conquer Jericho (Joshua 6), for example, or with Gideon to defeat a large Midianite army with only three hundred men (Judges 6–8), the great importance of human submission in such partnerships was evident. Joseph was submissive in partnering with God (Matthew 2) when he obeyed the instructions God gave him in a dream and took Mary and Jesus to Egypt, thus preventing Herod from killing the baby. Joseph was obedient to what God asked of him, and the partnership worked to avoid tragedy. A similar circumstance had occurred more than a thousand years earlier when God was able to enlist a princess with a mother's heart to partner with Him to rescue the baby Moses (Exodus 2). God had already partnered with the baby's mother and sister to set up the event by the river. These events, I believe, are the kinds of circumstances God is able to manipulate to appeal to humans to use our free will in obedience to Him.

Since Satan has to obey the same rules as God, partnering occurs on the other side of the fence as well. When "a new king, who knew nothing about Joseph, came to power in Egypt" (Exodus 1:8), Satan partnered with him to oppress the Israelites. When, after Joshua's great victory over Jericho, Achan disobeyed God and partnered with Satan, the Israelites were defeated at Ai (Joshua 7). And after God was able to use Gideon marvelously, Gideon chose to turn to idolatry, and partnered with Satan to mislead Israel into idolatry (Judges 8:27). King Saul also became a partner with Satan, as did Absalom and, in the divided kingdom, all the kings of Israel and many of the kings of Judah. In the New Testament, Herod, many of the Pharisees, Judas, Pilate, the Judaizers and many others partnered with Satan to accomplish his purposes.

It is not people unaided who do evil things. Behind them lie "the wicked spiritual forces in the heavenly world, the rulers, authorities, and cosmic powers of this dark age" (Ephesians 6:12). People who use their free will to partner with these invisible evil beings keep evil alive in the world. Satan, required to obey the same laws God obeys, cannot do things in the human sphere without human cooperation—human partnership.

Jesus, God's Ideal Partner

When Adam, who was expected to partner with God to run the world, failed, God had to look for other partners who would depend on Him and work with Him to carry out His plans for the world. But after Adam's failure, due apparently to a rule of inheritance, all potential human partners started with a sin nature. Thus, in working with these human partners, God always had to start "below zero," due to the sin nature we all inherited.

God's problem was how to find a human partner who would live in absolute obedience to and dependence on Him. With such a one, He could initiate a new humanity that would fulfill His original intention. If God had asked us how He should go about this, we might have advised Him to produce another innocent couple who, being aware of Adam's fall, would succeed in becoming perfect and then produce children and a new humanity. We might have advised Him to just forget about the old, sinful humans as He made this completely new start.

But God decided to do it differently. He was not content to allow us who are dead in sin to simply be thrown away. Instead He decided to create a partner who would not only meet His requirements but would also redeem the rest of us, or at least many of the rest of us. This partner would have to be fully human but start out sinless. He would then have to face all that Satan would throw at Him and succeed where Adam had failed.

First, Mary agreed to partner with God when she answered the angel God sent to her, saying, "I am the Lord's servant, may it happen to me as you have said" (Luke 1:38). Then her fiancé, Joseph, agreed to participate in God's plan by joining her as a partner with God when he chose to follow the angel's direction to proceed with his marriage to Mary (Matthew 1:20–25). Both decided to believe, obey and participate in this incredible scheme. God's partnership with Mary and Joseph resulted in the God-Man Christ Jesus, only the second sin-free man to be born on earth.

All God's hopes for the world and probably for the whole universe lay in His partnership with Jesus. If Jesus failed, as Adam had, God's rule over the universe would probably have ceased and His enemy, Satan, would have taken over.

One of the rules of this partnership seems to be that this partner, Jesus, could not carry out His mission as God. Though He was completely God as well as completely man, He had to do this task wholly as a man. The partner, working within the human context, had to be a human. Jesus was God, of course, and could theoretically have behaved like God. I say "theoretically" because, though He was fully God, He seems to have agreed with the Father never to use His deity on earth. So if He had asserted His "Godness," He would have broken that agreement, becoming disobedient to the Father and losing the universe to Satan in the process.

So, as we read in Philippians 2, Jesus put aside His deity during His time on earth, took everything Satan and his partners could throw at Him and survived without sin to defeat Satan and accomplish our redemption. This was the partnership God sought with Adam. But only through Jesus did God get the partner He needed, and only then did God's partnership system work to defeat Satan and accomplish our redemption.

The view that Jesus never used His deity while on earth may be new to you. But the evidence is indisputable: He worked totally out of His humanity, empowered by the Holy Spirit. To support this theory, we start by pointing to the fact that Jesus did no miracles before His baptism. If He had, the people of

His hometown, Nazareth, would have been aware of it. But no people were more amazed when He started His ministry than the people of Nazareth (Matthew 13:53–58; Luke 4:16–30). The people who would likely have trusted Him most had He grown up doing spectacular things among them rejected Him, referring to Him as merely a carpenter and a local boy (Matthew 13:55–57). He could not even do many miracles there because of their lack of faith (verse 58), not to mention the fact that they tried to kill Him (Luke 4:28–30).

When did He begin to do miraculous things? Immediately after His baptism (Luke 3:21–23). When Jesus received the Holy Spirit, having encapsulated His deity, He was empowered by God from outside Himself. Then and only then did He receive the ability to do miraculous things. And these He did in dependence on the Holy Spirit, not on His own deity.

In questioning this understanding, some would point to Jesus' appearance in the Temple at age twelve. Jesus did indeed impress the priests at that time, but it was, as William Barclay in his commentary on Luke points out, the impression of a sincere and well-studied young man. Nothing there suggests deity if we did not know the rest of Jesus' story.

What does suggest deity, a deity Jesus refused to use, is the way Satan went about tempting Him (Luke 4:1–13). In two of the temptations, Satan challenged Jesus to employ His deity to get out of difficult situations, saying, "If you are God's Son. . . ." Even in the third temptation it was Jesus' agreement with the Father to win the world as a human that was challenged. "I will give you all this power and all this wealth," our enemy said to Jesus—if only Jesus would take a shortcut to retrieving the world by bowing down and worshiping the devil (verse 6). Obedience to Satan at this point would, of course, have meant a temporary triumph for Jesus as a man at the cost of sacrificing His deity. Jesus' reply, though widely interpreted as a command to Satan, is probably a statement of His own commitment as an obedient man to "worship the Lord [my] God and serve only him" (verse 8).

So, in partnership with Jesus, God showed us what He intended for us. And at the end of His earthly sojourn, Jesus passed the baton to us, saying, "As the Father sent me, so I send you" (John 20:21). Then, to assure us that we have the same empowerment He had, "He breathed on them and said, 'Receive the Holy Spirit'" (verse 22).

Authority

Jesus said He came powerless (John 5:19), having in some mysterious way put aside His divine knowledge, power and other prerogatives (Philippians 2:6–8). He worked as God's partner, in total dependence on the Father and empowered by the Holy Spirit. Full of the Spirit and obedient to and dependent on the Father, He did His works as a human being. And when Jesus left, He promised the same Holy Spirit to His followers (Acts 1:4–5) to enable us to do the same and greater works than He did (John 14:12).

As with Jesus, the Holy Spirit is our Source of power. Jesus Himself is our authority-giver and our model.

The thing that startled people in Jesus' ministry was not simply the truths He spoke or the fact that He cast out demons. It was the fact that He spoke (Matthew 7:29) and cast out demons (Mark 1:27) with *authority*. The Pharisees are reputed to have had ways of coaxing demons out of people, and they quoted others as authorities as they spoke. But Jesus acted as if He owned the place.

During His ministry Jesus gave that authority to His disciples (Matthew 10:1; Luke 9:1). This is an amazing thing (as I pointed out in chapter 5), given the propensity of the disciples to misunderstand or to do the wrong thing. The fact that Jesus was willing to risk that authority with the disciples is good news for us. Could the risk be any greater with us than it was with the disciples?

When He left the earth, Jesus instructed His followers to teach their followers all that He had taught them, presumably including how to minister in His authority (Matthew 28:20; Luke 24:49). He gave His followers one more command—to wait until they had received the Holy Spirit's power before launching out in ministry (Luke 24:49; Acts 1:4, 8). They were to receive the same Holy Spirit who had empowered Jesus.

Earlier, perhaps to make sure they—and we—got the point, Jesus had said to His disciples, "I am telling you the truth: those who believe in me will do what I do—yes, they will do even greater things, because I am going to the Father" (John 14:12). *Just as Jesus did mighty works in partnership with the Father, now we get to do those same works in partnership with Jesus.*

It is as if Jesus came to earth with a credit card with God the Father's name at the top and Jesus' name under it. This meant Jesus had all the authority the Father's name would bring. When Jesus left, He passed the credit card on to His followers, including us, with His name at the top and ours beneath it. In doing so, Jesus gave us the authority to use His name to bring about His will (John 14:13–14). We have the authority, then, to regularly use the formula "In Jesus' name" to convey the power of God—not automatically, as in magic, but out of our relationship with Jesus and the authority that relationship gives us.

As I mentioned in chapter 1, the difference between magic and working under the authority of God is crucial to this discussion. With magic the use of formulas and rituals is believed to automatically bring about the desired result. If the process does not work, the conclusion is that a mistake has been made in the procedure. In actuality Satan works behind the scenes to empower or not empower the formulas, but he deceives people into thinking they are in control through correct use of the formulas and rituals. Beyond magic, animist priests often believe they can control spirits to do their bidding when, in actuality, it is they who are being used by the spirits.

Working in partnership with and under the authority of God—which we as servants of Christ are privileged to do—is quite another thing. We do not control God. We submit to Him, following Jesus' example. As Jesus modeled life in partnership with and under the direction of the Father, we are to listen to God as our first job, then do what we hear from Him as Jesus did (John 8:28; 5:19, 30). When we do this, finding His will and conforming to it, Jesus assures us that He will do what we ask (John 14:13–14). This is the proper exercise of the authority that has been graciously given to us by God. When formulas are used (e.g., "in Jesus' name"), the results flow from the relationship with and obedience to the personal Source of power behind the formula, not from the formula itself.

The sons of Sceva tried to use Jesus' name but without the authority given by the relationship with Jesus. They were exposed and beaten for their attempt to use an authority that was not theirs (Acts 19:11–16). We need fear no such outcome as long as we keep on good terms with Jesus, the Source of our authority.

It is an awesome thing to experience a demon's response both to the authority of Jesus and to our right to work in that authority. On several occasions I have seen the whole demeanor of a demon change in response to the question "Do you recognize that I come in the name of Jesus Christ?" Their arrogance fades, their tone of voice betrays submission and sometimes the demonized person actually begins to tremble. Demons recognize the presence of one who represents the Lord. One day they will be forced to bow their knees and "proclaim that Jesus Christ is Lord, to the glory of God the Father" (Philippians 2:11).

Those who work in partnership with Satan work under his authority and operate in his power—authority and power that have, ironically, come originally from God. As I mentioned, Satan has to obey the same rules that God set up for Himself. By obtaining legal rights, Satan and his hosts are permitted to live in or otherwise influence humans through the commitments people make to them, whether consciously or unconsciously.

So partnership and authority go together in God's working in the human sphere. We who are committed to Jesus are called by Him to partnership in working toward His causes and in using the authority He gave us to help free others.

The Purpose of the Authority

The authority God gives us is to be used in specific ways to carry out our Master's will. This is a delegated authority. It does not belong to us; it is delegated to us. We are to be stewards of the authority, therefore, not owners of it. And the authority can be used either rightly or wrongly.

Proper use is indicated in Luke 9:1, where Jesus states that He gave His apostles authority and power over all demons and all diseases. It is clear that He intended for them to use this authority for purposes of deliverance and healing. Isn't it interesting that He put deliverance first? Assuming from Matthew 28:20 and John 14:12 that Jesus intended for the authority He gave the apostles to be passed on to their followers, and thus to us, deliverance and healing are among the ministries for which He intended us to use His authority.

Although we have the authority to curse, we are not to use it for that purpose. James assumes such authority when he counsels us to bless, not to curse (James 3:9). Some words are obvious curses; others are less so—and often it is not overtly clear which words constitute curses. We find, however, that when people speak hatefully to themselves, such words should be treated as possible curses and the person should renounce them. Doing so produces evidence that something powerful has been broken.

Thus the purpose for which God gives us this authority is to use it to imitate Jesus. This fact is clear from Jesus' prediction that all who have faith in Him will do what He did, and more (John 14:12). Determining the purpose of the authority is, therefore, related closely to what Jesus did and how He did it.

We now turn to a discussion of how God-given authority is to be used.

ten

Using God-Given Authority

In chapter 9 we discussed the partnership into which God invites us, and the authority that comes with that partnership. In this chapter we will focus on the ways we are to partner with God in using that authority. As throughout this book, the insights into this subject are derived from the interaction between a study of Scripture and the ministry experiences God has given me.

Universal Authority Rules

Both God's Kingdom and Satan's, as we discussed in chapter 6, are bound by the rules God put into the universe. Many of these rules or principles seem to govern the relationships between God or Satan, on the one hand, and humans, on the other. I call these "authority relationships" (see Kraft, 1997, and

Kraft and DeBord, 2000, for more detail on this subject). Six principles, among others, govern these relationships:

1. There are conditions under which humans can give authority in their lives to either God or Satan. Human obedience to God or Satan, resulting in partnership with either, gives whichever master specific rights in a person's life. God purposed for Adam that he live a life of obedience to and partnership with Him. But not until Jesus, the second Adam, do we see what human life was intended to be. Disobedience to God (sin), which is automatically obedience to Satan, gives the satanic kingdom rights over a person. And when a person wallows in sin, thus partnering with Satan, the enemy has the right to send a demon to live in him or her.

2. Dedicating a person to God or Satan, whether self-dedication or dedication by someone in authority over that person, gives whichever master authority over the one dedicated. When people commit themselves or their children to God, a kind of spiritual label is put on that person that says, This one belongs to God. The same is true of any dedication to a satanic being. Many people in non-Christian religions or occult organizations dedicate themselves or are dedicated by those in authority over them to false gods or spirits. Thus they are put into partnership with and under the authority of a demon, cult leader or false religion. Others who belong to organizations such as Freemasonry or Scientology commit themselves unconsciously to the enemy. When a parent dedicates a child to Satan, the parent gives the enemy authority to work in and through that child's life.

3. The spirit world honors human authority, both natural and delegated. The spirit world operates in relation to the human world in terms of "natural" patterns—those relating to the authority of husband over wife, parents over children and the like. Such authority is given to humans so that we will partner with God in caring for those under our authority. Those who give themselves to Satan, of course, partner with him.

But delegated authority is also honored by the spirit world. As husbands we can delegate to our wives our total authority over home and children when we go on a trip. Likewise the leaders of organizations can delegate their authority for certain purposes. When they do so, the spirit world must listen to the one to whom authority is delegated, as if that person were the top authority figure.

Frequently I have been authorized by people to take authority over demons in them or in their houses. When I do so, I work in partnership with God, with their permission and under their—as well as God's—authority. Once I ministered to a man in his thirties who had carried a demon since he was five. That demon had been authorized by a caregiver who had taken care of that man daily when he was a child! When his parents turned him over to the caregiver, they had given her their authority, which she used to invite one or more demons.

4. *What leaders do with their authority affects those under them.* Those in authority over others need to be careful not to take their authority lightly because it always involves partnering with spirit world beings. We see in Scripture that disobedience on the part of those in spiritual or civic authority over others—for example, Israel's kings—affects the whole group over which they have authority. Many evangelical churches in our day are hindered spiritually by the fact that some of their leaders are partnering with Satan through immorality or occult involvement with such things as horoscopes, fortunetelling, Eastern mysticism, New Age or Freemasonry.

5. *Any commitment, dedication, curse or blessing made by a person in one generation may give authority to either master, God or Satan, over that person's descendants.* Commitment of people to God in one generation blesses their descendants, especially if they do not turn their backs on God. But satanic power also may enter the family line through conscious or unconscious commitments, such as those mentioned above or through cursing. If such commitments are not canceled, the interference is passed on to the following generation. Because of this rule, many children come into the world already demonized because of agreements their ancestors made with the enemy.

Exodus 20:5, part of the second of the Ten Commandments, may mean that such satanic interference is limited to four generations. I sincerely hope so. I have frequently found demons, however, that claim to have been in a family for many generations, stemming from such commitments or curses. One way or the other, we observe from Scripture a spiritual relationship between members of the same family, which means that children participate in commitments made by their parents.

God kept His commitments to Abraham for many generations, even after Israel ceased to be faithful to Him. God's blessing on David extended to Solomon and to one after another of his descendants (1 Kings 11:34–36), in spite of the fact that first Solomon and then many of his descendants were unfaithful to the Lord. In 2 Kings 8:19 "the LORD was not willing to destroy Judah, because he had promised his servant David that his descendants would always continue to rule." This they did until the fall of Jerusalem (2 Kings 25). When God curses, as He did in the Garden of Eden, those effects also continue from generation to generation.

6. *On the basis of relationship and obedience to either master, God or Satan, these spirit powers delegate authority to humans.* Spiritual empowerment in the human world can be granted by either God or Satan. On God's side, we note again that Jesus gave His disciples (His partners) authority and power over all demons and diseases (Luke 9:1) while He was on earth. After His ascension He sent the Holy Spirit to empower His partners (Acts 1:4–8) to do the works He did, and even more. With the Holy Spirit within us, Christians carry the authority and power of God Himself.

Satan, too, can give people authority to work in his power to do miraculous things. The amount of authority and power available to individuals on Satan's side depends on the rank of the inhabiting demons. Higher-ranking demons can give a person power to do signs and wonders, as with Elymas (Acts 13:8–11) or the demonized girl in Philippi (Acts 16:16), even to do such powerful and miraculous things as moving around out of body through astral projection.

Authority to Partner with God in Blessing

God gave us the authority to partner with Him in blessing. This is a huge area of authority given to us by Jesus by which we can actually use words that He empowers to bring good to people. The authority to bless (Matthew 5:44; Romans 12:14) is one of the most precious gifts God has given us. Genuine spiritual transactions take place when we speak blessing in Jesus' name. We must be careful who we bless, why and with what, but we can bless without shyness those He directs us to bless. I doubt, though, that He wants us to use our words indiscriminately to bless everyone (see 2 John 9–11).

As usual Jesus modeled this area of authority for us. In the Beatitudes He blessed people for specific behavior and attitudes (Matthew 5:3–12). Judging by Jesus' behavior after the resurrection (John 20:19, 21, 26), He blessed people regularly when He came into their presence with the lovely Hebrew greeting *Shalom,* "peace, well-being." Just as Jesus blessed, we are to bless.

When Jesus sent out His followers to minister in Luke 9 and 10, He told them to bless those who cared for them by blessing their households (Luke 10:5). He instructed the disciples—and us—to bless freely, before we even know how our recipients will react. But not everyone will accept us (Luke 10:6, 10–11). When this happens we are justified in taking back our blessing (verse 6), since the person who declares a blessing "owns" that blessing. Indeed, if we are rejected, we can go further and publicly shake the dust of the unreceptive town off our feet (verse 11).

The Bible is full of blessings. Not only did Jacob and other Old Testament fathers pronounce blessings on their sons (for example, Genesis 48–49), but Paul starts each of his letters with a blessing (for example, Romans 1:7; 1 Corinthians 1:3; 2 Corinthians 1:2; Galatians 1:3). Jesus was blessed before He was born (Luke 1:42) and afterward (Luke 2:34–35). Jesus blessed children (Mark 10:16), people who lived Kingdom values (Matthew 5:3–12), His disciples after His resurrection (John 20:19, 21, 26) and those present at His ascension (Luke 24:50–51). Further, He commands us to bless those who curse us (Luke 6:28).

We find about three hundred references to blessing in Scripture. Undoubtedly more examples of blessing would have been documented if blessing had not been so universally practiced by those with a Jewish worldview. The more familiar something is, the less it gets mentioned by those writing or speaking. Invoking God's blessing on those they favored was, for the Jews, almost as natural as breathing. The favorite Jewish blessing was, of course, "peace, well-being." In each of Paul's letters he spoke peace on his readers. And since he was working in the Greek world, he added a favorite Greek blessing, "grace." Thus his usual opening blessing was "grace and peace." In his letters to Timothy, he added "mercy," another favorite Jewish blessing (1 Timothy 1:2; 2 Timothy 1:2). In each case these are not to be taken as mere words of favor but as the invoking of God's spiritual power for the benefit of those addressed.

The authority to bless is a wonderful gift from God. As I have experimented with it, I have found that blessing someone is a form of ministry in and of itself. As I have blessed people with peace, many have experienced a noticeable peacefulness coming over them like a warm shower or mild electricity. I have blessed myself with peace many times when I have been upset, and found that it often works wonders. People blessed with joy often find their minds filled quickly with God's praises. Once I blessed a woman with joy, and a demon manifested itself! The demon could not stand the praise for God that welled up in the woman's heart. On one occasion I blessed a woman with "a deeper experience of the love of God than you have ever had before," and the Holy Spirit started a major work in her life.

I make it a practice in my classes and seminars to bless the students at the close of each session. I frequently bless them with things like peace, patience, protection, freedom from fatigue and good rest after they go home from an evening class. Many remark on the changes these blessings initiate in their lives.

Blessing is also an effective vehicle for initiating deep-healing prayer ministry. It is my practice to bless the person to whom I am ministering at the beginning of each session. Often he or she needs the peace of God to combat fear and discomfort. The blessing usually changes such fear to peaceful anticipation of what God is about to do.

I also use blessing to conclude ministry sessions. I bless the person with the opposite of whatever problems or demons we have tackled during the session. If we have prayed for inner healing for a damaged self-image, I bless the person with such things as new self-love and self-appreciation. If we have just kicked out a demon of anger, rage or violence, I bless that person with gentleness and self-control. If the problem or demon is fear, I bless the person with confidence or faith. Sometimes I just use a general blessing, saying, "I bless you with the opposite of each of the problems [or demons] we have dealt with."

We are not authorized to curse those who reject or offend us, although with the authority to use words to bless others comes the authority to curse. Instead we are commanded to bless and pray for others, even those who curse us (Luke 6:28; Romans 12:14; 1 Corinthians 4:12). But according to 2 John 9–11 we are not to bless heretics—"anyone who does not stay with the teaching of Christ, but goes beyond it." A heretic, says John, "does not have God." So we are not to "welcome [heretics] in [our] homes" or "even say, 'Peace be with you.' For anyone who wishes them peace becomes their partner in the evil things they do."

Authority to Partner with God in Breaking Bondages

Another important area, not entirely different from blessing, is the authority to join God in breaking bondages. Bondage to Satan can be due to such things as sin, "soul ties," contemporary or generational curses, self-curses and authority relationships.

A soul tie is a relationship in which one person is dominated by another. Such domination creates a bonding empowered by Satan. Any such bonding must be broken if the person is to be set free from the bondage Satan creates through such ties. We frequently find such ties between mothers and daughters, cult leaders and followers, or any other controlling relationship. Sexual relationships outside of marriage also create soul ties and resulting bondage.

Soul ties can usually be broken through asserting authority over them to cancel them. Once the person has repented of any sin involved and renounced any control Satan has been given through the soul tie, I usually say something like, "In the name of Jesus, I cancel any soul ties between [so-and-so] and [so-and-so]."

Curses are obvious bondage-creators. Bondage caused by curses can be brought on consciously or unconsciously by parents, people whom the person has offended or even by the person himself or herself. Missionaries are frequently the recipients of curses. They are often cursed by people resistant to their activities or by shamans who find their presence a threat to their occupation. Such curses can also be broken by having the person renounce anything that needs renouncing and then simply claiming Jesus' power to break the curses. Unwanted children are also frequent recipients of curses. Many people who were unwanted at conception by their parents received a curse of unwantedness.

Generational bondages are passed down from generation to generation through inheritance. These are often signaled by particular sins or compulsions that occur in each generation, often carried by inherited demons. In each case we have the authority to renounce such bondage if it is in us, and to cancel it in other people.

One type of generational bondage is the result of a dedication of an ancestor to gods or spirits. In many societies (e.g., Asian, African, Native American) it is normal for each child to be dedicated at or before birth to the gods of that people. In Chinese society, for example, a baby's name and date and time of birth are traditionally written on a paper and taken to a temple. This act dedicates the child to the god or spirit of the temple or that of the family. Even when a family fails to do this for their child, the family spirit invited through the dedication is passed on to the child for several generations. This type of bondage can be broken by speaking against the dedication, then casting out the demons representing both the father's and mother's family lines.

Authority over Places and Things

We can bless places and buildings with freedom from enemy activity, and with protection against any plans the devil might have for them in the future. As evangelicals we often use the authority Jesus gives us to dedicate places such as church buildings. In doing so we partner with Jesus to cleanse such places spiritually. Teachers have reported to me that they have done a similar thing with their classrooms and found that the children behaved better after they dedicated the room. The leader of a small Christian band reported to me that audiences turned much more responsive to their messages after they dedicated their instruments. Probably all of us have experienced the blessing that comes to us through music dedicated to God. We also have heard of—and perhaps experienced—the problems that occur when people listen to music dedicated to Satan.

A passing along of spiritual power seems to happen when we take authority over places and things. This power of God apparently extends even to influencing people who use or hear objects that have been blessed. This is what happens when we bless classrooms, churches, sacred objects, homes, specific rooms, furniture, offices or workplaces, computers and other objects.

With this in mind, we should take seriously the blessing of our food before we eat. We have the authority to empower food and drink to bring blessing to those who eat and drink it. I also use the authority of Jesus to cleanse food that may be contaminated, such as food I was offered in Africa, Papua New Guinea and other places.

A scriptural example of the empowerment of material objects is the use of Paul's handkerchiefs and aprons to bring healing and deliverance (Acts 19:12). People have told me of significant changes when they blessed letters and sent them to people. I assume that for such blessing to have effect, the receiver must be willing, but I am not sure what the rules are in this area. It cannot hurt, though, to experiment with using our authority to empower things used by or given to others.

Conversely we can use our authority—often quite unconsciously—in wrong ways to direct negative words toward people or objects. Many who have spoken such negative words toward themselves have found themselves, or parts of themselves, cursed. Often people who are sexually abused, for example, curse their sexual organs or their ability to enjoy sex. Such directing of spiritual power toward oneself is likely to develop into disease in one's sexual organs or dysfunction in one's sexual experience. I have seen dramatic changes in people who have asserted their authority to renounce the curses they put on themselves or parts of themselves. Once they renounce the curses, I ask them to begin blessing those parts of themselves that are now freed from curses. We can do this with the authority God gives us.

Authority to Partner with God to Heal and Deliver

In John 14:12—a verse I go back to again and again—we are told that we get to do the works that Jesus did. Among these works are healing and deliverance from demons. Unfortunately even those evangelicals who believe that healing gifts are for today often assume these are for a select few and that the rest of us must settle for less spectacular gifts.

This was my thinking when I began the course with John Wimber. I assumed God zapped some people with the gift of healing and left the rest of us out. Wimber pointed out, however, that I have the gift of teaching and asked how I got it.

"I worked at it," I replied.

His response was, "That's how you get the gift of healing."

This was a completely new idea to me, especially when he said we are to try and try again, testing God's promise that we would do what Jesus did. Through experiencing and experimenting with healing and deliverance, we discover whether or not we have the gift—or, rather, any of the healing gifts, since the word *gift* is in the plural in 1 Corinthians 12:9.

Note, again, the importance of experiencing and experimenting. In John 7:17 Jesus tells us to resolve to do the will of God in order to know for sure. With healing gifts this resolve must be accompanied by actually trying to do it. If we try a healing gift and fail fifty times in a row, we may conclude that we do not have that gift.

In my own case I prayed for many people for physical healing, with only moderate success; many headaches went away, several people had their legs lengthened and a few other things happened, including one healing from cancer. Half to two-thirds of the people for whom I prayed, however, did not experience any change, and four or five other people suffering from cancer died! Though I was diligent in trying, I was more often than not disappointed. So were the people for whom I prayed.

Things changed, however, when I began asking the two questions I mentioned earlier and basing my use of Jesus' authority on the answers. The questions are: "When did this [usually physical] condition start?" and "What was going on in your life at that time?" The answers to these questions usually help me know what emotional or spiritual issues are underlying the physical or emotional condition with which a person struggles.

I will return to this topic in more detail in chapter 12 on ground-level spiritual warfare. Suffice it to say, experience has demonstrated that healing and deliverance are in operation today if we are willing to experiment with partnering with Jesus to bring freedom to people in these areas. He has given us the authority to do so.

Authority to Partner with Jesus to Protect

An additional use of Jesus' authority is to protect ourselves and those under our authority. I believe God automatically grants us a certain amount of protection from enemy activity. But we do not seem to be completely protected. Why is not clear. It seems clear, though, that when we claim more protection for ourselves and those under our authority, more protection is granted. I have experimented with blessing myself with protection from disease and accident (especially in cars or planes), and it seems that much of what could have happened has not. Sometimes God's protection is obvious, as when a recent heart operation revealed that it was miraculous I had not had a heart attack before the operation, or on the two or three occasions when a plane I was on narrowly avoided colliding with another plane. At other times I am unaware of the ways I have been protected. I hate to think what could have happened if I had not exercised my right to regularly claim God's protection.

Those of us who are parents or leaders of organizations easily recognize our obligation to physically protect those under our authority. It is incumbent on us, then, to see our responsibility to protect them spiritually as well. We are the gatekeepers of our families and organizations. Any enemy that seeks to harm our people has to get past us.

In this regard, it is my practice to let the enemy spirit world know that if it wants to mess with my wife, children, their spouses or my grandchildren, those spirits have to deal with me. And I am not going to let them go over, under or around me. If they are to get into my family, they have to go *through* me, and I am not going to allow that either. We should claim such protection from accidents, diseases, even relational problems. In claiming such protection, I partner with Jesus in doing something He wants to do: protect my family. Meanwhile I invite the Holy Spirit to come into my family and do whatever He wants.

We should do the same with any organization or activity in which we have an official capacity. Pastors, teachers, CEOs, board members and anyone else with responsibility in the human realm (e.g., seminar leaders, youth leaders) should activate that responsibility in the spiritual realm by using the authority Jesus gives us to protect.

In addition we can claim Jesus' power to protect material objects such as our cars, computers and homes. I like to bless my cars and whoever is driving them with complete protection from accident or breakdown. I also claim protection for my computers. Neither of these practices is foolproof, but I do not like to think how bad things could get if I did not use the authority Jesus gave me to protect these things.

I regularly claim protection for my home and the homes of our children and grandchildren. I claim protection from natural problems (e.g., earthquake, fire, bad weather), from human problems (e.g., burglary) and from spiritual problems (e.g., whatever the enemy might seek to do directly). It is especially important to speak protection over our homes and goods when we go away on trips, lest the enemy attempt to take revenge on us while our homes are unguarded.

Claiming Authority over the Past

God gave us authority to cancel any claims the enemy makes on us due to events and agreements of the past. As with claims Satan may have stemming from things we do in the present, our aim is to be as "clean" as Jesus was. In John 14:30 Jesus referred to Satan as "the ruler of this world," but He stated that Satan "has no power over me." Or, as other versions translate it, "He has no hold on me" (NIV), "He has nothing in Me" (NKJV), "He has no rights over me" (NEB).

Some rights the enemy has over people come through inheritance. Believers have the authority, however, to cancel those rights. The place to start is with the recognition that God has planned and chosen each of us from before the creation of the world (Ephesians 1:4). We can then assume that He has superintended the coupling of each pair of our ancestors and the transmission of both genetic and spiritual influences down through the generations. Then, according to Psalm 139:13, He formed and framed us in our mothers' wombs so we would come out just right.

Nevertheless, the enemy has had ample opportunity through this process to influence—and often to intrude on—our ancestry by way of demonization. Through choices our ancestors made, doors often were opened into our bloodlines, permitting the enemy to cause damage and to insert his demons that are inherited from generation to generation.

To help free people from such bondages, I find it important to take authority over five major areas: *vows, curses, dedications, sin* or *trauma*. Whether by ourselves or with the help of another, it is important that we take authority over these issues in our ancestry in order to cancel any rights the enemy may have gained in our lives because of our family's past.

1. AUTHORITY OVER VOWS

Vows are assertions by which people bind themselves to do or not do things. Vows that fall in line with Satan's purposes in our lives are empowered by him. The enemy uses vows to establish strongholds in a person. Vows can be made by our ancestors or by ourselves and can be very damaging: "I will not be like my mother/father"; "I never want children"; "I will never allow myself to enjoy sex"; "I will never let a man/woman get close to me again"; "I refuse to grow old"; "I will never amount to anything"; "I will never get it right."

I ministered to a man once who had vowed at age five never to cry again. Many men and some women have made similar vows. I once heard about a woman who had actually written a letter to Satan, vowing to give him her firstborn son, and every firstborn son thereafter of her descendants, if he would make her rich and famous. She became rich and famous, but her descendant, a firstborn son, was in deep trouble.

To break the power Satan wields in our lives through ancestral vows, we simply claim authority in the name of Jesus to break their power. Doing this in a general way usually takes care of things. But sometimes the power of Satan through a given vow is so great that we must discover what the vow was and break it quite specifically. God can reveal what we have to know in order to break the vow, either through a word of knowledge or by forcing a demon to tell us.

I deal with ancestral vows—as well as curses, dedications and sins—by saying something like this: "In the name of Jesus, I take authority over all vows in the father's and the mother's lines to cancel any power given to the enemy, and to break his power through vows that may have been made by any one of [name's] ancestors." Vows made by the person also need to be broken and can be done in the same way. Again, it is helpful to be as specific as possible.

2. AUTHORITY OVER CURSES

The second kind of past event that needs to be canceled is cursing. Likely both we and our ancestors have been the target of curses, whether leveled at us formally (e.g., through a set ritual) or informally. This is especially likely if we or our ancestors have served in non-Western societies in which curses are commonplace. Missionaries and others attempting to witness for Christ are frequent targets of such cursing.

Unfortunately many curses that need to be broken come from parents or other close relatives through negative statements or thoughts. As I mentioned earlier, unwantedness carries a curse. By claiming the authority of Jesus to break curses aimed at them in the womb, many adults who were unwanted or whose parents wanted a baby of the opposite sex experience freedom. Adopted people almost always have such curses.

A common form of cursing is *self-cursing*. I have ministered to many who grew up with strong negative feelings toward themselves or some part of themselves. In addition to victims of abuse cursing their sex organs, many people curse their bodies during their teenage years. Women tell me they have cursed such things about themselves as their hair, faces, breasts, hips, minds and personalities. A man often curses such things as his emotions, his sex drive, his sex organ and his ability to perform tasks in jobs or athletics.

A curse that needs to be broken over people of Jewish ancestry is the one recorded in the New Testament when, at Jesus' crucifixion, the Jewish leaders said, "Let the responsibility for his death fall on us and on our children" (Matthew 27:25). A messianic friend of mine experienced a radical change in his life when the one ministering to him broke the effects of this curse on him. I am not sure whether this curse applies to all Jewish people, but as we have spoken against this curse in those of Jewish ancestry, we have often seen changes. In one of my recent ministry sessions, a Jewish believer experienced major physical as well as emotional and spiritual changes when this curse was broken and the demons attached to it were expelled.

Partnering with Satan in cursing, often through negative words or thoughts, gives Satan a right to a person, whether that person be oneself or another. But we have the authority by partnering with Jesus to take away all rights the enemy has obtained through cursing, whether these rights came through ancestors or through the person himself or herself. My ministry practice is first to claim God's power to cancel any rights over a person through cursing by his or her ancestors, and then to have that person renounce any self-curses. Finally I break the power of any curses leveled at the person from conception up to the present.

3. Authority over Dedications

Persons with Asian, African, Latin American or American Indian ancestry can count on the fact that they or their ancestors have been dedicated to false gods and spirits that are really demons. People who have belonged to false religions such as Buddhism, Hinduism, Islam, Shintoism (in Japan) or shamanism (in Korea and elsewhere), or to cults such as Freemasonry, Mormonism, Scientology, New Age, Christian Science and the like, or whose ancestors have belonged to such false religions or cults, also need to have the effects of dedications broken.

My practice is to cancel any power the enemy is able to wield through ancestral dedications, whether I suspect these are present or not—especially over non-Westerners, but over Westerners, too. It is better to be safe than sorry. I treat known specific dedications expressly, whether ancestral or in the person's life. To do this I simply assert the authority of Jesus Christ to cancel any enemy rights and to break all power gained through dedications to the specific god or spirit, if known. Then I speak the covering of any rituals used in these dedications with the blood of Jesus Christ.

In a recent ministry session dealing with a spirit of Freemasonry, the demon boasted, "You don't even know the curses [i.e., stemming from the Freemasonry dedications] that are on her!"

"I don't have to know those curses," I replied. "I cover them all with the blood of Jesus Christ."

After a pause the demon stated, "I don't have any power anymore."

And we were easily able to kick him out.

4. Authority over the Transmitted Effects of Sin

Often Satan has gained rights in our lives through sinful behavior on the parts of various ancestors. Many of us know of alcoholism, aberrant sexual behavior or even criminal activity in our family trees. Such behavior allows the enemy rights, on the basis of which he can make claims on us. Any wallowing in sin on our part can give the same rights.

With the authority we have in Christ, we can claim freedom from satanic interference in the area of sin as well. We simply assert the power of God to break any power Satan has gained in a person's generational line through sinful behavior. It is a good idea to precede such taking of authority with identificational repentance (see chapter 13), claiming the authority that is ours as the current representative of our family line and *repenting of the sins of our ancestors.* Like Nehemiah (Nehemiah 1:6–7) and Daniel (Daniel 9:5–11), we identify with our ancestors in their sinfulness, taking responsibility for their sins as if they are ours and confessing our participation with them. We then assert our authority to repent on their behalf to remove family guilt from ourselves—though not from them.

We do not have the right to grant any ancestors forgiveness, but we can free people for whom we are praying from any guilt that attaches itself to them and from any rights that the ancestors' sin gives the enemy over them. To do this we may have the person say something like, "As the current representative of my father's/mother's family, I assume responsibility for the sins of my ancestors and humbly repent for their disobedience in the name of Jesus Christ, who paid for their sins as well as mine." The act of identificational repentance breaks this dimension of the enemy's power over them.

5. Authority over the Effects of Trauma

We often find, in dealing with demonization in the present, that the enemy is able to enter when a person experiences trauma or abuse. Given the fact that such experiences may have happened to more than one ancestor, it is helpful to cancel any rights the enemy may have gained through trauma in the family line. This is done in the same way as recommended above for any of the other four areas.

Prayer as Partnership

For most of my Christian life I have been puzzled by prayer. I always saw prayer primarily as a way of requesting things from God. We are assured, however, that God knows what we are about to ask before we ask it (Matthew 6:8). So why ask? We also are told that if we ask anything according to God's will, our request will be granted (1 John 5:14–15). But how are we to know what God's will is?

I failed to see at least two things. The first is that *prayer is an act of partnership with God.* The second is that *prayer is primarily an act of spiritual warfare,* an enormous threat to Satan's plans. For when we take the authority God has given us to exercise the privileges of our relationship with Him by calling on Him in prayer, the enemy is in trouble.

Take the so-called "Lord's Prayer" as an example (Matthew 6). Jesus starts by assuming we have the authority of a family relationship that enables us to call God our Father. The prayer brings us into partnership with God by committing ourselves to Him in worship. He alone is to be the object of our worship and allegiance. To cement this partnership, God has adopted us into His family (1 John 3:1), even assigning us rights of inheritance (Romans 8:17; Galatians 4:7). Such allegiance and worship damage the enemy's cause and stifle his attempts to win us over.

Then, assuming as Jesus always did that this world is in captivity, He teaches us to position ourselves with God to bring about the victory of God's Kingdom over that of the usurper, Satan. This is a second act of defiance of the enemy and his schemes. From the overall teaching of Scripture, then, we learn that the seeking of God's Kingdom is a partnership. That is, God is not going to conquer without human participation. Our job is to seek that Kingdom above all else (Matthew 6:33) so that God's will may be done on earth just as it is in heaven.

Next we are to ask for our needs to be met. But this request is to be made in full assurance that God knows our needs and desires (Matthew 6:31–32) and meets them with our assistance. We are to partner with Jesus by taking on us a yoke that He claims is not heavy since He, like the strong ox of Jewish custom, carries the heavy end (Matthew 11:28–30).

Partnership in forgiving is the next thing we request. But this request involves a condition and a commitment. We are to forgive as Jesus forgives. This is our commitment. The condition is that if we do not forgive, Jesus will not forgive us. This is one of the most important and most warlike of the statements in this prayer. It is also the only part of the prayer on which Jesus elaborates (Matthew 6:14–15). In helping people deal with emotional wounds in inner healing ministry, we find that it is through unforgiveness that the enemy is most effective in crippling people. If Jesus' people are to be free to fight the enemy, we must forgive.

And finally we are to request protection from "hard testing" and that God "keep us safe from the Evil One" (Matthew 6:9–13). We are to ask God to protect us from temptation—but this, too, is partnership. We also know that our enemy, Satan, is behind temptation. So we ask our Master to work with us to defeat this enemy. And the enemy, knowing the power of our prayer partnership with God, does whatever he can to keep us from praying.

Conclusion

That God would invite us into partnership with Him and give us the authority we have been discussing is truly mind-boggling! But just about everything concerning God is mind-boggling, especially once we have broken through to the God side of the glass ceiling. With this partnership as our right and this authority as a gift from God, the tragedy is that so few of us evangelicals even know these opportunities exist, much less enter into them.

Our enemy is alive and well and very active in our world today. And according to Romans 16:20 God desires to crush him under *our* feet. To carry out His desire, we need all the authority God gives us and all the commitment to this partnership with Jesus that we can muster. We are at war, and powerless Christianity will not suffice.

With this introduction to partnership and authority, then, let us turn more specifically to the subject of spiritual warfare.

eleven

Spiritual Warfare

The subject of spiritual warfare or spiritual conflict is of major concern to many evangelicals. The popularity of Frank Peretti's books *This Present Darkness* (1986) and *Piercing the Darkness* (1989) raised the subject and has led to a good bit of discussion in many evangelical circles. The question in many people's minds is, "Since Peretti's books are fiction, how well does his portrayal of spiritual warfare correspond to what happens in real life?"

Though I cannot vouch for everything Peretti writes on this subject, my experience leads me to grant a high degree of credibility to his picture of the spirit world. He portrays an active, well-organized realm of evil spirits—a realm assumed by the authors of Scripture. He imagines what goes on between the inhabitants of the evil realm, the angels of God and human beings. He describes the great evil power that operates as a satanic conspiracy and attempts to defeat God by thwarting and attacking the people of God and our institutions. He observes the need for partnership between humans and God to counter that power. And he correctly views prayer as an act of warfare and the primary means of obtaining the spiritual power enabling us to attack the enemy and win.

Theologians and others with no experience in dealing with the spirit world have sought to discredit Peretti (e.g., Guelich, 1991). But they speak from a base of no experience. I question their right, therefore, to critique him. My experience leads me to believe that Peretti knows his subject more accurately than his critics, and I recommend that evangelicals read his books as a way of becoming sensitized to what probably goes on in the invisible spirit world.

In this chapter I will outline what is usually referred to as spiritual warfare. In the following chapters I will suggest some things we can do to participate with God in this warfare. But first . . .

Should Evangelicals Fear This Topic?

I once asked an evangelical pastor the following question: "If demons exist, would you rather know or not know?" He answered as probably many evangelicals would: "I'd rather not know!" What a sad commentary! Because the Holy Spirit lives within us, in the spirit world we are like elephants and demons are like mice. The myth (probably not true) is that mice actually terrify elephants—not because they have more power than elephants but only because they bluff them into fear. Thus it is with us and the satanic kingdom: We, in partnership with Jesus, carry infinitely more power than satanic "mice" do, but they are expert at bluffing us out of using that power against them.

Not surprisingly we fear the unknown and keep away from it gladly if we can. Evangelical pastors and other church leaders have enough to do without opening this can of worms! But the result is a sub-biblical Christianity—a Christianity without power. Our Christianity is so affected by Western secular assumptions that we deny in practice, if not in theory, the existence of the invisible supernatural world. And more and more, with widespread questioning of whether science has all the answers, people are looking for a faith with power as well as insight.

Evangelical theologians who tend to live in their heads feel justified in discussing whether or not demons exist today. Many pastors who also tend to live in their heads join them, especially since they, with the theologians, have bought into the secular assumption that emotional problems are all psychological. And they blame spiritual problems on the person and believe such problems can be solved through Bible reading, praying and just "gutting it out." *Jesus is trusted when He talks about love or sin, but not when He assumes demonic influence, as He often did.*

But what if Jesus was right about demons, as we believe He was right about love and sin? What if people in our churches (as in the synagogues of Jesus' day) are inhabited by demons? Can we assume that the battles waged by Jesus against satanic emissaries are over? Are all the demons gone? Or are they smart enough to not reveal themselves to people who question their existence so they can do their work unhindered, even in people (Christians) they know have more power than they do?

On the other hand, what about the excesses we talked about in chapter 5? What about those who blame everything on demons and spend a lot of time shouting at them? We certainly do not want to be associated with people that off-balance. These excesses, which do exist, affect our imaginations so that we cannot conceive of being involved in spiritual warfare without being, or at least perceived as being, loony.

When it comes to spiritual warfare, Jesus knew something we do not. He knew the world is full of enemy spirits and that they are very successful at victimizing people. He also showed us what to do about it. Not being secularized, as we are, He did not treat alien beings as psychological problems. Nor did He simply accommodate a prescientific worldview that believed psychological problems were the manifestation of demonic beings. He was dealing with capital *R*-Reality when He assumed alien beings that serve Satan exist and that they seek to disrupt whatever they are allowed. Such alien beings are very much part of the scene today.

Should we be afraid to follow Jesus in this area of Reality? We should not. But we need to learn a few things, in addition to the fact that we have more power than demonic forces. Jesus did not go into battle unprepared. Nor dare we. And we do not have to become like the hyperemotional people who, unlike Jesus, make spiritual warfare look so distasteful to us evangelicals.

The Bible Takes Satan and Demons Seriously

Satan and his forces are taken very seriously in Scripture. Throughout the Old Testament the evil kingdom is always lurking in the background and affecting what goes on in the human realm. But Satan is not omnipresent. He has to depend on his principalities, powers, rulers and ground-level demons (dark angels) to carry out his plans. Whether in the Garden of Eden or afflicting Job, whether in his activities during Israel's wars or influencing the pagan nations, these messengers of evil have been and are the agents of Satan.

In the New Testament, ground-level demonic spirits influenced those who killed the babies when Jesus was a child (Matthew 2:16–18). Though Satan himself confronted Jesus in the wilderness (Luke 4:1–13), he undoubtedly was accompanied by a host of demonic spirits. Dark angels were especially active during Jesus' ministry. Indeed we frequently see Him exposing and casting them out. Satan must have assigned some of his choicest ground-level spirits to work with the Pharisees and the other Jewish leaders to build up opposition to Jesus. Demonic beings were active in many of the events recorded in the book of Acts (e.g., Ananias and Sapphira, Acts 5:1–11; the demonized slave girl, Acts 16:16–18) and in activities recorded throughout the epistles and Revelation (e.g., the table of demons, 1 Corinthians 10:21; blinding those who do not believe, 2 Corinthians 4:4; the teachings of demons, 1 Timothy 4:1; and many of the activities throughout the book of Revelation).

Our struggle is not against flesh and blood, but against the rulers, against the authorities, against the powers of this dark world and against the spiritual forces of evil in the heavenly realms.

Ephesians 6:12, NIV

In spite of this, neither Jesus nor the leaders in the New Testament seemed alarmed by the satanic kingdom or its activities. They were not impressed by them at all. When confronted they dealt with them matter-of-factly, knowing that God's Kingdom and His power are infinitely greater. But they took the satanic kingdom seriously. While they were never afraid of evil spirits, they acknowledged their existence and used the power of the Holy Spirit to fight them.

A study of the gospels reveals that two of the most important things Jesus did were to speak about the Kingdom of God and to demonstrate that it was already present on earth. The fact that He drove out demons, as He stated, "proves that the Kingdom of God has already come to you" (Luke 11:20). Repeatedly Jesus operated in God-anointed spiritual authority. He came to defeat Satan both during His life and through the cross and resurrection. Time and time again Jesus exercised His spiritual authority over the enemy. More than half of the gospel of Mark is devoted to His demonstrations of this fact through healing and deliverance.

Jesus made it plain, however, that He did not limit this authority to Himself. During His earthly ministry He conferred on His apostles (Luke 9) and on the 72 (Luke 10) the "power and authority to drive out all demons and to cure diseases" (Luke 9:1). With this authority and power they were to heal the sick and let people know that "the Kingdom of God has come near you" (Luke 10:9). Then He said to His disciples and to us, "As the Father sent me, so I send you" (John 20:21). Jesus intended that His followers imitate His approach to witness, accompanying words with power (see Acts 1:8).

From Jesus' words in Matthew 28:20 we learn that He meant for His followers to teach their followers the things He had taught them. He stated that they are to teach their followers "to *obey everything I have commanded you.*" That this teaching was to include how to operate in the authority of Jesus to perform signs and wonders seems clear from His promise in John 14:12 that "those who believe in me will do what I do—yes, they will do even greater things, because I am going to the Father."

What Are Evil Spirits?

The fallen angels we call demons or evil spirits (I make no distinction between these terms) are the "ground-level" troops, as opposed to the "cosmic-level" principalities, powers and rulers of Ephesians 6:12. These are the ones we encounter most often during spiritual warfare. Scripture tells us that demons seek people to inhabit (Matthew 12:43–45). They apparently envy our bodies. They have distinct personalities, are destructive (Mark 9:17–29) and differ in power and wickedness (Matthew 12:45; Mark 5:4).

Since Satan can be in only one place at a time, the other members of his hierarchy execute his schemes throughout the universe. In addition to broader assignments such as governing territories and institutions, evil spirits bother humans—especially Christians. Satan does not like anything God likes. He picks on God's favorite creatures, therefore—us. I believe he has at least one demon assigned to each person.

Evil spirits, both ground- and cosmic-level, are especially interested in disrupting and, if possible, crippling anything or anyone that might threaten Satan's domination of the world. They aim their guns, therefore, at individuals, groups and organizations that in any way seek to serve God's purposes. They produce "strongholds" in people's minds (2 Corinthians 10:4) and probably in other places as well. They attack Christian ministries. They are agents of doctrinal aberrations (1 Timothy 4:1). They affect health (Luke 13:11), perhaps they affect weather (Luke 8:22–25), and they even have "the power over death"

(Hebrews 2:14)—though they have no power except that allowed them by God.

Within the hierarchy these evil beings, whatever their level, seem to respond only to those over them or to a greater power. They can be released from whatever they are assigned to do only by their supervisor or by a power (i.e., God) greater than that supervisor.

The satanic kingdom wants us to fear it. But when we realize how little power that kingdom has compared to the power of God, our fear evaporates. We should respect Satan and demons and never take them lightly. But most of what looks like power on their part is either deceit or bluff or both. *They really have little more power than that given them by the persons they inhabit.*

Satanic beings are involved in every kind of disruptive activity in human life. They can hinder earthly activities and delay answers to prayer (Daniel 10:12–13). They seem to have authority over places and territories (i.e., buildings, cities, temples). In addition they appear to have authority over social groups (e.g., organizations, people groups) and influence sinful behavior such as homosexuality, abortion, drug addiction, lust, incest, rape, murder and so forth.

Levels of Spirits

Evil spirits operate at different levels and types. I will describe the types as I understand them with more detail in the following chapters. We may diagram the types as follows:

Ground-Level Spirits (living in people)	Cosmic-Level Spirits (in the air, Ephesians 2:2)
1. Family spirits 2. Occult spirits (representing occult allegiances) 3. Ordinary spirits (attached to sinful attitudes and emotions)	1. Territorial spirits (over territories) 2. Institutional spirits (over organizations) 3. Vice spirits (over vices) 4. Object and household spirits (over objects and houses) 5. Ancestral spirits

Ground-Level Spirits

Spiritual warfare is waged on at least two levels. The lower level is what I call ground-level warfare. This type of warfare involves dealing with the spirits (demons) that are assigned by the demonic kingdom to live and work within people. Such demons (as we saw briefly in chapter 3) take at least three forms: *family spirits, occult spirits* and, for lack of a better name, *ordinary spirits*. Family spirits are stronger than occult spirits, and occult spirits are usually stronger than ordinary spirits.

1. *Family spirits* are those that are inherited through the generations in societies that routinely dedicate their children to gods and spirits. These can be found living in large numbers of Asians; in the tribal peoples of places like Africa, Melanesia and Latin America; and in indigenous peoples in Euro America such as Native Americans, Australian aborigines and gypsies. Unfortunately they are passed down from generation to generation, even to people who have not been dedicated personally. I do not know how many generations such demons can affect, but I have found them in people two generations after such dedication was practiced. I have found family spirits, one representing the father's line and another representing the mother's line, when ministering to Koreans, Chinese and Africans. I also have found, on occasion, that people with European backgrounds have family spirits, especially if their ancestry goes back to European royalty.

2. *Occult spirits* are those that come from membership in cults or occult organizations. Like family spirits these can be passed down to succeeding generations, even to children and grandchildren who are not dedicated. I have worked with well over a hundred people who have carried spirits of Freemasonry passed on to them by parents or grandparents, even though they themselves were never part of that organization.

3. *Ordinary spirits* are those that gain a legal right because the people hang onto unforgiveness, anger, hatred, fear and the like. These are the kinds of problems we see most in deep-level healing. A rule of the universe seems to be that when such

human problems are not addressed, the enemy has a legal right to implant his accomplices.

I have experienced numerous encounters with ground-level demons and can testify that they are real and are in the world in abundance. Though I seldom have been able to simply command them to leave, as the gospels portray Jesus doing, I have been successful in confronting them in Jesus' name and freeing people of them and their interference.

As we have discussed, demons are able to live in people because they have "legal rights"—rights that are theirs by laws of the universe and until someone with more power comes along to evict them. These rights are granted them by virtue of spiritual "garbage." Such garbage consists of rights given through inheritance, invitation, wallowing in sin, curses and a few other ways (see Kraft, 1992). *Demons are like rats, and rats live where there is garbage.* Dealing with the garbage, then, is the most important aspect of the process of fighting demons at ground level. We have found that an approach to demonized people that frees them from the garbage makes it possible to deal with the demons easily and effectively without violence.

A struggle may take place at first, if the person's will is not yet on God's side or if he or she has a lot of garbage. But as soon as the person is willing to deal with the garbage and partner with Jesus to confront the demons—usually with someone knowledgeable helping—the tough part is over. And most people who come for deliverance prayer have already chosen to turn to God for help.

Cosmic-Level Spirits

The upper level of spiritual warfare is ordinarily known as cosmic-level warfare (called "strategic-level warfare" by C. Peter Wagner). The term, as I stated earlier, is derived from Ephesians 6:12: "We are not fighting against human beings but against the wicked spiritual forces in the heavenly world, the rulers, authorities, and *cosmic* powers of this dark age" (emphasis added). At cosmic level we have to deal with at least five kinds of higher-level satanic spirits (as I explained in chapter 3):

territorial, institutional, vice, household and *ancestor spirits*. The order in which I list these spirits does not necessarily represent a hierarchical ordering. I am not sure, for example, that vice spirits are less powerful than institutional spirits, even though I have listed vice spirits below institutional spirits. It is probable, however, that territorial spirits are above the others.

Cosmic-level spirits are probably the spirits mentioned in Ephesians 2:2, in which Satan is called the ruler of the spirits in the air. The listing of spirit types in Ephesians 6:12 suggests a hierarchy that might correspond with some of the types listed below. As the author of the book of Daniel saw (and with which Frank Peretti concurs), God's own host of spirits (angels) counters those of the enemy. But the activity of both God's and Satan's emissaries depends at least partially on human partnership.

Some cosmic-level satanic spirits seem to be in charge of ground-level spirits, assigning them to people and supervising them as they carry out their assignments. For example, when people commit themselves to occult organizations such as Freemasonry, Scientology, Mormonism or the Jehovah's Witnesses, demons representing the higher-level spirits of these organizations inhabit the people. Likewise vices such as abortion and homosexuality bring automatic demonization.

1. TERRITORIAL SPIRITS

Territorial spirits are those assigned to nations, cities and regions. We read about two of those assigned to nations in Daniel 10:13 and 21. They are called "the Prince of Persia" and "the Prince of Greece." These spirits were powerful enough to hinder the delivery of God's answer to Daniel's prayer. Because Daniel was living in Persia, the picture emerges of a high-level spirit protecting that nation from a visitation by God. Fortunately God's spirits, called angels, countered the enemy's hindering activity. Thus the angel sent to Daniel went to the archangel Michael to obtain the help he needed to get through to Daniel. We read of a battle in the heavenlies between the emissaries of Satan and those of God. We do not know much about how this conflict was waged, but we gather that it both affected and was influenced by humans.

2. INSTITUTIONAL SPIRITS

Institutional spirits are the second type of cosmic-level spirits. We can infer from Scripture that such spirits are assigned to churches, governments, educational institutions, cults, occult organizations (e.g., Scientology, Freemasonry, Mormonism) and non-Christian religions (e.g., the gods of Hinduism, Buddhism, animism). Note that some are assigned to enhance occult activity while others are assigned to disturb churches, Christian institutions and other organizations committed to God. Again God's angels are available to counter occult and religious activity and to empower the activities of organizations committed to Him, if humans partner with Him (e.g., the angels of the churches in the book of Revelation, chapters 2 and 3).

3. VICE SPIRITS

Vice spirits are those assigned to oversee and encourage vices such as prostitution, abortion, homosexuality, gambling, pornography and war. Those of us involved in spiritual warfare often feel the presence of satanic spirits in and around establishments that propagate these activities. But when we partner with God to break the power of these spirits, interesting things happen. A former student of mine reported that she had once worked in an abortion clinic. As Christians prayed outside that clinic, what was going on inside was crippled. In fact, she said she felt the power of God so obviously that she left the clinic and never returned.

4. HOUSEHOLD AND CULTURAL ITEM SPIRITS

Household and cultural item spirits are the fourth type of cosmic-level spirits. These are spirits I believe inhabit households, rocks, trees, material items that have been dedicated, rituals, dedicated music and the like. In many societies people believe in "kitchen spirits" and spirits that inhabit other rooms of the house, as well as nature spirits that inhabit rocks, trees, water, etc. Many, including missionaries, who have purchased art items in other societies testify that obvious enemy activity began when those items were brought into their homes. In addition, much contemporary popular music is dedicated to Satan, either formally or informally. Christians should be aware of such realities and use the authority of God to counteract their effects.

5. ANCESTRAL SPIRITS

Ancestral spirits are demons assigned to deceive people into believing that their dead ancestors still participate in human life. Many of the peoples of the world are convinced that their dead ancestors are active in bringing blessing when they are honored or in taking revenge if they are not treated right by the living. Such belief is not scriptural. God does not have ancestral angels. I am sure, though, that people attempting to follow God's truth in ancestral matters will receive the help of ministering angels.

Discussions of spiritual warfare should take into account these levels and types of spirits and what to do about them. Although Jesus frequently encountered and cast out ground-level demons, He seemed not to take notice of higher-level spirits except in His encounter with Satan (Luke 4:1–13). In confronting and defeating Satan in his own territory (i.e., the wilderness was considered the property of Satan), Jesus likely broke much of Satan's power over at least that part of Palestine.

Some scholars have suggested that the demons afflicting the Gerasene demoniac (Mark 5:1–20) were territorial spirits. This interpretation is supported by the fact that the demons begged Jesus not to send them out of their region (verse 10). Furthermore, in spite of the freed man's begging to be allowed to join Jesus' followers, Jesus sent him back to testify to the people of the region concerning his deliverance (verses 18–20). A revival broke out as a result! If these were territorial spirits, they were concentrated in one man like ground-level demons. And though they seemed more difficult to cast out than other demons, Jesus dealt with them in the same way He dealt with purely ground-level demons.

In the following two chapters we will deal further with both ground-level and cosmic-level spirits and discuss how to deal with them.

Forms, Meanings and Empowerment

An important issue in any discussion of spiritual warfare is the matter of cultural forms. The form-meaning distinction is an important contribution of anthropology to our understanding of culture and life. We use the term *form* to label all the customs, structures and material objects (visible and invisible) that make up a culture. These items may be material objects (e.g., jewelry, houses, chairs, idols) or nonmaterial entities (e.g., words, rituals, baptism, songs). We label as cultural forms all the rituals, music, beliefs, furniture and millions of other things we use and participate in during the course of our lives. Individual items, whether visible (e.g., tools, kitchen utensils, gestures) or invisible (values, language structures), whether small (pins, pencils) or large (ceremonies, buildings), are all cultural forms. *All the visible and invisible items of a culture are called forms.* People observe and use these cultural forms.

People also interpret and assign *meanings* to these forms. Such meanings can affect people powerfully. The term *meanings* signifies the interpretations of these forms by the people who use them. We learn from communication theory that meanings exist—not in the cultural or linguistic forms themselves but in the people who use the forms. People attach meanings to cultural forms according to the customary agreements of the people who use them. For example, we can talk to each other intelligibly only if both of us agree to attach the same meanings to the noises (words, sentences) we make. These words and sentences are the language forms we use. We expect that the other person will interpret them to mean what we mean by them. The forms are the parts of culture and language; the meanings are created according to the agreements of the persons who use the forms.

In addition to being vehicles of meaning, cultural forms can be spiritually *empowered*, either by God's power or by Satan's. Contrary to what many of our critics contend, we do not wrestle simply over meanings but with real, live invisible beings that are able to inhabit cultural forms (Ephesians 6:12). This fact is important in dealing with spiritual warfare.

Even Western Christians show some awareness of this principle when we dedicate church buildings, the elements of Communion, anointing oil and babies to our God. In addition we bless individuals and, in benedictions, whole congregations in the name of Jesus Christ. Though our critics probably believe such dedications and blessings are merely rituals, significant only because of their meanings, I do not. I believe, of course, that these acts have meaning. But multiple experiences of blessing or anointing a person and witnessing an immediate and unexpected reaction have convinced me that we also are dealing with God's empowerment.

James recommends that we use anointing oil to bring healing to the sick (James 5:14). If the oil is to be effective, however, it must be dedicated in the name of Jesus and thus empowered. The elements used in the Lord's Supper, too, can and should be dedicated. This is undoubtedly what Paul meant in 1 Corinthians 10:16 when he referred to the Communion cup as "blessed" (KJV, NRSV, NASB). He intended for the elements to be thus empowered. This empowerment makes it dangerous to participate in the Lord's Supper unworthily (1 Corinthians 11:28–32). Paul's handkerchiefs and aprons were also empowered (Acts 19:12), as was Jesus' robe (Luke 8:43–48), so that people received healing through them.

God regularly flows His power through words such as *in Jesus' name* and the commands we give to demons. When such words convey God's power, we call them "empowered language forms." When we dedicate buildings or objects to Jesus, we are using His authority to empower them for His purposes. This use of cultural forms to convey God's power seems to be acceptable to our critics. But these critics often object to the fact that cultural objects (material forms) can carry evil spiritual power.

Many missionaries and travelers have experienced strange occurrences in their homes that stopped when they prayed over or destroyed certain objects. These objects usually come from non-Western societies and were bought or given as souvenirs. Always when God's authority was invoked to break that power, the strange things that were going on stopped.

Peter and Doris Wagner experienced this problem firsthand. After Doris experienced a demonic presence several times in their own home, they invited two people with spiritual discernment to come to their house to discern what needed to be done. At first these two were unable to enter the house, presumably because the spirits knew why they had come. When they finally came in, they identified some objects the Wagners had brought home from Bolivia as at least partially responsible for the problem. These objects were destroyed, and the Wagners have had no such problems for more than ten years (Wagner, 1988:63ff.).

I once foolishly visited a temple in Taiwan during an important festival honoring spirits of death, and came away with a severe pain in my chest that was not relieved until we prayed three weeks later. Perhaps it was chance. Perhaps the event is explainable on the basis of meaning alone. Perhaps. It is curious, though, that with me and with many others who have recounted similar experiences, the problem started at a specific time related to a place that just might have been empowered, and ended at a specific time related to the application of the greater power of God to the problem. It takes less faith to believe in this type of empowerment, which I believe is biblical, than to postulate that meaning or simply chance are sufficient to provide explanation. Naturalism requires great credulity.

Probably all of us who deal with demonized persons have had the experience of getting nowhere with a demon until the person removes some object from his or her person. Often this is a necklace, a ring, sometimes a Masonic ring or some other piece of jewelry or decoration. When the item is removed, our ability to deal with the demon is improved immediately. When we ask the person about the item, we usually find that it was blessed with satanic power and given by someone in an occult organization.

Priest and his colleagues, in their desire to explain naturalistically our contentions about the empowerment of cultural forms, attempt to attribute everything to the meanings people assign to them. Although, as I have stated, meaning can be a powerful thing, my experience leads me to recognize an empowerment component in addition to form and meaning. This component has to be taken into account with cultural forms that have been dedicated to spirit beings, whether God or Satan.

When an object is dedicated to God or to Satan—usually in the name of a god or spirit—a meaning is given to it. But meaning alone cannot explain the power in such an object to disrupt a household or to hinder the casting out of a demon. Seldom does the person who owns the object have any idea that it can affect his or her life. But such dedicated objects do affect people's lives. Indeed, they are intended to do so by those who dedicate them. They are dedicated with the expectation that the objects thereby receive some kind of ability to convey spiritual power. We call this ability "empowerment."

Meaning and Empowerment Interact in Spiritual Warfare

Spiritual warfare is as much a matter of dealing with meanings as it is dealing with power. Repeatedly I have raised the issue of spiritual blindness inherent in our Western worldview. This blindness is a matter of the meanings we have been taught to assign to the events of life. If we do not see the spiritual dimension because of our worldview blindness, we will not recognize the spiritual power that may be active in many of our life experiences. So we may have both a meaning blindness and a power blindness.

The problems raised by inadequate handling of the meaning and empowerment of cultural forms can be troublesome. The blindness of the people in our own families or congregations is one of these problems. In addition to those who are blind to spiritual warfare, many in our families and churches have been affected by occult involvements such as New Age, Freemasonry, Scientology, fortunetelling, Ouija boards, certain computer games (e.g., "Dungeons and Dragons") and even certain movies and books (e.g., the *Harry Potter* series). These people are often quite unaware of the spiritual power behind these involvements. They fall into the meaning problem, therefore, of considering such activities harmless.

Whether we are dealing with family members or friends or whether we are in positions of Christian leadership, it is important for us to learn how to handle both empowerment and meaning. This is especially crucial for those of us who seek to witness to or disciple those in or from non-Western societies, whether overseas or in the United States. Often the meaning problem is more difficult to deal with than the empowerment problem; but the two problems regularly coincide.

Once we learn to work in the authority Christ has given us, we recognize that breaking the power of empowered objects is usually not difficult. Since we have infinitely more power in Jesus Christ than such objects can convey, we simply have to claim His power to break the enemy's power in the object. I simply say, "I break any enemy power in this object in Jesus' name." Then I also bless it in His name. The problem with satanic empowerment is not that we do not have the power to break it; it is that we must overcome ignorance (i.e., a meaning problem) so that we recognize when it is there and know what to do to break it.

In many non-Western societies, implements used for seeking food, warfare, religious practices and other necessary activities are routinely dedicated to the spirits or gods of the society. Temples, homes, workplaces and whole nations (e.g., Japan) also are dedicated by priests with the authority of their gods behind them. In the South Pacific, for example, those who made the large canoes used for fishing or for warfare dedicated them regularly to their gods. I suspect they still do, even if they call themselves Christians. When such things are dedicated to satanic spirits, they are empowered by those spirits. And, as I mentioned, many missionaries or travelers who have taken dedicated cultural items home with them have unwittingly invited enemy spirits into their homes.

In the United States I have been asked from time to time to advise people who have had strange experiences in certain places. In one case a church was experiencing difficulties that most of its parishioners interpreted naturalistically. But when it was discovered that the church had been built on an American Indian burial ground, and the power of Christ was claimed to break the power of the Indian spirits, these problems stopped. In another situation a missionary to Native Americans observed that over a thirty-year period, everyone who lived in a certain house on their mission station had left that station in some sort of severe difficulty. Though many of the missionaries attributed this fact to chance, the leader of the mission decided to fast and conduct spiritual warfare prayer over the house. Things seem to be fine now.

When we suspect an object or place has been used for satanic purposes, it is important to disempower it before attempting to use it. Satanic power can and should be broken over rituals, buildings, carvings, songs and just about anything else people use. Those things should be captured for God's use. Despite the fact that many counsel us to refuse to use whatever the enemy has used (e.g., Hunt and McMahon, 1985), I believe we are to capture most cultural forms, not reject them merely because our enemy uses them (see my discussion of this unwise position in Kraft, 1989:211). My rule of thumb is to capture everything except those items that have no other purpose than to honor false gods and spirits (such as idolatrous statues, masks and other items used in religious rituals). Those things I destroy. But we should not try to use even the ones we can capture until the power is broken. That would be unwise in the extreme.

Many people who are used to dealing with spiritual powers still have a meaning problem even after the power is broken in formerly empowered items and places. They may continue to interpret disempowered items as still powerful. Converts to Christianity, for example, may have a difficult time using items and techniques within a Christian context that, in their pre-Christian days, they once used to experience satanic power (e.g., music, visualization). They may agree that the power is broken, but memories of past events in which these items or techniques were used may be a major hindrance to their being able to use them while living within Christianity.

For people converted out of non-Christian religions or occult organizations, it may take years, or a generation or two, before the pre-Christian meanings associated with given objects are fully replaced. Such people frequently want to throw away every vestige of their culture that reminds them of their old involvement with shamans, rituals and evil spirits. In their place they tend to borrow cultural forms from the West (e.g., music, monologue preaching) on the assumption (meaning) that these Western forms carry more spiritual power than their traditional forms. The Bible, in fact, is often interpreted as a fetish, and these borrowed items to mean that God wants Christians in non-Western societies to be foreigners in their own country rather than to capture their own traditions for Christ. But since we Westerners understand so poorly the spiritual power dimensions of our movement, we often go along with and even encourage such a desire to dissimulate. And this has enabled converted foreigners to produce a Christianity that is as powerless as ours in the West and unattractive to most of the people of their lands.

The point is, people come into Christianity with their own meaning system—a system or worldview that will continue to interfere with whatever changes in interpretation they attempt to make. And this regularly causes problems both for those who lack understanding of the power issues and for those who were once involved in satanic power and find it difficult to reinterpret customs and places that once conveyed evil power.

We should not, however, give up in attempting to deal with either the power problem or the meaning problem. With those who have not experienced God's power at work, we can demonstrate the love and power of God—as Jesus did— by inviting them to watch and experience healing and deliverance. For those who have experienced satanic power, though the process may be slower, we can demonstrate the same things and help them cross the bridge from working in satanic power (e.g., in animism or New Age) to working in God's power. This bridge is often a shorter one to empowered Christianity than the bridge from secular naturalism—or powerless Christianity—to a Christianity with power, since most of the principles are the same. The basic difference is not in the principles—both God and Satan obey the same rules—but in the fact that powerful Christianity is plugged into God as the source of power, while animism and New Age are plugged into satanic power.

I pray that, whether at home or abroad, we can learn that a secularized Christianity—the usual form both in America and in most missionized lands—is a long way from the Bible in the area of spiritual power. This fact is as much a meaning problem as a power problem. When people have learned to depend on secular medicine, secular psychology and secular education without the power of God, they have not experienced the spirituality of the Scriptures either in the power dimension or in the meanings they attribute to Christianity. It is an important part of spiritual warfare to fight powerless Christianity on both the power front and the meaning front.

Conclusion

We have surveyed the subject of spiritual warfare—a subject very much in view in the Bible—in an introductory way. In the following chapters, we will address the subject in more detail.

twelve

Ground-Level Spiritual Warfare

Ground-level spiritual warfare takes place in human contexts, in contrast with warfare that takes place largely in the air. It involves the battle against spirits living within people as well as several other types of activity. Ground-level spiritual warfare deals with three types of spirits: family, occult and ordinary.

Activities such as repentance, unity of spiritual leaders, reconciliation and intercessory prayer that are designed to break the power of cosmic-level demons are treated in the next chapter, even though they are ground-level activities.

Demonization

Demonization is the major focus of ground-level warfare. Experience leads us to conclude that in every society a high percentage of people host demons, especially in societies in which babies are dedicated to spirits. In such societies the percentage of demonized people carrying family demons is close to one hundred percent. Early Church history indicates that the first generations of Christians assumed that every convert was demonized and, therefore, needed to be delivered as a precondition to church membership. If this was true at that time, it certainly is true now. Few churches today, however, attempt to clean up their members. If they did, church life would be quite different!

Remember that demons are like rats. If we find rats in our houses, we know we have to do something about the garbage that has attracted them. Inside a human being, emotional or spiritual garbage provides just such a congenial setting for demonic rats. Wherever such emotional or spiritual garbage exists, demonic rats seek and often find entrance. But if we dispose of the garbage, the rats cannot remain strong and can be cast out easily. With people, as with homes, the solution to the rat problem is not only to chase away the rats but to dispose of the garbage. *The biggest problem is not the demons; it is the garbage.*

Demons are attached most frequently to damaged emotions, sin or inheritance. We usually call the demon by the name of the human problem to which it is attached. But this often confuses inexperienced people who think we are trying to cast out a human emotion such as anger, shame, fear or a human sin like lust. This is not true. What is true is that demons attach themselves to the human problem. For example, a person may have the human problem called anger and a demon attached to that problem that we call "spirit of anger." Such names are what we call demonic "function" names. Though demons also may have personal names, it is more useful to know their function names. Function names indicate the emotion or sinful attitude that needs to be handled in order to weaken or expel the demon.

Demons seldom come singly; they come most often in groups. They are, however, arranged hierarchically, with a leader demon in charge of a whole group. My practice is to discover which is the head "rat" and tie all others under his authority to him by the power of the Holy Spirit. This enables me to deal with the whole group at the same time. The head spirit speaks for the whole group. Usually several groups of spirits inhabit a person, with a head spirit over each group. Once the power of each group is broken and the group is bound together, they can be sent to Jesus immediately. Or they can wait until all the groups are discovered, disempowered and bound together. Then all the groups are sent to Jesus at the same time.

How Demons Can Live in People

In order for demons to live in a person, two conditions must be met:

1. They must discover an "entry point."
2. They must have a "legal right" to stay there.

The entry point could be an outright invitation, or it could be via inheritance, or an emotional or spiritual weakness. The legal right is a right that accords with the principles of the spiritual universe. Both are provided in one or more of the following ways:

1. Demons can enter a person by invitation. *Conscious invitation* to demonization happens when the person is deliberately involved with or actually worships gods or powers other than the true God. Those involved in non-Christian religions, Satanism, New Age, Freemasonry, Mormonism, Christian Science and other occult organizations are inviting demons. Such activities are conscious invitations in spite of the fact that our society's worldview blinds it to spirit world activities. Thus people usually do not realize they are inviting demons. But their decision to become involved in the occult is a conscious one, just as a decision to defy the law of gravity would be a conscious decision, whether or not one knew the law.

Unconscious invitation frequently happens when a person wallows in some negative attitude derived from a difficult past experience. People who are physically or emotionally mistreated, for example, are likely to get angry. If they hold onto this anger and foster permanent resentment, bitterness and unforgiveness, a weakness is created that gives demons the right to enter. The anger itself is not a sin, according to Ephesians 4:26–27, but when we stay angry the devil is given a chance to influence us. My experience with demonized people shows that this influence is usually demonization.

Demons actively encourage sins such as those listed in Galatians 5:19–21, and frequently find entrance through the weakening effect of increasing sinfulness. Scripture is clear that sins must be dealt with by repentance and self-discipline. No demonization was suggested for some of the greatest sinners referred to in Scripture (e.g., the adulteresses of John 8 and Luke 7 and the sinful Corinthians of 1 Corinthians 5). Demons cannot enter simply because people commit sin. They can enter, however, if a person chooses not to repent but to continue in the sinful behavior or attitude.

2. Demons can enter a person through the invitation of someone in authority over the person. I know a woman who was raised in a Satanist family and dedicated by her mother to Satan. At that point one or more demons entered the girl, having been invited by those in authority over her. Such dedication of children to spirits or gods is a common practice worldwide. Furthermore, adults who submit to the authority of others in cults can become demonized through dedication or through satanically empowered "blessings" uttered by those in authority over them.

3. A third source of demonization is through inheritance. I cannot understand why God allows this, but children may be born demonized (Exodus 20:5). We often refer to this condition as the passing on of *generational* or *bloodline* spirits. Typically family spirits gain entrance through some commitment made by an ancestor or some curse put on an ancestor. I frequently find inherited spirits in people whose parents or grandparents were involved in witchcraft or occult organizations such as Satanism, Freemasonry, Mormonism or Christian Science.

4. A fourth way demons may enter is through cursing. This is a very common phenomenon, and I frequently find curses to be major factors in the power that demons attain. Curses are often the result of hateful words aimed at a person by another or spoken by the person against himself or herself. Sometimes, though, the curse is more formal, involving a ritual performed by someone practicing witchcraft.

But cursing does not always result in demonization. Usually other conditions must be met as well (such as the presence of weaknesses or sins I just described). According to Proverbs 26:2, without something in a person to hook onto, a curse is like a bird that flutters around but cannot find a place to land. Curses that do land probably carry demons with them.

Can Demons Live in Christians?

Considerable discussion has taken place in the Church as to whether or not demons can live in Christians. Confusion about the topic stems from two sources: the unfortunate term *demon possession* and the lack of experience within the Christian community in delivering people from demons.

The use of the term *demon possession* complicates things greatly. This term is the inaccurate rendering of the two most frequently used Greek terms in Scripture, each of which means no more than "having a demon." The rendering *demon possession* has absolutely no support in the Greek, and it greatly overstates the influence wielded by the vast majority of demons. Most of us working in deliverance prefer the term *demonized* to refer to the fact that one or more demons live inside a person.

The lack of experience in dealing with demonization within our churches leads many to the idealistic belief that Christians cannot be demonized. Though all of us wish that Christians were impervious to demonic inhabitation, experience contradicts such belief. All of us who work in deliverance frequently have to cast demons out of Christians. C. Fred Dickason, whose book *Demon Possession and the Christian* (1987) treats the subject exhaustively, reports over four hundred cases of genuine Christians out of whom he cast demons. I can attest to well over a thousand. We could have been wrong in a few cases, of course, but not in a thousand. Our experience and that of countless others proves that Christians can be—and frequently are—demonized so conclusively that we can be dogmatic about asserting it. Only those who draw their conclusions theoretically, without experience, can deny this fact. And as Dickason points out, the burden of proof lies with those who deny this fact to come up with some theory other than demonization to explain our deliverances.

My theory is that demons can live in only those parts of a Christian where sin also dwells. That is, as sin cannot dwell in a Christian's new nature (see 1 John 3:9), so demons cannot dwell there. The invitation to God to live within one's spirit produces this sanctified innermost being—one's new nature—that evicts both sin and any demons that have taken up residence there. But we fight sin, and perhaps demons, in our other parts: body, mind, emotions and will. It is these parts of Christians that can be home to sin or demons.

I have tested this theory scores of times by commanding demons—under strong pressure from the Holy Spirit to tell the truth—to tell me if they live in the person's spirit. I ask, "Did you used to live in the person's spirit?"

They usually answer, "Yes."

Then I ask, "Do you live there now?"

They consistently answer, "No."

So I ask, "When did you have to get out?"

They reply something like, "When Jesus came in." Or they give the date of the person's conversion.

I conclude, therefore, that demons cannot live in that innermost part of a Christian, the spirit, since it is filled with the Holy Spirit (see Romans 8:16). That part of us becomes alive with the life of Christ and is inviolable by the representatives of the enemy. Sin and demons can, however, live in a Christian's mind, emotions, body and will. We regularly have to evict them from those parts of Christians. Furthermore, I suspect that one reason a demon can have greater control of an unbeliever is because it can invade even the unbeliever's spirit.

The Kinds of Things Demons Do

Demons encourage several kinds of activity. They prefer to do these things from inside of people, if possible, since they can do more damage that way. If they cannot get in, however, they attempt to do the same sorts of things from outside, often trying to fool people into believing they are inside.

1. A major activity of demons is to disrupt. Though they cannot create problems out of nothing, demons can aggravate existing situations. They push, prod, tempt and entice people to make poor or unwise decisions. They work to make bad things worse and to get people to overdo good things so that the once-good things are no longer positive (e.g., overeating, overcontrolling mates or children). Christians are special targets of the enemy. If it were not for the protective power of the Holy Spirit, we can only imagine what they would do to us.

2. Demons are the primary agents of temptation. They do Satan's bidding at his command (e.g., Genesis 3:1–7; Matthew 16:22–23; 26:69–75; Acts 5:3). They apparently can put thoughts into people's minds, though we are responsible for what we do with those thoughts. They tempt primarily in areas of a person's greatest vulnerability. They "tailor-make" the thoughts they put into a person's mind to be appropriate for that person. It is their job to hammer away at a person. They will do whatever it takes to tempt, in hopes that they can contribute to the person's failure.

3. Demons do their best to keep people ignorant of their presence and activity. This is a particularly successful strategy in Western societies. They love it when people do not believe they exist. Demons have told us this repeatedly during ministry sessions. During a recent session observed by a psychologist who was learning about demonization, a demon became so angry during the ministry that it yelled through its host, "I hate it that she [the psychologist] is learning about us. For years we have been hiding and making them think we are psychological problems!"

Because demons can only piggyback onto problems that already exist, they hide effectively from many people. Westerners reason that if they can explain the problem as resulting from natural causes, they do not need to look further. Thus the demon wins and the person becomes discouraged, stops fighting the problem and blames himself or herself for it. Many give up hope, thinking they were crazy or that nothing could be done about the problem anyway.

4. Demons often resort to persuading people to fear them. They do this in several ways. People have come to me fearing they had a demon and that there was something very wrong with them spiritually. They did not know that the presence or absence of a demon usually has little to do with their present spiritual condition, except to hinder it. Christians are often very good at suppressing demonic activity. They usually have become demonized through inheritance, some kind of abuse or pre-Christian involvement, rather than through spiritual failure and rebellion. But the demons have pushed them to fear the worst.

Conversely a number of people are afraid they do *not* have a demon! These are often people who want to avoid responsibility for their problems. They hope to blame demons for them. On the other hand, some have been accused of being crazy or otherwise permanently disabled and genuinely hope that a major part of the problem is demonic and can be eradicated. It usually can.

Many people fear the power of demons. They have heard stories, seen movies or talked to people who became involved in fear-inspiring physical battles with demonized people. They have not learned that most physical battles can be avoided through inner healing and by exercising the spiritual power we have through empowered words, not the power of muscles.

5. In all that demons do, deceit is a major weapon. Demons lie, often in our self-talk—about who we are, who God is, who they are and what they do. As in Eden, they deceive, sometimes through direct contradiction and sometimes through indirect questioning of truth. Then they lead people to think the false concepts or ideas are their own.

6. By whatever means possible, the job of demons is to hinder anything good. They try to keep people from God or from doing anything God wants. They hinder unbelievers from believing (2 Corinthians 4:4). They also influence Christians in the belief area. In addition, such activities as worship, prayer, Bible study and acts of love and compassion are high on the demonic hit list. They specialize in discovering and attacking weaknesses. The greater the weakness, the more often a person is likely to be attacked in that area.

Ground-level demons, often supported by cosmic spirits, attack Christians on Sundays, often from outside. They encourage conflict within families on Sunday mornings as they are preparing for or traveling to church. Demons like to push people's minds to wander during worship or the sermon. Headaches, babies crying and other means of breaking concentration in church can be demonic techniques. In addition, demons like to influence pastors to run churches as clubs rather than as hospitals, to focus on preaching and program rather than on ministering to people, to preach theoretically rather than practically, to perform rather than to communicate. They may push musicians to show off, prompt those who give announcements to interrupt the flow of worship and press ushers to be too obvious—all to weaken what God wants to do in church.

7. Demons specialize in accusing. The term *Satan* originally meant "accuser." Many such accusations are negative statements or thoughts against oneself or others. One of the enemy's favorite devices is to entice people to accuse God, others and themselves of disrupting truth, health, life, love, relationships and anything else that comes from God.

The self-rejection engendered by Western societies provides especially fertile ground for this aspect of demonic activity. In addition to self-accusation, demons plant in our minds thoughts that persuade us to accuse others or God. Demons encourage such things as rumors, disrupted relationships based on misunderstandings or anger at God, and blame of God for things He allows in our lives. They push people to retain guilt even after receiving God's forgiveness; convince people that something is incurably wrong with them; entice people into blaming themselves for abuse they received from others; and strongly suggest that the troubles they experience are from God and are deserved because of their failures.

8. Demons like to support compulsions. They delight in helping people develop a compulsive approach to both good and bad behavior. They reinforce compulsions relating to lust, drugs, alcohol, tobacco, overeating, undereating, pornography, gambling, materialism, competitiveness and the need to be in control. They also encourage exaggerated attention to "good" things such as work, study, attractive dress, religion, doctrinal purity, family, achievement, success and so forth. They delight in pushing people to build on weaknesses and exaggerate strengths. The roots of compulsions often lie in such attitudes as fear, insecurity and feelings of unworthiness. Knowing this, demons are quick to exploit their victims to produce compulsivity as fruit.

9. Demons are adept at harassment. Demons nip at our heels like angry dogs. Satan is referred to as "the ruler of this world" (John 14:30) and does not like it that those who belong to another King are wandering around in his territory. So he harasses us whenever and however he can. Demons often disrupt our lives in whatever ways God allows, influencing such things as traffic, weather, health, stress, relationships, worship, sleep, diet, mechanical things (especially cars and computers) and anything else that affects us.

I believe harassment was Satan's aim when he ordered demons to manifest themselves when Jesus was teaching in the synagogue (Luke 4:33–34). He probably also ordered them to stir up a storm while Jesus was in a boat on Lake Galilee (Luke 8:23–24) and to influence the Pharisees to bother Him continually. To counter such influences, when things begin to go wrong I am in the habit of saying, "If this is the enemy, stop it!" It amazes me how many things stop when I take that approach.

Demons do not seem to harass every Christian equally. They pay more attention to those who are the greatest threat to them and to those who do not have enough prayer support. Many Christians are so passive about their Christianity that they are no threat to the enemy, and get off with very little attention from him, while those who threaten the enemy without having enough prayer support are harassed regularly and effectively. But whether or not a person is a threat to the enemy, no strategy enables Christians to live completely free from demonic attention as long as we are in his territory.

Dealing with Ground-Level Demons

I have spoken of three types of ground-level demons:

Ground-Level Spirits (living in people)

1. Family spirits
2. Occult spirits (representing occult allegiances)
3. Ordinary spirits (attached to sinful attitudes and emotions)

1. *Family spirits* gain their power through the dedication of each generation of children to them. They are the first, and often the most powerful, of the types of spirits that inhabit people. These may be worshiped as gods or may masquerade as ancestors. They may be addressed by the father's or mother's family name or simply as "father's/mother's family spirit."

Recently I was working to bring inner healing, including freedom from some demons, to a Chinese Christian missionary of about fifty years of age. In addition to the fairly "normal" problems to which demons attach, such as hate and anger, she carried family demons that she had inherited from her parents. Some demons had also entered her when her parents dedicated her at a temple soon after her birth and when they took her to a temple as a child for healing. She also carried demons that entered when she practiced Chinese martial arts under a "master" who, without her awareness, dedicated all he did to demonic spirits. This woman had no idea these things that had happened long ago were responsible for the daily (and nightly) torment she experienced. She believed in demons but until recently had believed the lie that demons could not live in Christians, especially dedicated ones such as those who serve as missionaries.

I have discovered that just about every Asian, African or Native American child born into non-Christian families—and even many born into Christian families—are dedicated in traditional ways to family spirits. Though many in these societies claim not to believe in spirits anymore, often this is done "just in case."

These spirits may be strong and well hidden, but the power of Jesus is so great that claiming it to break all power passed down by ancestors usually renders them powerless. This involves canceling the rights given to the spirits through vows, curses, dedications, sins, violence and anything else the ancestors did. Any permission given by the person himself or herself, or anyone in authority over the person (e.g., by appealing to those spirits for healing or blessing), also needs to be canceled.

2. To deal with *occult spirits,* one must cancel the rights given to demons through dedications, vows and curses a person has brought on himself or herself through membership in an occult group. The initiatory rites of religions and secret societies—even some university fraternities and sororities—give demons the right to live in those who undergo them, whether they know it or not. Most do not know the price they pay to belong to such groups. People automatically give demons rights to inhabit them when they follow non-Christian religions such as Islam, Buddhism, Mormonism, Christian Science, Scientology and Jehovah's Witnesses. They also give demons those rights when they join secret societies such as Freemasonry or college fraternities and sororities where they take oaths.

When a person renounces his or her association with a religion or cult, the person leading the ministry session simply cancels all rights by covering every word or ritual with the power of the blood of Christ. In most cases this is all that is necessary. But in some cases the person may need to renounce specific things he or she has said.

3. *Ordinary spirits* gain rights through a person's wallowing in some negative emotion or sin, or through someone in authority over the person imparting such an emotion with the demon attached. As with the other ground-level demons, the

person is usually unconscious of their presence since they masquerade as the person's own voice.

Many acquire such demons soon after conception due to the fact that their parents did not want them or did not want a child of their sex. Spirits of shame and sometimes of anger can enter this way. Spirits like fear, anger, rebellion and a host of others usually enter during childhood. Dealing with such spirits is a function of inner healing (see chapter 8), since the presence and strength of these spirits is calibrated to the amount and kind of inner garbage the person carries.

Talking to Demons

Many of us who deal with demons are criticized, largely by the inexperienced (e.g., Priest, Campbell and Mullen, 1995), for asking demons for information to use in expelling them. The theory of such critics is that since demons are liars, they can never tell the truth and, therefore, can never be of help to us, even under pressure from the Holy Spirit. From the certainty with which these critics present their theory, one might be misled into thinking they themselves have tried extracting information from demons and have always been fooled. If they had, however, they would have changed their theory, for they would have discovered what we have—that God gives us a lot of useful information by forcing the demons to reveal their secrets to us.

These critics claim that demons *cannot* tell the truth. Yet whenever demons or Satan speak in the New Testament, they always speak truthfully even though they usually speak it at the wrong time. Demons often do try to lie. But when they do, the Holy Spirit usually reveals it to us right away. Once again experience proves that the Holy Spirit uses even demons to provide the information we need. Hundreds of times I have received information from demons that was accurate and helpful in casting them out.

Demons were not the only source of our information. In these cases God also gave us words of knowledge, and we derived information from experience.

In demonization the real problem is not the demons but the emotional and spiritual garbage in the person's life that gives the rats a legal right. Thus the information we seek concerns those root problems. I do not converse with demons for the fun of it or to obtain general data—though a good bit of such information, whether accurate or inaccurate, surfaces along the way. The purpose of talking to demons is to use them to obtain the information we need to get people healed and, in the process, to get rid of the demons. If they reveal something that enables us to defeat them, we are grateful for the way God uses this technique.

Our critics must respond not only to the practice of which they do not approve but also to the results of that practice. I can point to well over a thousand positive deliverance sessions—sessions in which demonized people were freed. If we counted the experiences of my associates, we could at least quadruple that number. To counter this practice, these authors need to explain away the fact that, over and over again, the Holy Spirit leads us to crucial insights through the statements He forces demons to make.

Another worthy result of forcing demons to give us information is the fact that receiving this information usually speeds things up. In comparison with ministries that refuse to talk to demons, we get more done in a shorter time. I have heard of one such ministry in which the usual time to expel demons is four to five hours, and this is without much attention to inner healing. We usually accomplish at least as much as they do in one-fourth to one-half the time, even though we spend about three-quarters of our time on inner healing. Perhaps one reason we derive so much help from demons is that we spend much time weakening them through inner healing. Those who tackle demons when they are stronger probably find that they are strong enough to lie, more so than when they are weak.

Using demons to help us parallels what happens in court when a hostile witness is put on the stand. By definition a hostile witness tries to support the other side. Thus the aim of the attorney who questions hostile witnesses is to entrap them into revealing information that will help the attorney's—not the witness's—cause. Nobody has suggested that our judicial system not make use of hostile witnesses simply because we cannot trust them. But everybody knows that they and their statements should be handled carefully. An important difference between using a human hostile witness and using a demon is that the power of the Holy Spirit adds to the pressure on demons in remarkable ways.

Our critics contend that God can tell us all we need to know about demons, so we should depend entirely on Him. God *can* indeed reveal all we need to know. But experience teaches us that often He does not do things according to our rules and expectations. Furthermore, our critics believe that Satan and his helpers are too much for God because they assume that even God does not have the ability to make demons tell the truth—ever! Our critics must learn that when we extract information from demons under the influence of the Holy Spirit, and that information checks out as the truth (as it usually does), the source of the revelation is not, as they contend, demonic. The demons are only the means. The source of the truth is God.

When we command demons to give us information, we put them completely under the authority of the Holy Spirit. A typical question I ask is, "Does this person need to forgive anyone?" When the answer is "Yes," I command the demons to tell me who it is. The demon usually tells us the name, and usually it is someone the person has forgotten to forgive. When the person forgives the one named, the demon's power is obviously lessened and we are able to free the person both from the sin of unforgiveness that gave the demon its rights and from the demon itself.

If we can get this kind of information in any other way, we do. Often God reveals such information to the person or to the ministry leader through a word of knowledge. But if not, getting it from the Holy Spirit through His pressure on the demon is a good second choice. So far, as I said, it has enabled at least several thousand people to be freed from demons who might not have been freed if we had refused to use this method. It reminds me of the story of someone who criticized Moody for some of the methods he used in evangelism. If I remember correctly, his reply was something like, "I don't always like my methods either, but I like the way I'm doing it better than the way you're not doing it."

Is this the way Jesus did it? No—at least as far as we can tell from the Scriptures. But Jesus did converse with Satan himself. On occasion I have been able to cast out demons His way—by simply commanding them to leave. More often, however, He leads me and my colleagues to obtain and use information provided by the demons themselves. If this method leads to a freedom smile on the victim's face afterward, I will gladly use it, whether or not the inexperienced theorists like it.

Generational Transmission of Demons

The inheritance of demons is a condition, as I have indicated, that I do not like at all. But I have been involved in casting out too many demons of Freemasonry and of other occult and non-Christian religions from people *who themselves have had nothing to do with those organizations* to avoid it. These are people whose fathers, grandfathers, mothers or grandmothers, or sometimes lineal relatives even farther back—not themselves—were members of the organization. I have had the most experience with Freemasonry. As part of the rituals they undergo to become members, Freemasons take vows, often unconsciously, dedicating themselves and their descendants to Lucifer (see Decker, 1992; Shaw and McKenney, 1988). Obviously these dedications result in demonization of the ones who dedicate themselves. Are these demons transmitted generationally? Or do the descendants of those Freemasons pick up the demons through family contact alone?

Some probably acquire certain demons through family contact. But for many, contact with a Masonic grandparent was minimal. The most likely theory, as distasteful as it may be, is that they inherited the demons at conception. This theory (as we discussed earlier) also lines up with Scripture.

A second bit of evidence is found when we take authority over the person's ancestry. When we use the power of Christ to break generational curses, vows, dedications and rights given to the enemy through sin by the person's ancestors, the demon's power is usually greatly diminished. This experience suggests either that the demon was inherited and has power through the family connection or that some tendency was inherited that gave rights to the demons.

Another thing we notice is that when a person inherits demons, additional demons are likely to have attached themselves either to the inherited demons or to the person's own emotional or spiritual garbage. The presence of one or more demons coming by inheritance seems to make people more vulnerable to becoming inhabited by additional spirits, such as those that can come through curses (Proverbs 26:2) or through contact with infested objects.

Conclusion

We simply call them as we see them in our experience. I invite anyone reading this, especially our critics, to enter into such experiences and see how they call them. Perhaps better theories are out there. I, for one, would welcome them, especially with regard to inherited spirits. But simply denying (as our critics do) that we are actually dealing with demons is an unacceptable answer, given the mountain of experiential data from which we draw our conclusions. The kinds of interactions we have with demons, including the interviews, are very convincing, even to those skeptics with open minds who have watched and listened as we have worked to set captives free.

thirteen

Cosmic-Level Spiritual Warfare

Spiritual reality is just as ubiquitous at the cosmic level as it is at ground level. Thus cosmic-level spiritual warfare is just as crucial. Scripture offers glimpses of this level of warfare in Job 1, again in Daniel 10 and again in Jude, as well as in other places. Ephesians 2:2, for example, speaks of Satan as the ruler of spiritual powers in space. Ephesians 6:12 gives names of such powers.

But beyond these few fairly clear references, we must theorize concerning cosmic-level spiritual activities. We can assume, based on Scripture, that God and Satan are at war at cosmic level as well as at ground level. But what is our involvement to be?

Second Corinthians 4:4 alerts us to the fact that our enemy blinds the minds of unbelievers lest they come to a knowledge (experience) of the truth. From a practical standpoint we can assume that Satan wants to keep us blind to cosmic-level reality so we cannot affect its outcome. The question is, Can we affect the outcome? Can we partner with Jesus in confronting the enemy at cosmic level? I believe we can. Can we, then, confront that blinding activity so that efforts at evangelism may be more successful? I believe the answer is yes, and the evidence is experiential.

Scripture endorses plenty of ground-level activity that can influence what goes on at higher levels. But we need to be wise and cautious, and work in dedicated groups rather than individually. There are rules for this kind of warfare which, if not followed, can result in tragedy (see Robb and Hill, 2000; Dawson, 1989; Wagner, 1991, 1993).

I presented different levels of cosmic spirits in chapter 11. Now I would like to address each one individually and in more detail. Remember that the order of the listing does not necessarily represent a hierarchical ordering of the spirits.

Cosmic-Level Spirits (in the air, Ephesians 2:2)

1. Territorial spirits (over territories)
2. Institutional spirits (over organizations)
3. Vice spirits (over vices)
4. Object and household spirits (over objects and houses)
5. Ancestral spirits

Territorial Spirits

The first of the cosmic-level spirits is the category of territorial spirits. I see these satanic principalities and powers as assigned to create a satanic "force field" influence over various peoples inhabiting specific territories such as Persia and Greece (Daniel 10:13, 21). Territorial spirits have legal rights to influence the people of the given territory and, as we see in Daniel, even to hinder God's workings in those territories. God assigns His angels to operate in these territories as well. But rules govern the power each type of spirit wields.

These rules relate primarily to partnership between humans and spirit beings. Thus when we refer to territories, we are referring to the people more than to the geography. It is *people* who give rights to *territory*. When they partner with God, they give rights to Him. When they partner with Satan, they give rights to him.

As throughout the Old Testament—starting with Adam's sin, continuing through the murder of Abel and on throughout Israel's history—the sinful acts of humans brought curses on the geography in which those sins were committed. Genesis 3:17 and 4:10–12 (as well as many passages thereafter) give references to spiritual damage to the land. So it is scriptural to assume that the geography is affected by the behavior of the people, both past and present. In keeping with the spiritual warfare theme of Scripture, the effect of such sinful behavior is to give a personal being (Satan) rights over the land. Just as the Fall gave the enemy certain territorial rights, so contemporary or past human sin—especially the sin of allegiance to Satan—gives him rights today.

The Fall gave the enemy general rights, as Satan himself points out to Jesus in Luke 4:6, referring to the kingdoms of the world and all their power and wealth: "It has all been handed over to me, and I can give it to anyone I choose." This is a territorial outcome, even though people handed over the territory. And these general rights of Satan continue, affecting generation after generation until Jesus comes to take it back.

So we recognize Satan's authority over the world and the organization of his kingdom into something like the hierarchy described in Ephesians 6:12. (It may be a hierarchy in spite of some of the commentators.) This leads many to postulate territorial satanic rulers that have been given rights by the people who inhabit the territories or, more likely, by their ancestors. Most of the animistic peoples of the world, including those in the Old Testament, assume that territorial spirits are in charge and can usually name the spirits that rule over various places.

This theory gains additional support from the observation that people often specialize in particular types of evil, as if a spiritual power is over them that encourages that sin. Likewise, concentrations of sinful institutions or organizations exist in particular localities. For example, businesses promoting such things as drugs, pornography, prostitution, gambling and occult bookshops often congregate in the same locales. I will deal with this issue further when addressing vice spirits.

As John Dawson (1989) and others (Wagner, ed., 1991) point out, a look at the history of many of these places draws attention to the fact that these very locales usually were committed specifically—even formally dedicated—to satanic influence in earlier generations. It seems reasonable, then, that such regularity would tell us something about how the spirit world interacts with the human world.

We are left to further speculate as to what God's angels do to counter Satan's servants. We can assume that angels implement the protection we receive from God to keep satanic spirits from doing their worst. I am sure we all have been protected over and over again from accidents through the activity of angels. Jesus refers to the fact that angels are assigned to children (Matthew 18:10).

Many of us involved in spiritual warfare have experienced satanic oppression in certain areas of the world. Through experience we assume that God's angels are able to counter such satanic activities when we assert the authority we have in Jesus and when we pray. In Israel, for example, I felt this type of oppression. But we prayed over the places where we did seminars, and God did some important things in these places. Another example was relayed to me by the wife of a colleague of mine who reported an unusual surge of sexual feelings while staying in a New York motel. But the feeling left when she took authority over the room in the name of Jesus Christ to cancel any rights the enemy had over that room.

On many occasions I have spoken in places in which I experienced a freedom in teaching that felt truly supernatural. These were occasions when the places were "cleaned out" spiritually through round-the-clock praying preceding the meeting. Also, primary schoolteachers have reported to me big differences in the behavior of children when the teachers pray authoritatively over the room(s) in which they teach. In such cases I believe God's angels carry out God's part of the partnership.

Institutional and Religion Spirits

Institutional and religion spirits are those assigned to churches, governments, educational institutions, cults and occult organizations. They have two types of assignments. Some are assigned to empower religions and occult institutions, and God's angels oppose them. Other satanic spirits are assigned to disrupt Christian institutions, while God's angels protect and aid any of the adherents who partner with God.

The religions of the world are counterfeits of what God seeks to do in the human context. They are clever counterfeits, masterminded by Satan to deceive humankind into partnering with him rather than with God. Much truth is incorporated into these religions, and adherents frequently manifest a high degree of commitment. But when people practice these religions, they unwittingly partner with Satan, giving him a legal right to influence them and to take over the territory in which they live. Whether it is Buddhism, Hinduism, Islam, animism, Mormonism, Jehovah's Witnesses, Church of Religious Science, Western naturalism or any of the other varieties of satanic deceit, high-level satanic spirits are assigned to aid and abet the deception.

When dealing with converts out of such religions, we almost always find ground-level demons that tell us they are under the authority of higher-level spirits. On occasion we find that a higher-level institutional spirit has taken residence in a person, whether temporarily or permanently. Such spirits are extremely difficult to cast out. I remember clearly the frustration of attempting to deal with such a spirit in a Lutheran pastor in Switzerland and with a similar one in a woman in Israel. To our dismay we were not able to cast out either of these spirits, though I later heard from the woman that she had finally become free. Could this be the kind of spirit Jesus identified as requiring more prayer and perhaps fasting (Matthew 17:21; Mark 9:29)? As I have mentioned, some scholars (including myself) think it was a cosmic-level (territorial) spirit that Jesus cast out of the Gerasene (Mark 5:1–20).

In occult organizations the same kind of deceit is attached to what are usually smaller groupings of people. Like those in false religions, these people commit themselves, either consciously or unconsciously, to Satan, partnering with him and participating in his deceit. Those who join Freemasonry organizations, for example, in the very first of their degrees (levels or ranks) renounce all light they have found in any other activity, and pledge themselves to seek "the light" in Freemasonry. Usually without knowing it, they commit themselves to Lucifer as the god of light, regarding the true God as the god of darkness. Since the Bible is used and many of the statements and rituals imitate Christianity, most of those involved in these organizations have no idea they have committed themselves to Satan.

As with false religions, the adherents of such organizations as Freemasonry, Scientology, many secret societies on university campuses (e.g., the Skull and Bones Society), New Age, Satanism and others become demonized. And like the demons of the religions, occult demons claim to be governed by higher-level spirits. Again using Freemasonry as an example, higher-level spirits would be assigned over a Masonic lodge with individual spirits of Freemasonry living within the members of that lodge. Individual demons of such occult organizations, most unfortunately, are passed down to later generations through inheritance, even to those who do not themselves become members of the organization.

From the fact that letters were written to the angels of the churches in Revelation 2 and 3, we can deduce that God assigns angels to His churches. These angels combat satanic beings assigned to harass these churches and other Christian organizations. Both theological liberalism and rigid fundamentalism portray some of the results of demonic activity in their theologies and practice. Nominalism and the ignorance of many evangelical churches about spiritual warfare also reflect such demonic activity. Paul's warning to Timothy against teachings encouraged by demons (1 Timothy 4:1) and his mention of a "table" of demons (1 Corinthians 10:21) certainly point to such cosmic-level demonic activity.

Again many ground-level spirits come in through church and theological avenues. Good examples of this are demons in persons controlled and manipulated by Christian leaders in such a way that their right to think for themselves is taken away. Further evidence of institutional spirits influencing Christians is the exclusivity based on the lifestyle or small doctrinal points of many very conservative groups. These demons also claim they are assigned by higher-level demons.

Does God assign angels to counter such satanic beings? Of course. And many Christian organizations demonstrate clearly that they are working in partnership with God and His angelic servants to honor Jesus Christ in a world where enemy activity is often very obvious.

Vice Spirits

High-level satanic beings are likewise assigned specifically to aid and abet establishments whose main purpose is to entice their adherents into sinful behavior. These spirits probably work under territorial and sometimes under institutional spirits. Examples of the latter might be temple prostitution or the prostitution and Satanism rings associated with certain Masonic lodges. Spirits are probably assigned to promote alcoholism or drugs in various institutions as well.

Places like Las Vegas and Atlantic City, not to mention the many Native American gambling establishments, are infested by vice spirits of gambling. Abortion establishments crawl with spirits of murder and death. Areas of our country are reigned by high-level spirits of homosexuality or pornography. High-level spirits of death are present wherever unjust killing takes place, as in theaters of war. Again, one of the major concerns of such cosmic-level spirits is to move their demonic underlings into the people who participate in these activities.

When people gather to pray for the disbanding or banishment of a sinful organization, it becomes evident that God makes His angels available to fight vice spirits. I have heard several reports of churches successfully using authoritative prayer to banish such activities from their neighborhoods. I wish more churches took such responsibility!

Household, Cultural Item and Nature Spirits

I am not sure whether this group of spirits should be regarded as a single category or several categories, or if it should be considered cosmic-level or a separate ground-level type. But we will treat it as a single type and at cosmic level. Under this heading we focus on such things as household spirits, the music of satanic music groups, certain computer games, dedicated items brought home from overseas by travelers and missionaries, certain medicines (e.g., bought at certain health food stores), martial arts (e.g., Tae Kwan Do) and the spirits that inhabit certain lakes and forests.

In animistic societies people regard anything out of the ordinary as the work of spirits. If someone drowns in a pond, for example, the likely interpretation is that the spirit of that pond took the person's life. Such animists then offer sacrifices or conduct rituals intended to change the spirit's attitude from harmful to kindly. Even though too many such occurrences in many societies are attributed to demons, we should be open to the possibility that such spirits exist and that they are very active in these societies.

Examples of household spirits are the gods in Taiwan that are attached to stoves, furniture, clothing and other household goods. These are the spirits in focus in Hiebert's important article on the "excluded middle" (1982). Hiebert points out that we Westerners believe in ground-level things like nature and humans, and as Christians we believe in God high above us. But we miss the fact that an enormous number of invisible spirit beings are between us and God—in a kind of middle zone. These spirits are active in the human sphere and are assumed to exist by the peoples of most societies outside of the West, as well as in the Bible. They are ignored and disbelieved by Westerners. Though these spirits are active in, around and among humans, they are quite separate from those ground-level demons that live inside of humans.

Music dedicated to Satan such as that of Marilyn Manson, Eminem, the Grateful Dead and others is very dangerous, especially since Western young people have no idea what lies beneath it. Another dangerous pastime that affects our young people is computer games, the best known of which is "Dungeons and Dragons"—though I am told that many worse computer games exist. Even books can be very dangerous, such as the *Harry Potter* series, in which at least seventy high-level witchcraft techniques are described. Through such dedicated music, computer games or books, or through dedicated items brought home from overseas, the enemy sneaks into many homes, and often into the people themselves.

Through the activity of spirits such as these, people become demonized. The number of young people carrying demons as a result of their engagement with certain music and computer games is probably staggering. Dedicated items in homes do not always result in demonization, but if such objects are present, households can be disrupted. Disturbing dreams, accidents and family arguments can become common. Many health food stores are New Age outlets, and it is standard for martial arts masters to dedicate their activities to their gods. Christians need to claim the power of Jesus' protection when going into places dedicated to New Age or pagan gods. Furthermore, we should be discerning in our choices of which of such places to enter at all.

Christians can combat household, cultural item and nature spirits through building dedications, Christian rituals (including worship and preaching), anointed music and blessings on items like anointing oil and the Communion elements. I do not know if these dedications mean that angels actually live in these items and places, as demons do in items and practices dedicated to Satan. But we can be sure God sends angels to empower our blessings and dedications.

Ancestral Spirits

As I pointed out in chapter 11, many of the world's peoples (e.g., most African and Asian societies) assume that their dead ancestors remain part of the living community. The visibly alive, then, are obliged to honor or even worship these "living dead" by doing such things as setting up altars, performing certain rituals to honor or worship them, providing them with food and even, on occasion, offering sacrifices to them to "keep them happy." The assumption is that when the ancestral spirits are happy, the family will be blessed. When any family member displeases the ancestors, however, the family can expect revenge.

We can assume that those who believe in ancestral spirits do have experiences with spirits that reinforce their belief. But since the Bible speaks of judgment (not ancestorhood) following death (Hebrews 9:27), I conclude that it is not the spirits of ancestors that those who honor or worship their departed loved ones experience. It seems clear to me that this belief and the experiences that go with it constitute a form of satanic deceit carried out by demons. We can assume that Satan assigns certain demons to keep this lie alive.

The issue of ancestral spirits is relevant to anyone seeking to bring spiritual freedom to people with ancestral reverence or worship in their background. These spirits relate to ground-level family spirits that need to be cast out of Asians, Africans, American Indians and others. Sometimes belief in ancestral spirits is incorporated into their Christian belief system, too. A prominent Korean pastor with an important deliverance ministry believes that when he does deliverance, he is releasing people from the spirits of dead ancestors. I believe he is wrong in his analysis. I do not believe the spirits he casts out are ancestral spirits, although he apparently has success in freeing people from the real alien beings—demons.

As I have said, I do not believe God has a category of angels parallel to this satanic category as He has for the other categories. God's angels are, however, always on hand to assist us in ministry to people for whom this is part of their belief system. With such people we will have to deal with both the power and the meaning issues that we discussed in chapter 11.

Ground-Level Activity to Deal with Cosmic-Level Spirits

The question of what to do about cosmic-level spirits is, once again, a controversial one. Many notice that Jesus seems never to have dealt with demons above ground level and suggest that we should not be concerned with cosmic-level beings. Such people believe we should continue simply to do what Jesus did by freeing people from ground-level spirits. This argument has good logic. And though I believe we can legitimately challenge cosmic-level spirits, I am happy to continue to focus almost entirely on ground-level spirits in my own ministry.

I suggest, however, that we think of cosmic-level spirits in terms of the rats and garbage analogy used to describe ground-level spirits. If the higher-level spirits are like rats, we should look for the human garbage that gives them legal rights and deal primarily with that. Such garbage is anything that enables cosmic-level rats to gain control over groups of people, their land and other meaningful things that keep them captive to cosmic-level spirit influence.

Garbage that gives demonic principalities rights in the human arena falls into the same two basic categories as for ground level: spiritual stuff and sin stuff. Spiritual garbage includes curses directed at people and the things that pertain to them. Thus curses against youth that come from satanic music, and curses leveled at Christian families and organizations, need to be taken seriously. Cosmic-level spiritual dimensions of activities such as war, pornography, homosexuality, drugs, gambling, abortion, prostitution and slavery also fall into this category.

The sin stuff pertains to choices made by people to participate in sinful activities. When people agree to participate in such activities as the above—and especially when officials use their authority to allow and encourage them—they are entering into sinful behavior that gives the enemy rights. When sizable numbers of people in a given area sin in one or more of these ways, cosmic demons gain substantial power over them and the places they inhabit. The demonic strength of homosexual principalities over parts of San Francisco and other locales are a case in point.

To counter both kinds of garbage, we must do several things, most of which are clearly taught in Scripture. A key verse is 2 Chronicles 7:14:

If my people, who are called by my name, will humble themselves and pray and seek my face and turn from their wicked
ways, then will I hear from heaven and will forgive their sin and
will heal their land.

NIV

In this verse God identifies several of the requirements for
His people if they are to win or regain His favor. It is, I believe,
a divine message to churches and all other groups that claim
to follow Jesus.

The first of these requirements is that we humble ourselves.
This involves a whole people giving up their pride and, thus,
their right to challenge God and His ways of doing things.
Repentance is certainly a major part of our humbling. Though
this humbling is on a group level, it needs to involve each individual repenting, especially the leadership. As I have pointed
out in my discussions of authority (e.g., Kraft, 1997), human
authority is honored in the spirit world. Thus, if those in authority give up their pride and repent, the enemy army takes a major
hit.

The next thing mentioned in this verse is that we should
pray and seek God's face. Prayer is one of the supreme acts of
partnership with God. It is hard to understand prayer unless
we connect it with spiritual warfare. God would like many
great things to happen, but He often finds no partner to enable
Him to follow His rules and bring them about. Intercessory
prayer is especially important. God wants us all to be continually in prayer (1 Thessalonians 5:17), but He especially
works when those with the gift of intercession pray. These are
people who love to pray and hear from God what they should
be praying for as they pray. Though everyone should seek
God's face, gifted intercessors seem to make better contact
more often.

Turning from our wicked ways needs to accompany these
other things. We must first turn to God, then deal with our own
problems. The requirement is group righteousness. Such righteousness is abhorrent to our enemy and wounds him deeply.

On the other hand, this and all other obedience to God enhances God's cause, empowering His angels to accomplish what He wants in the human sphere.

As mentioned above, it is especially important for the leaders in authority to lead in doing the things that bring victories over the cosmic spiritual forces. When the spiritual leaders (e.g., pastors) of a community get together in unity, giving up their competitiveness and criticisms of each other, God is greatly empowered to defeat satanic principalities and powers. And when these leaders take the lead in reconciliation between people who have been oppressed or otherwise mistreated and members of the community or their forebears who have oppressed them, the enemy is put to flight.

Christian leaders have participated in what seem to be great victories through identifying with those who perpetrated past wrongs and apologizing to God and to representatives of those who were hurt. We call this "identificational repentance." It is what Daniel (chapter 9) and Nehemiah (also chapter 9) did when they took on themselves the blame for the sins of their ancestors, asking God to forgive them as if they had been the perpetrators. The rule seems to be that the guilt for communal sin remains until persons from that community who have authority in the present take responsibility for the past sin and repent. We see this rule in effect in 2 Samuel 21:1–14, in which King David was held accountable for King Saul's sin in breaking the covenant made by Joshua years before with the Gibeonites.

To discover things that went on in history, those specializing in cosmic-level spiritual warfare have developed a research technique called "spiritual mapping." Spiritual mapping consists primarily of research into the spiritual history of a community. The aim of such research is to discover what Satan and God have been doing in that community. Researchers seek to find out the kinds of things Satan has done, what allowed him to do those things and what the results are now. On God's side the quest is to discover what He has been doing and what resources are available if a spiritual attack is to be attempted.

Spiritual mapping is a contemporary form of spying out the land (Numbers 13). Just as God instructed Moses to send spies into the Promised Land to gather information that would help them later when they attempted to take it, so the advocates of spiritual mapping suggest that we "spy out" whatever we can, to discover the ways in which the enemy is working in any given area. Though some make unwarranted claims for this approach, common sense suggests that we investigate and experiment in seeking to discover whatever we can to aid us in promoting the cause of our King. We believe God would rather have us experiment with new approaches than retain our present level of ignorance. Whatever the outcome of the investigations, and whatever the claims made for this approach, we learn from Scripture that prayer integral to a spiritual mapping approach is the right thing to do.

In seeking to discover what God has been doing, John Dawson (1989) suggested we seek to find the "redemptive gift" of each community. This is God's reason for allowing the community to be formed. From such research, strategy is developed for attacking cosmic-level satanic forces and encouraging the exercise of a community's redemptive gift.

Our approach to dealing with cosmic-level satanic forces is to focus on the garbage in order to weaken the higher-level spirits. Dealing with this garbage involves us in several activities that are unquestionably right. Few—even the most severe critics of cosmic-level spiritual warfare—will argue against such things as prayer, unity of believers and leaders, repentance and reconciliation. These are actions that can and should be done even if we do not believe they have anything to do with weakening the spirits in the air. Though some of the critics do not like terms like *identificational repentance* and *spiritual mapping,* these are simply relatively new terms for old biblical ideas. As I mentioned, both Daniel and Nehemiah identified with the sins of their ancestors, taking responsibility for them even though they had no part in committing them. And spiritual mapping is simply research and reconnaissance, similar to Moses' instructions to the spies in Numbers 13.

Examples from Experience

Quite a bit of experimenting in the area of cosmic-level spiritual warfare is taking place. People regularly go to places that have been under satanic control for a long time to do what they call "prayer initiatives." These prayer initiatives usually involve those with intercessory gifts traveling to the places for which they are praying. Such intercession is designed to reclaim or to start the process of reclamation from the enemy of the places where these initiatives take place. During and after such prayer initiatives, numerous things happen in the human realm that indicate God is doing something special in response to the faithfulness of His people.

In an exciting book entitled *The Peacemaking Power of Prayer* (Robb and Hill, 2000), the authors record prayer initiatives and their results in Bosnia, Kosovo, Cambodia and Rwanda. To secular minds, the fact that things changed politically in each of these places is attributed to changes in circumstances and expertise in negotiation. It is interesting to note, however, that in each case the major changes occurred immediately after the prayer initiatives.

The *Transformations* videos put out by George Otis Jr. (1999b; 2001) record several situations that were radically changed as a result of taking cosmic-level spiritual warfare seriously. A spectacular example of spiritual transformation has taken place in a Guatemalan town of about twenty thousand, Almolonga. Over the past twenty years that town has changed from a carousing, drunken place whose four jails could not hold all those who violated the law into a peaceful place with only one tavern and no jails. It has been eight years since they needed a jail. By confronting the territorial spirit of the area and breaking its power, the people have brought about a radical transformation that has occurred even in their agriculture. Whereas they used to send out one truckload of produce per week, now they send out forty per day! The size of the produce is almost beyond belief. Otis's *Transformations* videos also document significant transformations that have taken place in Cali, Colombia; Hemet, California; and Kiambu, Kenya.

But Argentina is in some ways an even more powerful demonstration of how cosmic-level spiritual warfare can enhance the work of Christ. For years evangelists such as Carlos Annacondia and Omar Cabrera have used an approach to evangelism that involves several weeks of warfare praying prior to an evangelism crusade. Annacondia conducts open, visible challenges to the cosmic spirits at the beginning of each meeting (see Annacondia, 1998). Then, when the evangelist senses that the covering of Satan's power is broken, he preaches. The response rate is incredible.

Other exciting examples of the success of warfare evangelism in Argentina are recorded in the book *The Rising Revival* (Wagner and Deiros, eds. 1998) and a chapter by Ed Silvoso in *Behind Enemy Lines* (Kraft, ed., 1994). Silvoso reports on the success of this approach in the city of Resistencia, where he led a three-year comprehensive spiritual attack aimed at breaking the power of the territorial spirits over the city and opening the people up for evangelism. This approach involved persuading the pastors (the spiritual "gatekeepers") to repent of their sins and disunity and to unite. It also involved training pastors and lay church leaders in spiritual warfare prayer, repentance, reconciliation, prayer marching and eventually all-out evangelism. The results have been spectacular.

Conclusion

Such experiments in Argentina and elsewhere in the world suggest that a direct approach to warring against cosmic-level spirits can be successful. But just as it is more important to deal with the spiritual garbage in ground-level warfare, so it is at cosmic level. Dealing with corporate garbage through such activities as confession of sin, repentance, reconciliation and the uniting of the spiritual gatekeepers (pastors) is the first order of business if prayer against territorial bondage is to be successful.

Though the critics of this approach can be harsh, again, they usually work from theory alone. They have not taken into proper account the results of this approach in Argentina and, lately, in several other places through Ed Silvoso's seminars.

In spite of the criticisms, could the Holy Spirit simply be leading us in our day (the last days?) into more of the "all truth" Jesus promised in John 16:13? Or could it be that Jesus was showing us that dealing with ground-level garbage automatically weakens cosmic spirits? Perhaps His approach was to break satanic power at the cosmic level by cleaning up ground-level garbage and praying continually both in private and in public, as in John 17? Either way, those engaged in cosmic-level warfare are discovering that most of what it takes to confront higher-level spirits takes place effectively at ground level through dealing with "cosmic garbage." And it seems to be paying off.

fourteen

I Want to Finish Well

I have a son who, at the time of this writing, has run eighteen marathons—26.2 miles each! He has punished his body both in the races and in the training. Between races he averages running five or more miles each day to keep in shape. He even made himself run every day for more than a year just to prove to himself that he could do it.

I once asked Rick what his goal was in running marathons. Did he ever hope to win one?

"No," he answered, "I never hope to win a marathon. I just want to finish!"

Once Meg and I went to a marathon with him, along with his wife and children, providing him with water a couple of times along the way and enjoying with him his conquest of the finish line. He was spent, but he finished. His time was not what he hoped it would be, but he finished. His legs were stiff and it took him a few days to recuperate, but he finished. And both he who did the running and we who cheered him on are satisfied that he finished well.

A major encouragement, Rick tells me, is the fact that his wife, Tanya, has always been waiting at the finish line of each of his races. And usually fans are cheering him and the others on, both at the starting point and as they finish. In fact, it is tempting for a runner to exert himself too much at the start, responding to the cheering of the fans but using up too much energy at the start. The toughest part of the race is the middle, where few fans cheer and you are nearly overwhelmed with the awareness of how tired your body is.

The Footrace of Christianity

Several times in the New Testament, the Christian life is likened to a footrace. In Hebrews 12:1–3 we are first alerted to the fact that a "cloud of witnesses" watches us. Then we are encouraged to get rid of whatever hinders us and to run the race with determination, eyes fixed on Jesus, "the author and finisher of our faith; who for the joy that was set before him endured the cross, despising the shame" (KJV), and finish well.

Many stories are recorded in Scripture of those who finished well. Hebrews 11 lists several. Among my favorites are Joseph, Moses, Elijah, Samuel, John and Paul. But many did not finish well. Some started well but turned aside. Among these are Gideon, Samson, King Saul, Solomon and Judas. Some never even started well. All the kings of Israel and many of those of Judah fall into this category. The concept of finishing well divides people into three categories: those who do not finish well, those who do finish well and those who start well and stumble but get up and finish well.

Stumbling

Marathoners frequently stumble as they are running. Rick told me once of a time when he stumbled, barely avoiding landing face-first on the pavement by catching the surprised runner in front of him around the waist. But he was able to regain his balance and continue the race. He finished and even finished strong, pushing himself to make up for his stumble and responding to the cheering of the crowd along the final miles of the race.

Biblical characters also stumbled on their way to the finish line. Perhaps David and Peter are the most easily recognized. David, though called by God "a man after my own heart" (1 Samuel 13:14), stumbled badly when he used his power to steal Bathsheba from her husband and then to have her husband killed. But God, through His partner Nathan the prophet, convicted David of his sin. And David got up, repented and kept running the race—finishing well.

When Peter stumbled by denying his Lord, he needed the help of Jesus, the very One whom he had let down. He learned that, though Jesus is the goal, He also runs with us. When Peter stumbled, it was as if he hit the ground but Jesus lifted him to his feet again and sent him on his way. Tradition has it that Peter finished so well that they had to crucify him to shut him down.

The Christian life started for me on August 6, 1944. It started well and I am satisfied with my life over the distance from that time to this. But I have stumbled a few times. I am not proud of these times, but with a lot of help from God, I have been able to pick myself up and continue the race.

Worldview Stumbling

We stumble in a variety of ways—stumblings from which we may or may not recover. One, of course, is morally. Some start well but stumble morally and never get back on track with God. Another type of stumble is doctrinal—where one goes off the tracks doctrinally. We might call another type vocational, where a person whom God calls to one vocation disobeys and goes into another.

Still another type of stumbling is "worldview stumbling." This is when a person God leads into a paradigm shift, with new spiritual experiences, turns back to the old understanding, refusing to grow and continue at the level into which God has led him or her.

This is what happened in Gideon's life (Judges 6–8). God led Gideon into the most incredible of experiences, using him to defeat Israel's enemies against unbelievable odds. God was so determined to lead Gideon to a higher plane that He deliberately cut Gideon's army to a size so small that they could not possibly interpret any victory as a human thing. God wanted Gideon and his people to know for certain that the victory was because of God's help, not because of their own abilities (Judges 7:2).

In keeping with the partnership rule that I discussed in chapter 9, God enlisted Gideon to work with Him to defeat the Midianites. God refused to do it alone. But whenever God enlists humans to assist Him, there is a risk—the risk that when good things happen, we will take credit for them. Yet if we learn the lesson of partnership, working together with God leads us to new heights, paradigm shifts, practice shifts and experiences that take us far beyond what we once knew as normal. We grow, we learn, we change, we become more than we once were. And even if we stumble at times along the way, we hope we will continue growing in our experience with God until the end—and finish well.

But Gideon, in spite of all he had experienced in working with God to rescue His people, stumbled, fell, never recovered and finished badly. And because of him, "all the Israelites abandoned God" and worshiped the idol Gideon set up (Judges 8:27).

Gideon's stumble involved a return to his previous worldview. His family members were idol worshipers, and apparently his father's idols were of high significance to their community (Judges 6:25–30). Perhaps Gideon's father was the leader of his community's worship of the Baal and Asherah idols, since their altars are referred to as belonging to him. Whatever the case, Gideon had been brought up in a household where Baal, not Yahweh, was worshiped. Assumptions concerning Baal and Asherah would have been part of his worldview, then—until the angel of God met him as he was threshing wheat in a winepress (Judges 6:11) and started him on a paradigm shift.

But later in Gideon's life, after a period of growth-producing experiences, during which he was forced to work out of a new set of worldview assumptions, his old worldview resurfaced. Like a bungee cord, the old worldview that he had apparently never fully replaced snapped him back to the familiar comfort of old idolatry.

Our God brings experiences into our lives that are intended to move us from where we are, with respect to worldview, to higher levels of understanding and experience. He challenges us to grow, and expects us to keep growing spiritually until He calls us home.

Often the challenge is embodied in a crisis experience such as the apostle Paul had on the road to Damascus (Acts 9:1–19). In such a crisis a person is challenged to radically change direction in life. Or, as with Peter, God may challenge us after a notable failure (John 21:15–19). When the challenges come, we can—like Paul, Peter, King David and any number of scriptural personalities—grow, thrive and with all our strength press forward toward the finish line and finish well. Or we can, like Gideon, King Saul (1 Samuel 18) and Judas, crumble in response to the challenge and finish badly.

With that "cloud of witnesses" looking on, God intends that we rise to the challenge and, like marathoners, push on to finish well.

What Is the Point?

I began this book with five purposes, all relating to the "normal" Christian experience of most American evangelicals. That experience characterized my own Christian life for the first 38 years after I accepted Christ as my Savior. In light of where God has led me since 1982, however, I have come to see that part of my Christian experience, when compared with Scripture, as subnormal.

1. Demonstrating Spiritual Power

As evangelicals we are committed to practicing and pro-claiming a fully biblical Christianity. If we are to be true to that commitment, however, we need to get beyond what passes for normal evangelical Christianity and into the forefront of demonstrating biblically balanced spiritual power. This is the first of my purposes in writing this book. Jesus was a healer and promised we would do what He did (John 14:12). When He commissioned us to go into all the world to communicate the Gospel (Mark 16:15), He also commissioned us to work in His authority and power to demonstrate His willingness to heal and bring spiritual freedom, as well as to save (Mark 16:17–18; Luke 9:1; John 20:21).

I took a powerless Christianity to Nigeria—a Christianity that offered only secular answers to spiritual problems. With this kind of Christianity, I was unaware of the glass ceiling between it and fully biblical Christianity, much less able to see through it. I regret this deeply and wish with all my heart that I had been led before 1957 into the kind of Christianity I now know. Now that I am experiencing more of what Jesus promised us and seeing people regularly blessed, healed and freed, I am determined to finish with this kind of Christianity rather than with the kind on which I cut my teeth. Though I am grateful for the solid foundation that kind of evangelicalism gave me, I want *this* kind at the end of the race.

2. Freeing Christians from Bondage

My second purpose has to do with freeing Christians from spiritual and emotional bondage. Through most of my life, the best I could do was sympathize with those who knew Christ but just could not get their spiritual and emotional acts together. I, like most evangelicals, frequently recommended that these people go to professional counselors for help. And many did, often with disappointing results. Not knowing the power of God to heal, I thought that was the best we could do.

Again I was offering a powerless, secularized form of Christianity, and again I regret very much that I was not able to help people. Discovering that God is still in the healing business and that He is willing to use me to bring freedom to hurting people has taken me through the glass ceiling and transformed my understanding and experience of Christianity. As I near the end of my race, it is this kind of Christianity that I want to carry across the finish line—a Christianity like that in the gospels and Acts.

3. Responding to the Critics

A third purpose is to respond to some of our critics. It both interests and disturbs me to see how adamant certain people are in critiquing the perspectives and practices of those of us who have moved into powerful Christianity. They usually work from an intellectualized understanding of Christianity that eliminates the possibility that God would do things outside their narrow and secularized paradigms. It is not enough for them that people are healed and freed through our ministry, just as in Jesus' day. They do not seem to want to look at results (e.g., Priest et al., 1995; Lowe, 1998). Since what we do does not fit into their theories and since they refuse to take our results seriously, they fight what we do.

Our critics have reason to critique some of the examples of Christian power ministries prominent in our day. But they do not come to us to find out whether we are guilty of the excesses of such ministries and, therefore, properly to be condemned along with them. Instead they insist on reacting against their own stereotypes of healing ministries on the assumption that we are guilty of the excesses in those ministries to which they can rightly point.

I choose, however, to continue to work with Jesus in the power of the Holy Spirit to set captives free—as He promised we would. And I want to finish my course, as Jesus finished His, bringing freedom from our enemy to as many people as possible—in spite of the critics.

4. Recognizing the Validity of Experience

A fourth purpose has been to speak a good word for the place of experience in Christian life. I, like many evangelicals, have been strongly warned against trusting experience as opposed to trusting what God has said in the Scriptures, as interpreted logically by theologians. This warning is warranted if the only alternatives are trusting the Bible or trusting experience. Those who have turned completely to trusting experience have often gone astray. Fortunately the extremes are not the only option. It is possible (as I have tried to show) to be both Scripture-based and experience-oriented.

But to accept as scriptural the kinds of experience of which I speak here may require a paradigm shift away from a largely academic, "knowledge-about" understanding of God and the Scriptures. Western evangelicals tend to be negative toward any Christian experience that involves more than a modicum of emotion—especially that of Pentecostals and charismatics. Indeed, in their condemnation of emotion, many make the mistake of equating experience with emotion and regarding them both as invalid. In so doing they fail to note that emotional expression is scriptural (including the attribution of emotion to God and to Jesus) and that all aspects of Christianity are validated in experience.

Personally I want my experience of this incredible relationship with God to be up to scriptural standards. "Knowledge-about" and "faith-without-feeling" Christianity is no longer acceptable to me, though before I knew that there was more, I was content with it. I am, happily, no longer experiencing that kind of Christianity, and I want to finish well at the new level to which the Holy Spirit has brought me.

5. Continuing to Discover and Grow

The fifth purpose of this book involves the possibility of experimenting with our Christian experience in order to discover and grow in relationship and ministry. All agree that the Bible provides a mere outline of what our life in Christ is supposed to be. There is much to flesh out in real life that, though allowed by the Bible, is not specifically mentioned or illustrated there. Thus I make no apology for the fact that no specific biblical precedent exists for some of the techniques we use in deep healing ministry. The biblical accounts show Jesus healing and banishing demons with a word or gesture. We are not told what preceded or followed those actions. Though we have found that we usually need to do much more than the scriptural accounts of Jesus' ministry portray, when we achieve similar results we are satisfied.

Our critics, on the other hand, like to suggest that if we do not do it exactly Jesus' way, our approach is invalid. But they are not setting captives free. We are. To again quote Moody's response to similar criticism, "I like the way I'm doing it better than the way you're not doing it."

The life in Christ, if authentic, involves growth, change, experimentation and discovery, especially in the all-important relationship dimension. Ministry, too, involves growth in working with Jesus to accomplish whatever His purposes are. Listening to Him and working in sync with Him often involves doing things we have never planned or even previously considered. Such activity seems out of bounds to those whose Christianity is more intellectual than relational. Though the Scriptures are full of examples of people hearing directly from God, intellectual theologizing assumes that such relational interaction between God and humans no longer occurs. Those caught in that kind of Christianity cannot imagine a relationship or ministry activity that involves hearing from God directly. For them, closely relating to God, ministering to people to set them emotionally and spiritually free, and hearing directly from God are all on the other side of the glass ceiling.

Though it is important to test what we think we hear from God, and to be constantly aware of the possibility of being misled, we lose a lot if we refuse to allow God to lead us directly and in ways appropriate to the immediate situation. When we learn that God still communicates with us and we learn to listen to Him, we enter a new dimension of Christian experience. I want to end my days on earth in that dimension.

My Intent for Finishing the Race

I intend for this book to carry a message to evangelicals concerning why and how we can move into a Christianity more biblical than has ordinarily characterized evangelicalism. We have committed ourselves to the Bible but refused to learn from charismatics what God has taught them concerning what the Christian life is intended to be. Yet if we look closely at the Scriptures, we must notice that the only kind of Christianity shown there is charismatic Christianity. Because it does not fit into our worldview categories, we have been put off by what we see on the other side of the glass ceiling—a Christianity into which God wants to take us. Many evangelicals have turned away from what we could learn about Scripture from charismatics without even trying it. And some have moved a bit into it and then allowed the bungee cord of their old worldview to snap them back.

I plan to do neither because I believe it is God who has brought me into a richness of biblical Christian experience that I hardly imagined possible a few years ago. I want to finish my race continuing to experience and grow in this direction.

Like most evangelicals I was taught to reason my faith and my approach to ministry, and to be very suspicious of anything based on experience. Yet I have strongly advocated here that we give higher—though not total—priority to the experiential dimension of our faith. As I have said, we are to *experience* the truth (John 8:32), not just *know* it intellectually. Experiencing the truth is a relational thing, not an intellectual thing.

Rather than be suspicious of experience, we should embrace it, as long as it is biblical. For many of us this requires gaining the freedom that working in the power of the Holy Spirit enables, and then partnering with God to do the kinds of things we see in Scripture. As I have written, Jesus wants us to go beyond salvation into freedom and to become His partners in doing what He did in the days of His flesh. We have learned the intellectual part of biblical Christianity. Let us now grow in the experiential part.

To do this, many evangelicals will have to move backward into parts of the Bible they have treated as superseded by other parts. We have tended to agree with the pastor who once told me, "Mine is a Christianity of the epistles, not of the gospels and Acts." Unfortunately he, like most evangelicals, failed to see that the context of the epistles is one of spiritual warfare, of power against power, where righteousness on the part of the human partners is not only good for us, but empowers God to do what He wants in opposition to the enemy.

When, like this pastor, we focus merely on the need for human morality (as taught in the epistles) and on the fact that God wins in the end, we lose the overall picture—a picture of a cosmic battle, or series of battles, that God wins only when humans partner with Him. In short, the context on which the epistles depend is provided by the gospels and Acts. We must not separate the epistles from that relational warfare context, or all we will have left is an intellectualized, powerless Christianity.

As evangelicals we have rightly focused on conversion as the essential first step for Christians. To climb beyond that step, orthodox evangelicalism gives the impression that we must emphasize correct intellectual belief (doctrine) based primarily on the epistles, especially Romans. While paying little attention to the fact that the letters (epistles) are experiential, relational and context-specific, we have treated them as if they were written as theological treatises. Which of our own personal letters would we like to have analyzed and picked apart word by word as we have done with the New Testament epistles?

With this as our ethos, many marvelously converted, sincere young Christians have died spiritually because nobody helped them first to get free from internal strongholds and then to grow strong in their relationship with Jesus. Their attention was turned to doctrine and they soon became containers of information-based, intellectual understanding of the faith with precious little development of their relationship with Christ and little or no experience of the power of Christ.

I was taught this way. And I attended Christian college and seminary with many other "true-blue" evangelicals who also were taught this way. We looked through the glass ceiling but found no way to get through it; and many of us died spiritually along the way and did not finish well. I thank God that I was introduced to both the power and the relational dimensions of Christianity—to a God who is much more alive than I ever imagined, a God who meets me regularly in love and power as I partner with Him in bringing freedom by ministering deep-level healing to those who need it. I have learned to experience the Scriptures relationally, as a place to meet God and relive with Him events that are similar to those in my own life. The gospels have not been the same for me since I discovered that I can, with Jesus, do all that stuff, too!

Heading Toward the Finish Line

So I want to keep growing till I die, to keep experiencing His presence moment by moment in life and ministry. It is good to have a solid intellectual foundation as I move toward finishing well. But the intellectual stuff is to be foundation, not super-structure. The experience of growth in relationship is the super-structure. And participating with Jesus in partnership to do what He said we would do—that is what fills the rooms of this relational superstructure.

As I reflect on my life and focus on what I have learned of the Christian experience of fellow classmates in college, I note that many have defected from the knowledge-oriented, secular, powerless Christianity we were taught. As I glance through my class yearbook, I can point to several who have left the faith altogether. I feel sorry for them because they never discovered the real thing before they abandoned it.

I, too, have defected from powerless Christianity, but in a different direction than most of them (though there are some who have turned in the same direction as I). I have broken through the glass ceiling into a Christianity with power. And in spite of the worldview pull to return to comfortable, staid, dignified, academic evangelicalism, I choose to continue in the direction God has taken me. For I am determined to finish well.

Bibliography

Annacondia, Carlos
    1998   *Listen to Me, Satan.* Orlando, Fla.: Creation House.
Arnold, Clinton
    1992   *Powers of Darkness.* Downers Grove, Ill.: InterVarsity.

Barclay, William
    1956   *The Gospel of Luke.* Philadelphia: Westminster.
Beckett, Bob, and Becky Wagner Sytsema
    1997   *Commitment to Conquer.* Grand Rapids: Chosen.
Bennett, Rita
    1982   *Emotionally Free.* Old Tappan, N.J.: Fleming H. Revell.
    1984   *How to Pray for Inner Healing.* Old Tappan, N.J.: Fleming
            H. Revell.
Blue, Ken
    1993   *Healing Spiritual Abuse.* Downers Grove, Ill.: InterVarsity.
Boyd, Gregory A.
    1997   *God at War.* Downers Grove, Ill.: InterVarsity.

Dawson, John
   1989   *Taking Our Cities for God.* Lake Mary, Fla.: Creation
          House.
Decker, Ed
   1992   *What You Need to Know About Masons.* Eugene, Ore.:
          Harvest House.
   1994   (ed.) *The Dark Side of Freemasonry.* Lafayette, La.: Hunt-
          ington House.
Dickason, C. Fred
   1987   *Demon Possession and the Christian.* Chicago: Moody.

Flynn, Mike, and Doug Gregg
   1993   *Inner Healing.* Downers Grove, Ill.: InterVarsity.

Guelich, Robert
   1991   "Spiritual Warfare: Jesus, Paul and Peretti," in *Pneuma*
          13:33–64.

Hiebert, Paul
   1982   "The Flaw of the Excluded Middle," in *Missiology*
          10:1:37–47, reprinted in *Anthropological Reflections on
          Missiological Issues.* Grand Rapids: Baker, 1994, pp.
          189–201.
Hunt, Dave, and T. A. McMahon
   1985   *The Seduction of Christianity.* Eugene, Ore.: Harvest
          House.

Jacobs, Cindy
   1995   *The Voice of God.* Ventura, Calif.: Regal.

Kallas, James
   1966   *The Satanward View.* Philadelphia: Westminster.
   1968   *Jesus and the Power of Satan.* Philadelphia: Westminster.
Kraft, Charles H.
   1989   *Christianity with Power.* Ann Arbor, Mich.: Servant.
   1991a "What Kind of Encounters Do We Need in Our Christian
          Witness?" in *Evangelical Missions Quarterly* 27:3,
          reprinted in *Perspectives on the World Christian Move-
          ment: A Reader,* 3rd edition. Pasadena, Calif.: William
          Carey, 1999.

1991b   *Communication Theory for Christian Witness.* Maryknoll, N.Y.: Orbis.

1992   *Defeating Dark Angels.* Ann Arbor, Mich.: Servant.

1994   *Deep Wounds, Deep Healing.* Ann Arbor, Mich.: Servant.

1995a   *Behind Enemy Lines.* Ann Arbor, Mich.: Servant (Pasadena, Calif.: Wipf & Stock, reprint).

1995b   "'Christian Animism' or God-Given Authority," in Rommen, Edward (ed.), *Spiritual Power and Missions.* Pasadena, Calif.: William Carey.

1996   *Anthropology for Christian Witness.* Maryknoll, N.Y.: Orbis.

1997   *I Give You Authority.* Grand Rapids: Chosen.

2000   (with David DeBord), *The Rules of Engagement.* Colorado Springs: Wagner.

Linn, Dennis and Matthew

1974   *Healing of Memories.* New York: Paulist.

1979   *Healing Life's Hurts.* New York: Paulist.

1985   *Healing the Greatest Hurt.* New York: Paulist.

Lowe, Chuck

1998   *Territorial Spirits and World Evangelisation.* Sevenoaks, Kent: OMF.

MacArthur, John F. Jr.

1992   *Charismatic Chaos.* Grand Rapids: Zondervan.

McAll, Kenneth

1982   *Healing the Family Tree.* London: Sheldon.

Otis, George Jr.

1999a   *Informed Intercession.* Ventura, Calif.: Renew.

1999b   *Transformations,* a video. Lynnwood, Wash.: Sentinel.

2001   *Transformations II,* a video. Lynnwood, Wash.: Sentinel.

Peretti, Frank E.

1986   *This Present Darkness.* Westchester, Ill.: Crossway.

1989   *Piercing the Darkness.* Westchester, Ill.: Crossway.

Priest, Robert J., Thomas Campbell and Bradford A. Mullen

1995   "Missiological Syncretism: The New Animistic Paradigm," in Rommen, Edward (ed.), *Spiritual Power and Missions.* Pasadena, Calif.: William Carey.

Robb, John, and James A. Hill
2000   *The Peacemaking Power of Prayer.* Nashville: Broadman & Holman.

Sandford, John and Paula
1982   *The Transformation of the Inner Man.* South Plainfield, N.J.: Bridge.
1985   *Healing the Wounded Spirit.* Tulsa: Victory House.
Scanlan, Michael
1974   *Inner Healing.* New York: Paulist.
Schacter, Daniel
1996   *Searching for Memory.* New York: Basic.
Seamands, David
1981   *Healing for Damaged Emotions.* Wheaton: Victor.
1985   *Healing of Memories.* Wheaton: Victor.
1988   *Healing Grace.* Wheaton: Victor.
Shaw, James D., and Tom C. McKenney
1988   *The Deadly Deception.* Lafayette, La.: Huntington House.
Silvoso, Ed
2000   *Prayer Evangelism.* Ventura, Calif.: Regal.

Tapscott, Betty
1975   *Inner Healing Through Healing of Memories.* Kingwood, Tex.: Hunter.
1987   *Ministering Inner Healing Biblically.* Houston: Tapscott.

Wagner, C. Peter
1988   *The Third Wave of the Holy Spirit.* Ann Arbor, Mich.: Vine.
1991   (ed.) *Engaging the Enemy.* Ventura, Calif.: Regal.
1993   *Breaking Strongholds in Your City.* Ventura, Calif.: Regal.
1998   (with Pablo Deiros, eds.) *The Rising Revival.* Ventura, Calif.: Renew.

Wardle, Terry
2001   *Healing Care, Healing Prayer.* Orange, Calif.: New Leaf.

Index

abortion, 39, 60, 186, 189–90, 223, 227
Abraham, 91, 153, 164
academic theological training, 17, 29, 33,
    47, 51–52, 54–55, 61–62, 74, 78, 90, 103,
    117, 119–21, 124, 128, 134, 149, 241,
    244–45
Adam, 34, 153–55, 162, 219
Africa, 169, 187, 211, 226
alcoholism, 176, 223
Ananias and Sapphira, 183
ancestral spirits, 60, 186, 189, 191–92, 218,
    225–26
angels of God, 22, 108, 155, 180, 189–90,
    218, 220–21, 222–23, 226, 237
anger, 39, 57, 59, 145, 147, 167, 187, 201–3,
    208, 210, 212
animism, 19–25, 29, 43–46, 65–66, 77–81,
    111–14, 190, 198–99, 219, 221, 224
animist, 21, 23–24, 116, 158, 168
Annacondia, Carlos, 232
anthropology, 61, 192
anti-Pentecostal, 7
apostleship, gift of, 95–96
Argentina, 60, 65, 76, 232–33
Ark of the Covenant, 23
armor of God, 66
arrogance, 85
Asherah, 237
Asia, 187, 211, 226
Atlantic City, 223
Australian aborigines and gypsies, 187
authority, God-given, 19–20, 22, 24–26,
    30–31, 48, 50, 65, 68–69, 85, 96–97,
    109–10, 112–13, 128, 135, 150, 157–79,
    184–85, 191, 193–94, 214, 220, 239

Baal, 237
Barclay, William, 156
Bathsheba, 33, 85, 236
Beatitudes, 165
behavior (correct), 9
Behind Enemy Lines, 107, 232
Bennett, Rita, 144
Bermuda Triangle, 77
biblical, 16, 20, 22–23, 32, 34, 36, 75, 80,
    81, 100, 106, 239, 241, 243
blessing, 21, 23, 34, 45, 85, 87, 92, 110–11,
    160, 163–67, 169–72, 191, 193, 239
Blue, Ken, 97
bondage, 8, 118, 126, 142, 145, 167–68,
    232, 239
books, occult, 196, 220, 225
Buddhism, 19, 59, 176, 190, 211, 221
Bultmann, Rudolf, 30, 47

Cabrera, Omar, 232
California, 7, 76, 231
Campbell, Thomas, 64–65, 67, 77–78, 212
charismatic Christianity, 12, 16, 54–55, 83,
    86, 91, 103–4, 144, 241, 243
Chinese martial arts, 210, 224–25
"Christian animism," 24, 112
Christian growth, 73, 139, 241–43
Christian Science, 176, 202–3, 211
Christianity with Power, 15
Christianity, 12, 15, 55, 66, 116–25,
    123–27, 129–34, 136, 143, 149, 181,
    199, 222, 239–45
church growth, 13, 14, 36, 55, 76, 127
Church of Religious Science, 221
college fraternities/sororities, 211
Colombia, 76, 231

Columbia International University, 18, 19
commitment, 7, 12, 40, 47, 52, 57, 59, 63,
    92, 100, 117–18, 123–25, 139, 141, 156,
    159, 163–64, 178–79, 203, 221, 239
communication, theory and practice of, 14,
    51, 139, 239
communion/Lord's Supper, 23, 124, 193,
    225
computer games, 196, 224–25
conflict between God and Satan, 46, 51
contextualization, 51, 120
control, abuse of, 95–96
cosmic-level (strategic-level) spirits, 58–61,
    185, 189–92, 208, 217–33
counseling, secular, 57, 61–62, 143–47, 239
counterfeits (deceits) of Satan, 19–24, 44,
    49, 108–9, 112–13, 132, 158, 186, 207,
    221–22, 226
covenant relationship, 91
cross-cultural ministry, 20, 51, 56, 121,
    124, 130–31
cultural forms, 109–10, 114, 192–95, 198
curses, 21, 34, 39, 67, 69, 102, 110–11, 160,
    163–64, 167–70, 173–75, 203–4, 211,
    216, 227

Daniel, 33, 34, 151, 177, 189, 229–30
data analysis, 28, 31, 70, 75–77, 111, 151,
    213, 216
David, 33, 34, 85, 153, 164, 229, 236, 238
Dawson, John, 218, 220, 230
DeBord, David, 162
Decker, Ed, 215
dedication of people and objects, 66, 111,
    163, 168–69, 172–74, 176, 190–91,
    193–99, 210–11, 216, 220, 224–25
Deep Wounds, Deep Healing, 147–48
Defeating Dark Angels, 58, 148
deity of Jesus Christ, 155–56
delegated spiritual authority, 24, 81, 109,
    159, 162–64
deliverance ministries, 53, 57
deliverance, 13, 50, 54–55, 127, 130, 160,
    170, 188, 198
Demon Possession and the Christian, 204
demonic beings, 18, 22, 29–30, 36–37, 39,
    47–48, 52, 57, 66, 77–78, 80, 89, 96,
    102–3, 108, 110–11, 118, 128, 134–35,
    141, 147–48, 157, 159–60, 162–64,
    166–68, 174–76, 181–85, 194, 200–16,
    220, 221–23, 226
demonic presence (activity), 69, 74

demonization, 31, 47, 49–50, 57–59, 63,
    68–69, 79, 111, 135, 141, 148, 163, 173,
    177, 189, 200–6, 213–15, 225
demonization, dual causation, 37–38,
    41–43
demonization of Christians, 70, 106, 194,
    204–5, 210
demons, inheritance of, 67, 69
demon-under-every-bush, 53–54
Dickason, C. Fred, 204
disciples of Jesus, 16, 24, 34, 47, 62, 87,
    96–97, 122, 128, 157–58, 160, 164–65,
    184
discipleship, 53, 61, 118, 121, 125, 138
dispensationalism, 13, 54
Dissociative Identity Disorder (DID), for-
    merly Multiple Personality Disorder
    (MPD), 49–50
doctrine (belief) based on experience, 8–9,
    61, 71, 119
doctrine (belief) based on knowledge, 8–9,
    99, 119–20, 182
drugs, 219, 223, 227
dual allegiance Christianity, 130
Dutch Calvinism, 98

Eastern mysticism, 27, 163
Elijah, 34, 235
Eminem, 224
empowerment, 45, 74, 113, 157, 164, 169,
    192–96
enlightenment rationalism, 48, 62, 65, 67
Ethiopian eunuch, 44
evangelical Christian counseling, 62–63
Evangelical Missiological Society, 18
evangelicalism, traditional Western, 35,
    46–48, 53–54, 62, 78, 83, 100, 105, 115,
    125, 127, 131
evangelism, 36, 60, 215, 218, 232
evil spirits, 21, 66–67, 112, 116–17, 127,
    130, 154, 180, 185–86, 190, 198. See
    also demons
exorcism, 66, 96
experiencial exercises (faith picturing), 44,
    146

faith, 84, 86–87, 91, 93, 156
family spirits, 58, 59, 186–87, 200–1, 210.
    See also ground-level spirits
fasting, 94, 221
fear, 57, 59, 69–70, 73, 187, 201, 212

feelings (as part of experience), 28, 32, 71, 105, 126, 146, 241
Flynn, Mike, 144
food dedicated to idols, 72–73
footrace, 235–36, 243
forgiveness, 37, 178–79
fortunetelling, 163, 196
freedom (from bondage), 8, 10, 17, 48, 51, 109, 111, 127–28, 130, 139, 141–49, 167, 173, 239–40, 242–43, 245
freemasonry, 19, 59, 162–63, 176, 187, 189–90, 196, 202–3, 211, 215, 222–23
fruits of the Spirit, 84
Fuller Evangelistic Association, 13, 14
Fuller, School of World Mission, 7, 14
Fuller Theological Seminary, 14, 46–47, 50, 55–56, 75, 120, 136

Galileo, 99, 101–2
gambling, 39, 60, 190, 209, 219, 223, 227
garbage, spiritual/emotional, 37–39, 56–57, 61, 148, 188, 201, 212–13, 216, 227, 230, 232–33
Garden of Eden, 164, 183, 207
generational/bloodline spirits, 201, 203, 207, 215–16. See also cosmic-level spirits
Gerasene demoniac, 191
Gideon, 153, 235, 237–38
glass ceiling, 15–17, 33, 45, 65, 81, 103, 119, 125, 149, 179, 239–40, 242–43, 245
Godward view, 40, 128
Grateful Dead, 224
Great Commission, 139
Gregg, Doug, 144
ground-level demonic spirits, 58, 60, 183, 185, 187–89, 191–92, 200–216, 221–24, 226–27, 232–33
Guatemala, 60, 76, 231
Guelich, Robert, 181
guilt, 57, 59, 208

harassment, 209–10
hate, 57, 59, 187, 210
Hayford, Jack, 50, 62, 136
healing, 13–17, 23–24, 26, 34, 36, 38–39, 45, 50, 53–55, 57, 61–63, 74, 83–89, 90, 93, 96, 99, 110–11, 118, 126–27, 130, 142–45, 147–48, 160, 166–67, 170–71, 179, 184, 193, 198, 210–13, 239–40, 245
hell, 139
heresy, 91, 129

hermeneutics, 30–31
Herod, 43, 154
hexes, 20
Hiebert, Paul, 224
Hinduism, 19, 176, 190, 221
Holy Spirit, 35, 38, 50, 55, 57, 63, 65, 79, 84, 91, 101, 111, 122, 128, 131, 135, 139, 142, 145, 155–58, 164, 166, 172, 181, 184, 205–6, 212–14, 233, 240, 243
homosexuality, 39, 52, 60, 186, 189–90, 223, 227
horoscopes, 163
human realm, 44, 47, 61, 99, 104, 108–10, 150, 172, 183, 231
human world, 107–8, 110
hymns, 127, 140
hyperemotionalism, 53

identificational repentance, 60, 177, 229–30
idols, 23, 72, 153–54, 197, 237–38
imitation of Jesus, 51, 121, 160, 184
incarnation of Jesus, 50–51
insecurity, 89–90, 95–96
institutional and religion spirits, 59, 186, 189–90, 218, 221–23. See also cosmic-level spirits
intercessory prayer, 37, 60, 200, 228
interpretation of spiritual truth, based on experience, 32, 36, 71, 75
Islam, 176, 211, 221
Israel, 59, 153–54, 164, 220–21, 235
Israelite army, 41

Jacob, 34, 153, 165
Jacobs, Cindy, 93
Jehovah's Witnesses, 189, 211, 221
Jewish Christians, 90–91
Jewish law and custom, 33, 90, 112
Job, 33, 42, 43, 108
John, apostle, 47, 235
Joseph, 152–53, 235
Joseph and Mary, 43, 153, 155
Joshua, 153, 229
joy, 126, 143, 149, 166, 235
Judaizers, 154
Judas, 154, 235, 238
Judeo-Christian understanding, 112

Kallas, James, 40, 128, 140
Kingdom of God, 46–47, 161, 178, 184

Kingdom of Satan, 34–35, 46–47, 73–74, 79–80, 111, 161–62, 178, 181, 183–84, 196

knowledge, 71, 75–77, 82, 106–7, 122, 134, 146

knowledge of the Bible, 16, 31, 49, 92, 129–30, 141, 241

Kraft, Charles H., 51, 80, 115, 161–62, 188, 228, 232, 234

Kraft, Meg, 14, 115, 234

Kraft, Rick, 234–35

Kraft, Tanya, 235

Latin America, 19, 66, 68, 187

legalism, 90–93, 95

legal rights of spirit beings, 39, 59, 109–11, 148, 150, 159, 187–88, 202, 213, 216, 218, 221, 227

Linn, Dennis and Matthew, 144

logical (straight) thinking, 9, 117, 244

Lowe, Chuck, 18, 100, 240

lust, 57, 201

MacAll, Kenneth, 77

MacArthur, John F. Jr., 18, 100

MacNutt, Francis, 144

MacNutt, Judith, 144

magic, 21, 43, 45, 81, 87, 112, 114, 158

Manson, Marilyn, 224

marathons, 234–35, 238

McKenney, Tom C., 215

medical doctors, 44, 130, 135

medicine, 78, 199

memory, 146–47

Michael, the archangel, 189

ministry, 14, 52–53, 56, 67, 73, 83, 124, 126, 140, 142, 147–48, 240

miracles, 29, 74, 155–56

missiology: definition of, 12; problems facing, 20, secular approach, 13, 55, 80–81, 135

missionaries, 61, 68, 80, 115–16, 120–21, 127, 135, 139, 168, 174, 190, 194, 196–97, 210, 224

Moody, Dwight L., 215, 242

Mormonism, 19, 176, 189–90, 202–3, 211, 221

Moses, 65, 153, 230, 235

Mullen, Bradford A., 64–65, 67, 77–78, 212

murder, 52, 223

Muslims, 19

Naboth, 34

"name-it, claim-it" (word-faith) movement, 53, 85–88

Nathan, 85, 236

National Association of Evangelicals, 55

Native Americans, 187, 211, 223, 226

Nehemiah, 177, 229–30

New Age, 19, 20, 21, 22, 24, 27, 44, 136, 163, 176, 196, 198–99, 202, 222

New Testament, 7, 15, 35, 40–41, 47–48, 51–52, 69–71, 95, 123, 135, 151, 154, 175, 183–84, 212, 235, 244

Nigerian church, 12, 13, 115–17, 120, 127, 239

nominalism, 52, 63

obedience, 48, 92, 154, 156–57, 159, 162, 164, 185, 229

object and household spirits, 60, 186, 189–91, 218. See also cosmic-level spirits

objects with satanic power, 67–69, 73, 113, 186

occult music, 224–25, 227

occult spirits, 58–59, 186–87, 195, 200, 210–11. See also ground-level spirits

occultism, 20, 29, 39, 77, 130, 162–63, 196, 198, 202–3, 215, 222

Old Testament, 21–22, 35, 41, 46–47, 71, 112, 152, 165, 183, 219

ordinary spirits, 58–59, 186–87, 200, 210–11. See also ground-level spirits

Otis, George, Jr., 36, 65, 76, 231

Ouija boards, 196

Papua New Guinea, 169

paradigm and practice shift, 80, 103

partnership with God, 17, 89, 111, 126–27, 150–65, 170–71, 178–79, 181, 188–90, 199, 217–18, 220–21, 223, 228, 237, 243, 245

partnership with Satan, 158–59, 162–64, 175, 189, 218–19, 221–22

Paul (apostle), 19, 23, 41, 42, 47, 66, 73–74, 86, 90–91, 129, 135–37, 165–66, 222, 235, 238

Peacemaking Power of Prayer, The, 231

Pentecost, day of, 97

Pentecostal Christianity, 12, 16, 54–55, 83, 103–4, 241

Peretti, Frank E., 180–81, 189

Peter, 33, 41, 135–36, 236, 238

Pharisees, 40, 74, 134, 154, 209
physical illness, 47, 87, 92–94, 98, 145, 160,
   164, 171
pornography, 39, 52, 60, 190, 209, 219,
   223, 227
prayer marches/walks, 60, 232
prayer minister, 142, 144, 147
prayer, 23, 44, 63, 77, 88, 99, 144–45, 179,
   181, 221, 228, 230, 232
prayer, intercessory, 37, 60, 200, 228, 231
Priest, Robert J., 18, 31, 37, 38, 43, 64–67,
   69, 72, 76–80, 100–1, 112, 195, 212, 240
principalities and powers (higher-level
   satanic spirits), 19, 39, 110, 218, 229
prisoners of war, 138, 140–42
prophecy, gift of, 93–95
prostitution, 60, 190, 219, 223, 227
protection from physical harm, 171–73
psychological problems, 37, 48–49, 57, 126,
   141, 182
psychology, 9, 44, 51–52, 55, 61, 130, 135,
   143, 199, 206

Rapture, the, 140
rationalism, 54, 64, 66–67
reality-based methods, 67, 70, 81–82
reconciliation, 37, 124–25, 200, 229–30,
   232
Reformed theology, 47, 54
relational aspect of Christian life, 92–93,
   117–19, 121–28, 139, 142–43
relationship, elements of, 92
repentance, 37, 39, 60, 124, 200, 228, 230,
   232
research, 105–7
righteousness, 35, 60, 228, 244
Rising Revival, The, 232
rituals, 22, 109, 158, 176, 193,196–98,
   224–26
Robb, John, and James A. Hill, 218, 231
Rules of Engagement, The, 107–8

sacrifices in the Bible, 22–23, 92
salvation (conversion), 48, 70, 119, 123,
   125, 138–42, 148–49, 154–55, 205, 244
Sanford, John and Paula, 144
Satan (Lucifer), 19, 21–22, 25, 30, 33–34,
   40–45, 47–48, 52, 66, 70, 96, 103, 106,
   109, 118, 128–29, 131, 137–42, 153,
   155–56, 158–59, 168, 173–74, 177–80,
   185, 188–89, 191, 206, 208–9, 212, 215,
   217, 221–22, 226

satanism, 20, 202–3, 222–23
satanist blessings, 203
satanward view, 40
Saul, 154, 229, 235, 238
Scanlan, Michael, 144
Schacter, Daniel, 146
science, 44, 61, 75, 78, 99, 101, 103–5, 107
scientific laws (principles), 9, 74, 99, 101–2
scientific process, 102–3, 110
Scientology, 19, 59, 162, 176, 189–90, 196,
   211, 222
Scripture, nature of, 33, 102
Seamands, David, 144
secular, 57, 63, 199
seed-faith money, 86
self-cursing, 175, 208
sexual abuse, 49, 52, 145, 175, 177, 207–8
shalom, 165–66
shame, 57, 59, 201, 212, 235
Shaw, James D., 215
Shintoism, 176
Silvoso, Ed, 36, 65, 232–33
sin nature, 38, 41, 154
sin, 33–34, 37, 42, 47, 57–58, 70, 74, 78, 92,
   105, 111, 138, 154, 162, 167, 173–74,
   176–77, 182, 188, 201, 203–5, 211, 214,
   216, 219, 227–29, 232, 236
skepticism, 7, 13, 29, 65, 74–76, 216
slavery, 227
Solomon, 164, 235
soul tie, 167–68
spells, 20, 21
spirit beings, 9, 45, 52, 113, 224
spirit world, 18, 21, 31, 32, 33, 74, 77–79,
   99–101, 107–8, 110–11, 134, 141,
   162–63, 172, 180, 202, 228
Spiritual Power and Missions, 18, 112
spiritual reality, 29, 52, 62, 74, 81, 100–4,
   107, 116, 134, 136, 150, 217
spiritual realm, 29, 30, 45, 61, 104, 108,
   112, 172
spiritual warfare ("cosmic- or strategic-
   level"), 19, 37, 39, 60, 110, 131, 188,
   217–33
spiritual warfare ("ground-level"), 18, 37,
   38, 39, 60, 110, 131, 171, 187, 200–16
spiritual warfare, 17, 18, 19, 23, 37, 43, 45,
   48, 52–54, 56, 61–66, 69, 72, 100–1, 103,
   129, 141, 178–83, 187, 191–93, 195–97,
   199–216, 228, 244
strongholds, demonic, 56, 174, 185, 244
stumbling in Christian life, 236–38

Sunday schools, 35, 36

Tapscott, Betty, 144
temptation to sin, 47, 96, 139–40, 156, 179, 206
Ten Commandments, 163
territorial spirits, 36, 59, 67, 69, 110, 113, 186, 189, 191, 218–23. *See also* cosmic-level spirits
Timothy, 166, 222
Transformations, 231
trauma, 173, 177
travelers (tourists), 196–97, 224
truth (from knowledge and experience), 9, 16, 30, 32, 35–36, 50, 56, 68, 70–72, 76, 78–79, 88, 101, 106, 117–24, 131–35, 147, 158, 191, 205, 207–8, 212, 214, 217, 221, 233, 243

unforgiveness, 57, 187, 203
unity of spiritual leadership, 37, 60, 200, 230, 232

validity of Experience, 71, 75–76, 78, 80–82, 102, 110–11, 120, 123, 127, 241
vice spirits, 60, 186, 189–90, 218, 220, 223. *See also* cosmic-level spirits
vows, 39, 173–74, 211, 215–16

Wagner, C. Peter, 13, 14, 15, 36, 58, 188, 194, 218, 220
Wagner, C. Peter, and Pablo Deiros, 232
Wagner, Doris, 14, 194
warfare, 52, 190, 223, 227
Western naturalism, 221
Wimber, John, 13, 14, 15, 94, 170
witchcraft, 203–4
word of knowledge, 65, 94, 174, 213–14
world religions, 19, 93
worldview, 27–30, 45, 48–49, 69, 81, 141, 166
Western, 28, 29, 30, 31, 34, 37, 45, 100, 103–4, 106, 195, 206–7
worship, 23, 45, 126, 178

Dr. Charles H. Kraft has since 1969 been a professor at the School of World Mission, Fuller Theological Seminary, in Pasadena, California, where he teaches anthropology, communication, prayer ministry (inner healing) and spiritual warfare. He holds degrees from Wheaton College (B.A., anthropology), Ashland Theological Seminary (B.D., theology) and Hartford Seminary Foundation (Ph.D., anthropological linguistics). He is the president of Deep Healing Ministries and conducts seminars in the United States and around the world on deep-level (inner) healing, deliverance and spiritual warfare.

Chuck is the author of 23 books and numerous articles dealing with the relationship of Christianity to culture and spiritual warfare. Among the books are *Christianity in Culture; Communication Theory for Christian Witness; Communicating Jesus' Way; Anthropology for Christian Witness; Christianity with Power; Deep Wounds, Deep Healing; Defeating Dark Angels; Behind Enemy Lines; I Give You Authority; The Rules of Engagement;* and *Culture, Communication and Christianity.*

Chuck and his wife, Marguerite, have been missionaries in Nigeria. Before joining the faculty of Fuller Seminary, Chuck taught for five years each at Michigan State University and UCLA in African languages with a specialization in the Hausa language of northern Nigeria. Chuck and Meg are the parents of four children and grandparents of fourteen.